A Programmer's Introduction to C#, Second Edition

ERIC GUNNERSON

Apress™

A Programmer's Introduction to C#, Second Edition

ISBN (pbk): 1-893115-62-3

Printed and bound in the United States of America 12345678910

Editorial Directors: Dan Appleman, Gary Cornell, Karen Watterson, Jason Gilmore

Technical Reviewers: David Staheli, Shawn Vita, Gus Perez, Jerry Higgins, Brenton Webster

Copy Editor: Kim Wimpsett

Managing Editor: Grace Wong

Production Editor: Janet Vail

Page Compositor and Soap Bubble Artist: Susan Glinert

Artists: Karl Miyajima and Tony Jonick

Indexer: Valerie Perry

Cover Designer: Karl Miyajima

Distributed to the book trade in the United States by Springer-Verlag New York, Inc., 175 Fifth Avenue, New York, NY, 10010

and outside the United States by Springer-Verlag GmbH & Co. KG, Tiergartenstr. 17, 69112 Heidelberg, Germany

In the United States, phone 1-800-SPRINGER; orders@springer-ny.com; http://www.springer-ny.com

Outside the United States, contact orders@springer.de; http://www.springer.de; fax +49 6221 345229

For information on translations, please contact Apress directly at 901 Grayson Street, Suite 204, Berkeley, CA, 94710

Phone: 510-549-5937; Fax: 510-549-5939; info@apress.com; http://www.apress.com

Contents at a Glance

Contents

Foreword

WHEN YOU CREATE a new programming language, the first question you're asked invariably is, why? In creating C# we had several goals in mind:

- *To produce the first component-oriented language in the C/C++ family.* Software engineering is less and less about building monolithic applications and more and more about building components that slot into various execution environments; for example, a control in a browser or a business object that executes in ASP+. Key to such components is that they have properties, methods, and events, and that they have attributes that provide declarative information about the component. All of these concepts are first-class language constructs in C#, making it a very natural language in which to construct and use components.

- *To create a language in which everything really is an object.* Through innovative use of concepts such as boxing and unboxing, C# bridges the gap between primitive types and classes, allowing any piece of data to be treated as an object. Furthermore, C# introduces the concept of value types, which allows users to implement lightweight objects that do not require heap allocation.

- *To enable construction of robust and durable software.* C# was built from the ground up to include garbage collection, structured exception handling, and type safety. These concepts completely eliminate entire categories of bugs that often plague C++ programs.

- *To simplify C++, yet preserve the skills and investment programmers already have.* C# maintains a high degree of similarity with C++, and programmers will immediately feel comfortable with the language. And C# provides great interoperability with COM and DLLs, allowing existing code to be fully leveraged.

We have worked very hard to attain these goals. A lot of the hard work took place in the C# design group, which met regularly over a period of two years. As head of the C# Quality Assurance team, Eric was a key member of the group, and through his participation he is eminently qualified to explain not only how C# works, but also why it works that way. That will become evident as you read this book.

I hope you have as much fun using C# as those of us on the C# design team had creating it.

Anders Hejlsberg
Distinguished Engineer
Microsoft Corporation

Dedication

To Tony Jongejan, for introducing me to programming and being ahead of his time.

Acknowledgments

THOUGH WRITING A BOOK is often a lonely undertaking, no author can do it without help.

I'd like to thank all those who helped me with the book, including all those team members who answered my incessant questions and read my unfinished drafts. I would also like to thank my managers and Microsoft, both for allowing me to work on such a unique project and for allowing me to write a book about it.

Thanks to the Apress team for making a bet on an unproven author and for not pestering me when I waited to turn in content.

Thanks to all the artists who provided music to write to—all of which was commercially purchased—with special thanks to Rush for all their work.

Finally, I'd like to thank all those who supported me at home; my wife Kim and daughter Samantha who didn't complain when I was working, even when it was during our vacation, and for my cat for holding my arms down while I was writing.

About This Book

C# IS ONE OF THE MOST EXCITING projects I've ever had the privilege to work on. There are many languages with different strengths and weaknesses, but once in a while a new language comes along that that meshes well with the hardware, software, and programming approaches of a specific time. I believe C# is such a language. Of course, language choice is often a "religious issue."[1]

I've structured this book as a tour through the language, since I think that's the best and most interesting way to learn a language. Unfortunately, tours can often be long and boring, especially if the material is familiar, and they sometimes concentrate on things you don't care about, while overlooking things you're interested in. It's nice to be able to short-circuit the boring stuff and get into the interesting stuff. To do that, there are two approaches you might consider:

To start things off quickly, there's Chapter 3, "C# QuickStart," which is a quick overview of the language, and gives enough information to start coding.

Chapter 34, "C# Compared to Other Languages," offers language-specific comparisons for C++, VB, and Java for programmers attuned to a specific language, or for those who like to read comparisons.

As I write this, it's early August 2000, and the Visual Studio version that will contain C# has yet to reach beta. The language syntax is fairly stable, but there will undoubtedly be some items changed "around the edges." See Chapter 35, "C# Futures," for some information on what is in store for the future versions.

If you have comments about the book, you can reach me at `gunnerso@halcyon.com`. All source code can be downloaded from the Apress Web site at `http://www.apress.com`.

1. See the Jargon File (`http://www.jargonfile.org`) for a good definition of "religious issue."

Introduction

Why Another Language?

AT THIS POINT, you're probably asking yourself, "Why should I learn *another* language? Why not use C++?" (or VB or Java or whatever your preferred language is). At least, you were probably asking yourself that before you bought the book.

Languages are a little bit like power tools. Each tool has its own strengths and weaknesses. Though I *could* use my router to trim a board to length, it would be much easier if I used a miter saw. Similarly, I could use a language like LISP to write a graphics-intensive game, but it would probably be easier to use C++.

C# (pronounced "C sharp") is the native language for the .NET Common Language Runtime. It has been designed to fit seamlessly into the .NET Common Language Runtime. You can (and, at times, you should) write code in either Visual C++ or Visual Basic, but in most cases, C# will likely fit your needs better. Because the Common Language Runtime is central to many things in C#, Chapter 2, "The .NET Runtime Environment," will introduce the important parts of it—at least, those that are important to the C# language.

C# Design Goals

When the C++ language first came out, it caused quite a stir. Here was a language for creating object-oriented software that didn't require C programmers to abandon their skills or their investment in software. It wasn't fully object-oriented in the way a language like Eiffel is, but it had enough object-oriented features to offer great benefits.

C# provides a similar opportunity. In cooperation with the .NET Common Language Runtime, it provides a language to use for component-oriented software, without forcing programmers to abandon their investment in C, C++, or COM code.

C# is designed for building robust and durable components to handle real-world situations.

Component Software

The .NET Common Language Runtime is a component-based environment, and it should come as no surprise that C# is designed to make component creation easier. It's a "component-centric" language, in that all objects are written as components, and the component is the center of the action.

Component concepts, such as properties, methods, and events, are first-class citizens of the language and of the underlying runtime environment. Declarative information (known as attributes) can be applied to components to convey design-time and runtime information about the component to other parts of the system. Documentation can be written inside the component and exported to XML.

C# objects don't require header files, IDL files, or type libraries to be created or used. Components created by C# are fully self-describing and can be used without a registration process.

C# is aided in the creation of components by the .NET Runtime and Frameworks, which provide a unified type system in which everything can be treated as an object, but without the performance penalty associated with pure object systems, such as Smalltalk.

Robust and Durable Software

In the component-based world, being able to create software that is robust and durable is very important. Web servers may run for months without a scheduled reboot, and an unscheduled reboot is undesirable.

Garbage collection takes the burden of memory management away from the programmer,[1] and the problems of writing versionable components are eased by definable versioning semantics and the ability to separate the interface from the implementation. Numerical operations can be checked to ensure that they don't overflow, and arrays support bounds checking.

C# also provides an environment that is simple, safe, and straightforward. Error handling is not an afterthought, with exception handling being present throughout the environment. The language is type-safe, and it protects against the use of variables that have not been initialized, unsafe casts, and other common programming errors.

Real-World Software

Software development isn't pretty. Software is rarely designed on a clean slate; it must have decent performance, leverage existing code, and be practical to write in terms of time and budget. A well-designed environment is of little use if it doesn't provide enough power for real-world use.

---

1. It's not that C++ memory management is conceptually hard; it isn't in most cases, though there are some difficult situations when dealing with components. The burden comes from having to devote time and effort to getting it right. With garbage collection, it isn't necessary to spend the coding and testing time to make sure there aren't any memory leaks, which frees the programmer to focus on the program logic.

C# provides the benefits of an elegant and unified environment, while still providing access to "less reputable" features—such as pointers—when those features are needed to get the job done.

C# protects the investment in existing code. Existing COM objects can be used as if they were .NET objects.[2] The .NET Common Language Runtime will make objects in the runtime appear to be COM objects to existing COM-based code. Native C code in DLL files can be called from C# code.[3]

C# provides low-level access when appropriate. Lightweight objects can be written to be stack allocated and still participate in the unified environment. Low-level access is provided via the `unsafe` mode, which allows pointers to be used in cases where performance is very important or when pointers are required to use existing DLLs.

C# is built on a C++ heritage and should be immediately comfortable for C++ programmers. The language provides a short learning curve, increased productivity, and no unnecessary sacrifices.

Finally, C# capitalizes on the power of the .NET Common Language Runtime, which provides extensive library support for general programming tasks and application-specific tasks. The .NET Runtime, Frameworks, and languages are all tied together by the Visual Studio environment, providing one-stop-shopping for the .NET programmer.

Second Edition Updates

If you already own the first edition of this book, you're probably asking yourself whether the second edition is worth the money. This section should give you enough information to make that choice.

The first thing I did was go through the book and update all the samples to conform to the compiler's Beta 2 release. Most of these changes are fairly minor, mostly due to naming changes in the Frameworks, though some of the samples did require a bit of re-architecting.

The second set of changes typically involve the addition of small sections or new examples. (These minor changes are listed below by chapter.)

As for the major changes, I heavily revised the chapters on delegates and events and developed a sample application using Windows Forms. There is a new chapter on threading and asynchronous operations, which details two different ways of getting things to occur simultaneously. Finally, there's a new chapter on execution-time code generation, which details how to write a self-modifying application.

The following are the major differences:

---

2. Usually. There are details that sometimes make this a bit tougher in practice.

3. For C++ code, Visual C++ has been extended with "Managed Extensions" that make it possible to create .NET components. More information on these extensions can be found on the Microsoft web site.

- Chapters 22 and 23, covering delegates and events, respectively, have been rewritten.
- Chapter 29 covers threading and asynchronous operations.
- Chapter 30 covers execution-time code generation using several techniques.
- Chapters 33–35 describe the development of a Windows Forms (formerly known as "WinForms") application.

There are also a number of minor differences in existing chapters:

- Chapter 8 covers deterministic finalization, `IDisposable`, and the `using` statement.
- Chapter 9 discusses immutable classes.
- Chapter 10 covers structs that implement interfaces.
- Chapter 11 provides more detail about versioning.
- Chapter 14 discusses checked and unchecked expressions.
- Chapter 17 covers string encodings, string interning, and regular expression options.
- Chapter 18 covers virtual properties.
- Chapter 19 now covers strongly typed enumerators, disposable enumerators, and multidimensional indexers.
- Chapter 20 now covers some nice things enums get from the `System.Enum` class.
- Chapter 25 presents a complex number class.
- Chapter 27 has design guidelines for overriding `object.Equals()`.
- Chapter 28 covers synchronized and case-insensitive collections.
- Chapter 31 provides interop design guidelines and more examples.
- Chapter 32 contains information on starting processes, doing custom serialization, and accessing environment strings.
- Chapter 38 describes the new default compiler response file.

The C# Compiler and Other Resources

THERE ARE TWO WAYS of getting the C# compiler. The first is as part of the .NET SDK.

The SDK contains compilers for C#, VB, C++, and all of the frameworks. After you install the SDK, you can compile C# programs using the `csc` command, which will generate an .exe that you can execute.

The other way of getting the compiler is as part of the Visual Studio.NET. The beta of Visual Studio.NET will be available in the fall of 2000.

To find out more about getting the .NET SDK or the Visual Studio.NET beta, please consult this book's page on the Apress Web site at

```
http://www.apress.com
```

Compiler Hints

When compiling code, the C# compiler must be able to locate information about the components that are being used. It will automatically search the file named `mscorlib.dll`, which contains the lowest-level .NET entities, such as data types.

To use other components, the appropriate .dll for that component must be specified on the command line. For example, to use WinForms, the system.winforms.dll file must be specified as follows:

```
csc /r:system.winforms.dll myfile.cs
```

The usual naming convention is for the .dll to be the same as the namespace name.

Other Resources

Microsoft maintains public newsgroups for .NET programming. The C# newsgroup is named `microsoft.public.dotnet.csharp.general`, and it lives on the `msnews.microsoft.com` news server.

There are numerous Web sites devoted to .NET information. Links to these resources also can be found at the Apress Web site.

CHAPTER 1

Object-Oriented Basics

THIS CHAPTER IS AN INTRODUCTION to object-oriented programming. Those who are familiar with object-oriented programming will probably want to skip this section.

There are many approaches to object-oriented design, as evidenced by the number of books written about it. The following introduction takes a fairly pragmatic approach and doesn't spend a lot of time on design, but the design-oriented approaches can be quite useful to newcomers.

What Is an Object?

An object is merely a collection of related information and functionality. An object can be something that has a corresponding real-world manifestation (such as an `employee` object), something that has some virtual meaning (such as a window on the screen), or just some convenient abstraction within a program (a list of work to be done, for example).

An object is composed of the data that describes the object and the operations that can be performed on the object. Information stored in an `employee` object, for example, might be various identification information (name, address), work information (job title, salary), and so on. The operations performed might include creating an employee paycheck or promoting an employee.

When creating an object-oriented design, the first step is to determine what the objects are. When dealing with real-life objects, this is often straightforward, but when dealing with the virtual world, the boundaries become less clear. That's where the art of good design shows up, and it's why good architects are in such demand.

Inheritance

Inheritance is a fundamental feature of an object-oriented system, and it is simply the ability to inherit data and functionality from a parent object. Rather than developing new objects from scratch, new code can be based on the work of other programmers[1], adding only the new features that are needed. The parent object that the new work is based upon is known as a *base class, and the child object is known as a derived class.*

---

1. At this point there should perhaps be an appropriate comment about standing "on the shoulders of giants..."

Inheritance gets a lot of attention in explanations of object-oriented design, but the use of inheritance isn't particularly widespread in most designs. There are several reasons for this.

First, inheritance is an example of what is known in object-oriented design as an "is-a" relationship. If a system has an `animal` object and a `cat` object, the `cat` object could inherit from the `animal` object, because a `cat` "is-a" `animal`. In inheritance, the base class is always more generalized than the derived class. The `cat` class would inherit the `eat` function from the animal class, and would have an enhanced `sleep` function. In real-world design, such relationships aren't particularly common.

Second, to use inheritance, the base class needs to be designed with inheritance in mind. This is important for several reasons. If the objects don't have the proper structure, inheritance can't really work well. More importantly, a design that enables inheritance also makes it clear that the author of the base class is willing to support other classes inheriting from the class. If a new class is inherited from a class where this isn't the case, the base class might at some point change, breaking the derived class.

Some less-experienced programmers mistakenly believe that inheritance is "supposed to be" used widely in object-oriented programming, and therefore use it far too often. Inheritance should only be used when the advantages that it brings are needed[2]. See the coming section on "Polymorphism and Virtual Functions."

In the .NET Common Language Runtime, all objects are inherited from the ultimate base class named `object`, and there is only single inheritance of objects (i.e., an object can only be derived from one base class). This does prevent the use of some common idioms available in multiple-inheritance systems such as C++, but it also removes many abuses of multiple inheritance and provides a fair amount of simplification. In most cases, it's a good tradeoff. The .NET Runtime does allow multiple inheritance in the form of interfaces, which cannot contain implementation. Interfaces will be discussed in Chapter 10, "Interfaces."

Containment

So, if inheritance isn't the right choice, what is?

The answer is containment, also known as aggregation. Rather than saying that an object is an example of another object, an instance of that other object will be contained inside the object. So, instead of having a class look like a string, the class will contain a string (or array, or hash table).

The default design choice should be containment, and you should switch to inheritance only if needed (i.e., if there really is an "is-a" relationship).

2. Perhaps there should be a paper called "Multiple inheritance considered harmful." There probably is one, someplace.

Polymorphism and Virtual Functions

A while back I was writing a music system, and I decided that I wanted to be able to support both WinAmp and Windows Media Player as playback engines, but I didn't want all of my code to have to know which engine it was using. I therefore defined an abstract class, which is a class that defines the functions a derived class must implement, and that sometimes provides functions that are useful to both classes.

In this case, the abstract class was called `MusicServer`, and it had functions like `Play()`, `NextSong()`, `Pause()`, etc. Each of these functions was declared as abstract, so that each player class would have to implement those functions themselves.

Abstract functions are automatically virtual functions, which allow the programmer to use polymorphism to make their code simpler. When there is a virtual function, the programmer can pass around a reference to the abstract class rather than the derived class, and the compiler will write code to call the appropriate version of the function at runtime.

An example will probably make that clearer. The music system supports both WinAmp and Windows Media Player as playback engines. The following is a basic outline of what the classes look like:

```
using System;
public abstract class MusicServer
{
    public abstract void Play();
}
public class WinAmpServer: MusicServer
{
    public override void Play()
    {
        Console.WriteLine("WinAmpServer.Play()");
    }
}
public class MediaServer: MusicServer
{
    public override void Play()
    {
        Console.WriteLine("MediaServer.Play()");
    }
}
class Test
{
    public static void CallPlay(MusicServer ms)
    {
        ms.Play();
    }
```

```
    public static void Main()
    {
        MusicServer ms = new WinAmpServer();
        CallPlay(ms);
        ms = new MediaServer();
        CallPlay(ms);
    }
}
```

This code produces the following output:

```
WinAmpServer.Play()
MediaServer.Play()
```

Polymorphism and virtual functions are used in many places in the .NET Runtime system. For example, the base object `object` has a virtual function called `ToString()` that is used to convert an object into a string representation of the object. If you call the `ToString()` function on an object that doesn't have its own version of `ToString()`, the version of the `ToString()` function that's part of the `object` class will be called,[3] which simply returns the name of the class. If you overload—write your own version of—the `ToString()` function, that one will be called instead, and you can do something more meaningful, such as writing out the name of the employee contained in the employee object. In the music system, this meant overloading functions for play, pause, next song, etc.

Encapsulation and Visibility

When designing objects, the programmer gets to decide how much of the object is visible to the user, and how much is private within the object. Details that aren't visible to the user are said to be encapsulated in the class.

In general, the goal when designing an object is to encapsulate as much of the class as possible. The most important reasons for doing this are these:

- The user can't change private things in the object, which reduces the chance that the user will either change or depend upon such details in their code. If the user does depend on these details, changes made to the object may break the user's code.

3. Or, if there is a base class of the current object, and it defines `ToString()`, that version will be called.

- Changes made in the public parts of an object must remain compatible with the previous version. The more that is visible to the user, the fewer things that can be changed without breaking the user's code.

- Larger interfaces increase the complexity of the entire system. Private fields can only be accessed from within the class; public fields can be accessed through any instance of the class. Having more public fields often makes debugging much tougher.

This subject will be explored further in Chapter 5, "Classes 101."

CHAPTER 2

The .NET Runtime Environment

IN THE PAST, WRITING MODULES that could be called from multiple languages was difficult. Code that is written in Visual Basic can't be called from Visual C++. Code that is written in Visual C++ can sometimes be called from Visual Basic, but it's not easy to do. Visual C++ uses the C and C++ runtimes, which have very specific behavior, and Visual Basic uses its own execution engine, also with its own specific—and different—behavior.

And so COM was created, and it's been pretty successful as a way of writing component-based software. Unfortunately, it's fairly difficult to use from the Visual C++ world, and it's not fully featured in the Visual Basic world. And therefore, it got used extensively when writing COM components, and less often when writing native applications. So, if one programmer wrote some nice code in C++, and another wrote some in Visual Basic, there really wasn't an easy way of working together.

Further, the world was tough for library providers, as there was no one choice that would work in all markets. If the writer thought the library was targeted toward the Visual Basic crowd, it would be easy to use from Visual Basic, but that choice might either constrain access from the C++ perspective or come with an unacceptable performance penalty. Or, a library could be written for C++ users, for good performance and low-level access, but it would ignore the Visual Basic programmers.

Sometimes a library would be written for both types of users, but this usually meant there were some compromises. To send email on a Windows system, there is a choice between Collaboration Data Objects (CDO), a COM-based interface that can be called from both languages but doesn't do everything,[1] and native MAPI functions (in both C and C++ versions) that can access all functions.

The .NET Runtime is designed to remedy this situation. There is one way of describing code (metadata), and one runtime and library (the Common Language Runtime and Frameworks). The following diagram shows how the .NET Runtime is arranged:

1. Presumably this is because it is difficult to translate the low-level internal design into something that can be called from an automation interface.

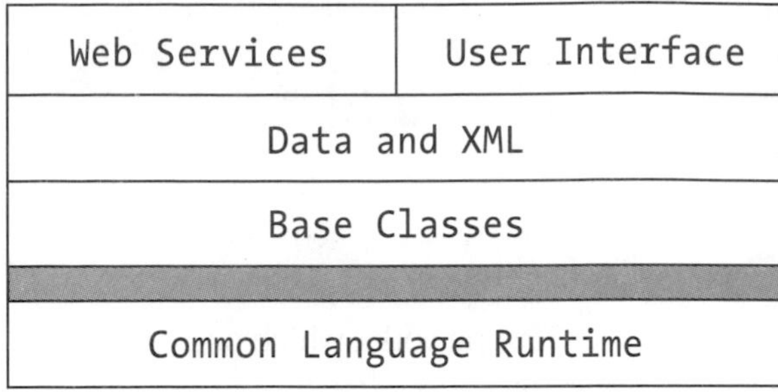

Figure 2-1. .NET Frameworks organization

The Common Language Runtime provides the basic execution services. On top of that, the base classes provide basic data types, collection classes, and other general classes. Built on top of the base classes are classes for dealing with data and XML. Finally, at the top of the architecture are classes to expose web services[2] and to deal with the user interface. An application may call in at any level and use classes from any level.

To understand how C# works, it is important to understand a bit about the .NET Runtime and Frameworks. The following section provides an overview; and more detailed information can be found later in the book in the Chapter 36, "Deeper into C#."

The Execution Environment

This section was once titled, "The Execution Engine," but .NET Runtime is much more than just an engine. The environment provides a simpler programming model, safety and security, powerful tools support, and help with deployment, packaging, and other support.

A Simpler Programming Model

All services are offered through a common model that can be accessed equally through all the .NET languages, and the services can be written in any .NET language.[3] The environment is largely language-agnostic, allowing language choice. This makes code reuse easier, both for the programmer and the library providers.

2. A way to expose a programmatic interface via a web server.

3. Some languages may not be able to interface with native platform capabilities.

The environment also supports the use of existing code in C# code, either through calling functions in DLLs, or making COM components appear to be .NET Runtime components. .NET Runtime components can also be used in situations that require COM components.

In contrast with the various error-handling techniques in existing libraries, in the .NET Runtime all errors are reported via exceptions. There is no need to switch between error codes, HRESULTs, and exceptions.

Finally, the environment contains the .NET Frameworks, which provide the functions traditionally found in runtime libraries, plus a few new ones. The Frameworks is divided into different categories.

`System`

The `System` namespace contains the core classes for the runtime. These classes are roughly analogous to the C++ Runtime Library and include the following nested namespaces:

NAMESPACE	FUNCTION
`Collections`	Collection objects, such as lists, queues, and hash tables
`Configuration`	Configuration and installation objects
`Diagnostics`	Debug and trace execution of code
`Globalization`	Globalize your application
`IO`	Input and output
`Net`	Network operations
`Reflection`	View the metadata of types and dynamically load and creating objects
`Security`	Support the .NET Security System
`ServiceProcess`	Create and manage windows services
`Text`	Encoding and conversion classes
`Threading`	Threads and synchronization
`Runtime`	Interop, remoting, and serialization

System.Data

The `System.Data` namespace contains the classes that support database operations.

SECTION	FUNCTION
ADO	ADO.NET
Design	Design-time database support
SQL	SQL Server support
SQLTypes	Data types for SQL server

System.Xml

The `System.Xml` namespace contains classes to manage XML.

System.Drawing

The `System.Drawing` namespace contains classes that support GDI+, including printing and imaging.

System.Web

The `System.Web` namespace contains classes for dealing with web services and classes for creating web-based interfaces using ASP.NET.

System.Windows.Forms

The `System.Windows.Forms` namespace contains classes to create rich-client interfaces.

Safety and Security

The .NET Runtime environment is designed to be a safe and secure environment. The .NET Runtime is a managed environment, which means that the Runtime manages memory for the programmer. Instead of having to manage memory allocation and deallocation, the garbage collector does it. Not only does garbage collection reduce the number of things to remember when programming, in a server environment it can drastically reduce the number of memory leaks. This makes high-availability systems much easier to develop.

Additionally, the .NET Runtime is a verified environment. At runtime, the environment verifies that the executing code is type-safe. This can catch errors, such as passing the wrong type to a function, and attacks, such as trying to read beyond allocated boundaries or executing code at an arbitrary location.

The security system interacts with the verifier to ensure that code does only what it is permitted to do. The security requirements for a specific piece of code can be expressed in a finely grained manner; code can, for example, specify that it needs to be able to write a scratch file, and that requirement will be checked during execution.

Powerful Tools Support

Microsoft supplies four .NET languages: Visual Basic, Visual C++ with Managed Extensions, C#, and JScript. Other companies are working on compilers for other languages that run the gamut from COBOL to Perl.

Debugging is greatly enhanced in the .Net Runtime. The common execution model makes cross-language debugging simple and straightforward, and debugging can seamlessly span code written in different languages and running in different processes or on different machines.

Finally, all .NET programming tasks are tied together by the Visual Studio environment, which gives support for designing, developing, debugging, and deploying applications.

Deployment, Packaging, and Support

The .NET Runtime helps out in these areas as well. Deployment has been simplified, and in some cases there isn't a traditional install step. Because the packages are deployed in a general format, a single package can run in any environment that supports .NET. Finally, the environment separates application components so that an application only runs with the components it shipped with, rather than with different versions shipped by other applications.

Metadata

Metadata is the glue that holds the .NET Runtime together. Metadata is the analog of the type library in the COM world, but with much more extensive information.

For every object that is part of the .NET world, the metadata for that object records all the information that is required to use the object, which includes the following:

- The name of the object
- The names of all the fields of the object, and their types
- The names of all member functions, including parameter types and names

With this information, the .NET Runtime is able to figure out how to create objects, call member functions, or access object data, and compilers can use them to find out what objects are available and how an object is used.

This unification is very nice for the both the producer and consumer of code; the producer of code can easily author code that can be used from all .NET-compatible languages, and the user of the code can easily use objects created by others, regardless of the language that the objects are implemented in.

Additionally, this rich metadata allows other tools access to detailed information about the code. The Visual Studio shell makes use of this information in the Object Browser and for features such as IntelliSense.

Finally, runtime code can query the metadata—in a process called reflection—to find out what objects are available and what functions and fields are present on the class. This is similar to dealing with IDispatch in the COM world, but with a simpler model. Of course, such access is not strongly typed, so most software will choose to reference the metadata at compile time rather than runtime, but it is a very useful facility for applications such as scripting languages.

Finally, reflection is available to the end-user to determine what objects look like, to search for attributes, or to execute methods whose names are not known until runtime.

Assemblies

In the past, a finished software package might have been released as an executable, DLL and LIB files, a DLL containing a COM object and a typelib, or some other mechanism.

In the .NET Runtime, the mechanism of packaging is the *assembly.* When code is compiled by one of the .NET compilers, it is converted to an intermediate form known as "IL". The assembly contains all the IL, metadata, and other files required for a package to run, in one complete package. Each assembly contains a manifest that enumerates the files that are contained in the assembly, controls what types and resources are exposed outside the assembly, and maps references from those types and resources to the files that contain the types and resources. The manifest also lists the other assemblies that an assembly depends upon.

Assemblies are self-contained; there is enough information in the assembly for it to be self-describing.

When defining an assembly, the assembly can be contained in a single file or it can be split amongst several files. Using several files will enable a scenario where sections of the assembly are downloaded only as needed.

Language Interop

One of the goals of the .NET Runtime is to be language-agnostic, allowing code to be used and written from whatever language is convenient. Not only can classes written in Visual Basic be called from C# or C++ (or any other .NET language), a class that was written in Visual Basic can be used as a base class for a class written in C#, and that class could be used from a C++ class.

In other words, it shouldn't matter which language a class was authored in. Further, it often isn't possible to tell what language a class was written in.

In practice, this goal runs into a few obstacles. Some languages have unsigned types that aren't supported by other languages, and some languages support operator overloading. Allowing the more feature-rich languages to retain their freedom of expression while still making sure their classes can interop with other languages is challenging.

To support this, the .NET Runtime has sufficient support to allow the feature-rich languages full expressibility[4], so code that is written in one of those languages isn't constrained by the simpler languages.

For classes to be usable from .NET languages in general, the classes must adhere to the *Common Language Specification* (CLS), which describes what features can be visible in the public interface of the class (any features can be used internally in a class). For example, the CLS prohibits exposing unsigned data types, because not all languages can use them. More information on the CLS can be found in .NET SDK, in the section on "Cross-Language Interoperability."

A user writing C# code can indicate that it is supposed to be CLS compliant, and the compiler will flag any non-compliant areas. For more information on the specific restrictions placed on C# code by CLS compliance, see the "CLS Compliance" section in Chapter 36, "Deeper into C#."

Attributes

To transform a class into a component, some additional information is often required, such as how to persist a class to disk or how transactions should be handled. The traditional approach is to write the information in a separate file and then combine it with the source code to create a component.

4. This isn't quite true for Managed C++, which loses some expressibility over C++.

The problem with this approach is that information is duplicated in multiple places. It's cumbersome and error-prone, and it means you don't have the whole component unless you have both files.[5]

The .NET runtime supports custom attributes (known simply as *attributes* in C#), which are a way to place descriptive information in the metadata along with an object, and then retrieve the data at a later time. Attributes provide a general mechanism for doing this, and they are used heavily throughout the runtime to store information that modifies how the runtime uses the class.

Attributes are fully extensible, and this allows programmers to define attributes and use them.

5. Anybody who has ever tried to do COM programming without a typelib should understand the problem with this.

CHAPTER 3

C# QuickStart and Developing in C#

THIS CHAPTER PRESENTS a quick overview of the C# language. This chapter assumes a certain level of programming knowledge and therefore doesn't present very much detail. If the explanation here doesn't make sense, look for a more detailed explanation of the particular topic later in the book.

The second part of the chapter discusses how to obtain the C# compiler, and the advantages of using Visual Studio.NET to develop C# applications.

Hello, Universe

As a supporter of SETI,[1] I thought that it would be appropriate to do a "Hello, Universe" program rather than the canonical "Hello, World" program.

```
using System;
class Hello
{
    public static void Main(string[] args)
    {
        Console.WriteLine("Hello, Universe");

            // iterate over command-line arguments,
            // and print them out
        for (int arg = 0; arg < args.Length; arg++)
            Console.WriteLine("Arg {0}: {1}", arg, args[arg]);
    }
}
```

As discussed earlier, the .NET Runtime has a unified namespace for all program information (or metadata). The `using System` clause is a way of referencing the classes that are in the `System` namespace so they can be used without having to put `System` in front of the type name. The System namespace contains many useful

1. Search for Extraterrestrial Intelligence. See `http://www.teamseti.org` for more information.

classes, one of which is the `Console` class, which is used (not surprisingly) to communicate with the console (or DOS box, or command line, for those who have never seen a console).

Because there are no global functions in C#, the example declares a class called `Hello` that contains the static `Main()` function, which serves as the starting point for execution. `Main()` can be declared with no parameters, or with a string array. Since it's the starting function, it must be a static function, which means it isn't associated with an instance of an object.

The first line of the function calls the `WriteLine()` function of the `Console` class, which will write "Hello, Universe" to the console. The `for` loop iterates over the parameters that are passed in, and then writes out a line for each parameter on the command line.

Namespaces and Using

Namespaces in the .NET Runtime are used to organize classes and other types into a single hierarchical structure. The proper use of namespaces will make classes easy to use and prevent collisions with classes written by other authors.

Namespaces can also be thought of as way to specify really long names for classes and other types without having to always type a full name.

Namespaces are defined using the `namespace` statement. For multiple levels of organization, namespaces can be nested:

```
namespace Outer
{
    namespace Inner
    {
        class MyClass
        {
            public static void Function() {}
        }
    }
}
```

That's a fair amount of typing and indenting, so it can be simplified by using the following instead:

```
namespace Outer.Inner
{
    class MyClass
    {
        public static void Function() {}
    }
}
```

Each source file can define as many different namespaces as needed.

As mentioned in the "Hello, Universe" section, `using` imports the metadata for types into the current program, so that the types can be more easily referenced. The `using` keyword is merely a shortcut that reduces the amount of typing that is required when referring to elements, as the following table indicates:

USING CLAUSE	SOURCE LINE
<none>	System.Console.WriteLine("Hello");
using System	Console.WriteLine("Hello");

Collisions between types or namespaces that have the same name can always be resolved by a type's fully qualified name. This could be a very long name if the class is deeply nested, so there is a variant of the `using` clause that allows an alias to be defined to a class:

```
using ThatConsoleClass = System.Console;
class Hello
{
    public static void Main()
    {
        ThatConsoleClass.WriteLine("Hello");
    }
}
```

To make the code more readable, the examples in this book rarely use namespaces, but they should be used in most real code.

Namespaces and Assemblies

An object can be used from within a C# source file only if that object can be located by the C# compiler. By default, the compiler will only open the single assembly known as `mscorlib.dll`, which contains the core functions for the Common Language Runtime.

To reference objects located in other assemblies, the name of the assembly file must be passed to the compiler. This can be done on the command line using the `/r:<assembly>` option, or from within the Visual Studio IDE by adding a reference to the C# project.

Typically, there is a correlation between the namespace that an object is in and the name of the assembly in which it resides. For example, the types in the `System.Net` namespace reside in the `System.Net.dll` assembly. Types are usually placed in assemblies based on the usage patterns of the objects in that assembly; a large or rarely used type in a namespace might be placed in its own assembly.

The exact name of the assembly that an object is contained in can be found in the documentation for that object.

Basic Data Types

C# supports the usual set of data types. For each data type that C# supports, there is a corresponding underlying .NET Common Language Runtime type. For example, the `int` type in C# maps to the `System.Int32` type in the runtime. `System.Int32` could be used in most of the places where `int` is used, but that isn't recommended because it makes the code tougher to read.

The basic types are described in the following table. The runtime types can all be found in the `System` namespace of the .NET Common Language Runtime.

TYPE	BYTES	RUNTIME TYPE	DESCRIPTION
`byte`	1	`Byte`	Unsigned byte
`sbyte`	1	`SByte`	Signed byte
`short`	2	`Int16`	Signed short
`ushort`	2	`UInt16`	Unsigned short
`int`	4	`Int32`	Signed integer
`uint`	4	`UInt32`	Unsigned int
`long`	8	`Int64`	Signed big integer
`ulong`	8	`UInt64`	Unsigned big integer
`float`	4	`Single`	Floating point number
`double`	8	`Double`	Double-precision floating point number
`decimal`	8	`Decimal`	Fixed-precision number
`string`	n/a	`String`	Unicode string
`char`	2	`Char`	Unicode character
`bool`	n/a	`Boolean`	`Boolean` value

The distinction between basic (or built-in) types in C# is largely an artificial one, as user-defined types can operate in the same manner as the built-in ones. In fact, the only real difference between the built-in data types and user-defined data types is that it is possible to write literal values for the built-in types.

Data types are separated into value types and reference types. Value types are either stack allocated or allocated inline in a structure. Reference types are heap allocated.

Both reference and value types are derived from the ultimate base class `object`. In cases where a value type needs to act like an `object`, a wrapper that makes the value type look like a reference object is allocated on the heap, and the value type's value is copied into it. This process is known as boxing, and the reverse process is known as unboxing. Boxing and unboxing let you treat *any* type as an `object`. That allows the following to be written:

```
using System;
class Hello
{
    public static void Main(string[] args)
    {
        Console.WriteLine("Value is: {0}", 3);
    }
}
```

In this case, the integer `3` is boxed, and the `Int32.ToString()` function is called on the boxed value.

C# arrays can be declared in either the multidimensional or jagged forms. More advanced data structures, such as stacks and hash tables, can be found in the `System.Collections` namespace.

Classes, Structs, and Interfaces

In C#, the `class` keyword is used to declare a reference (heap allocated) type, and the `struct` keyword is used to declare a value type. Structs are used for lightweight objects that need to act like the built-in types, and classes are used in all other cases. For example, the `int` type is a value type, and the `string` type is a reference type. The following diagram details how these work:

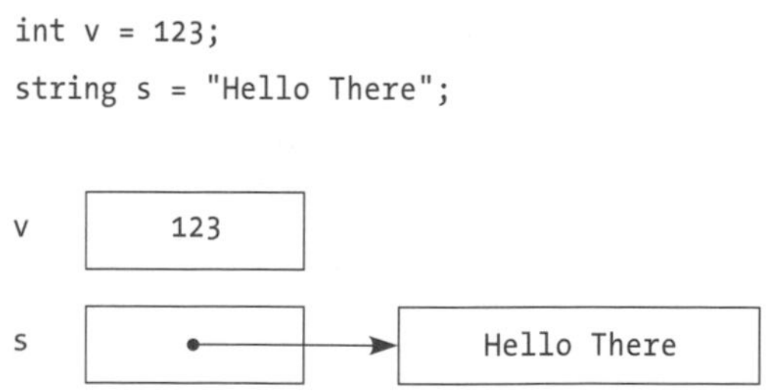

```
int v = 123;
string s = "Hello There";
```


Figure 3-1. Value and reference type allocation

C# and the .NET Runtime do not support multiple inheritance for classes but do support multiple implementation of interfaces.

Statements

The statements in C# are close to C++ statements, with a few modifications to make errors less likely, and a few new statements. The `foreach` statement is used to iterate over arrays and collections, the `lock` statement is used for mutual exclusion in threading scenarios, and the `checked` and `unchecked` statements are used to control overflow checking in arithmetic operations and conversions.

Enums

Enumerators are used to declare a set of related constants—such as the colors that a control can take—in a clear and type-safe manner. For example:

```
enum Colors
{
    red,
    green,
    blue
}
```

Enumerators are covered in more detail in Chapter 20, "Enumerations."

Delegates and Events

Delegates are a type-safe, object-oriented implementation of function pointers and are used in many situations where a component needs to call back to the component that is using it. They are used most heavily as the basis for events, which allow a delegate to easily be registered for an event. They are discussed in Chapter 22, "Delegates."

Delegates and events are heavily used by the .NET Frameworks.

Properties and Indexers

C# supports properties and indexers, which are useful for separating the interface of an object from the implementation of the object. Rather than allowing a user to access a field or array directly, a property or indexer allows a statement block to be specified to perform the access, while still allowing the field or array usage. Here's a simple example:

```
using System;
class Circle
{
    public int Radius
    {
        get
        {
            return(radius);
        }
        set
        {
            radius = value;
            Draw();
        }
    }
    public void Draw()
    {
    }
    int radius;
}
class Test
{
    public static void Main()
    {
        Circle c = new Circle();
        c.Radius = 35;
    }
}
```

In this example, the `get` or `set` accessor is called when the property `Radius` is referenced.

Attributes

Attributes are used in C# and the .NET Frameworks to communicate declarative information from the writer of the code to other code that is interested in the information. This could be used to specify which fields of an object should be serialized, what transaction context to use when running an object, how to marshal fields to native functions, or how to display a class in a class browser.

Attributes are specified within square braces. A typical attribute usage might look like this:

```
[CodeReview("12/31/1999", Comment="Well done")]
```

Attribute information is retrieved at runtime through a process known as reflection. New attributes can be easily written, applied to elements of the code (such as classes, members, or parameters), and retrieved through reflection.

Developing in C#

To program in C#, you're going to need a way to build C# programs. You can do this with a command-line compiler, VS.NET, or a C# package for a programming editor.

The Command-Line Compiler

The simplest way to get started writing C# code is by using the .NET Runtime and Frameworks SDK. The SDK contains the .NET Runtime and Frameworks and compilers for C#, Visual Basic.NET, the Managed Extensions to C++, and JScript.NET. The framework can be downloaded from:

```
http://msdn.microsoft.com/net
```

Using the SDK is easy; write your code in an editor, compile it using `csc`, and then run it. But easy doesn't necessarily mean productive, however. When writing with just the SDK, you'll spend a lot of time looking at documentation and trying to figure out simple errors in your code.

You can find details about using the command-line compiler in Chapter 38, "The Command Line Compiler."

Visual Studio.NET

Visual Studio.NET provides a full environment to make programming in C# easy and fun. Beta versions of Visual Studio.Net are available at the same URL as the SDK:

```
http://msdn.microsoft.com/net
```

If you're a subscriber to MSDN Universal, you can download Visual Studio.NET; if not, you'll be able to order it for a nominal charge.

Visual Studio.NET provides some real help for the developer.

The Editor

The most important feature of the Visual Studio.NET editor is the IntelliSense support. One of the challenges of learning C# and the Frameworks is simply finding your way around the syntax of the language and object model of the Frameworks. Auto Completion will help greatly in finding the proper method to use, and syntax checking will highlight the sections of code with errors.

The Form Designer

Both Windows Forms and WebForms applications are written directly in code, without separate resource files, so it's possible to write either application without Visual Studio.NET.

Doing layout and setting properties by hand isn't very fun, however, so Visual Studio provides a Form Designer that makes it easy to add controls to a form, set the properties on the form, create event handlers, and so on.

The form editing is two-way; changes made in the form designer show up in the form code, and changes made in the form code show up in the designer.[2]

The Project System

The project system provides support for creating and building projects. There are predefined templates for most types of projects (Windows Forms, Web Forms, Console Application, Class Library, and so on).

The project system also provides support for deploying applications.

Class View

While the project system provides a view of the files in a project, class view provides a view into the classes and other types in a project. Rather than writing the syntax for a property directly, for example, class view provides a wizard to do it for you.

The Object Browser

The object browser provides the same sort of view that class view does, but instead of looking at the code in the current project, it lets you browse the components in other assemblies that the project is using. If the documentation for a class is

2. Within reason.

incomplete, the object browser can show the interface of the class as defined by the metadata for the component.

The Debugger

The debugger in Visual Studio.NET has been enhanced to provide cross-language debugging facilities. It's possible to debug from one language to the other, and it's also possible to debug code executing remotely on another machine.

Other Tools of Note

The SDK comes with a number of utility programs, which are detailed in the .NET Framework Tools section of the documentation.

ILDASM

ILDASM (IL Disassembler) is the most useful tool in the SDK. It can open an assembly, show all the types in the assembly, what methods are defined for those types, and the IL that was generated for that method.

This is useful in a number of ways. Like the object browser, it can be used to find out what's present in an assembly, but it can also be used to find out how a specific method is implemented. This capability can be used to answer some questions about C#.

If, for example, you want to know whether C# will concatenate constant strings at compile time, it's easy to test. First, a short program is created:

```
using System;
class Test
{
    public static void Main()
    {
        Console.WriteLine("Hello " + "World");
    }
}
```

After the program is compiled, ILDASM can be used to view the IL for `Main()`:

```
.method public hidebysig static void Main() cil managed
{
  .entrypoint
  // Code size       11 (0xb)
  .maxstack  8
  IL_0000:  ldstr      "Hello World"
  IL_0005:  call       void [mscorlib]System.Console::WriteLine(string)
  IL_000a:  ret
} // end of method Test::Main
```

Even without knowing the details of the IL language, it's pretty clear that the two strings are concatenated into a single string.

The details of the IL language can be found in `ILinstrset.doc`, which can be found in `C:\Program Files\Microsoft.Net\FrameworkSDK\Tool Developer Guide`.

ILDASM can be used on any assembly, which raises some questions over intellectual property. Although having code stored in IL does make disassemblers easier to write, it doesn't create an issue that didn't exist before; x86 assembly language can also be disassembled and decoded.

Microsoft is aware of the issue and will be providing some tools to make it more difficult to reverse-engineer assemblies.

NGEN (PreJIT)

NGEN is a tool that performs the translation from IL to native processor code before the program is executed, rather than doing it on demand.

At first glance, this seems like a way to get around many of the disadvantages of the JIT approach; simply PreJIT the code, and then performance will be better and nobody will be able to decode the IL.

Unfortunately, things don't work that way. PreJIT is only a way to store the results of the compilation, but the metadata is still required to do class layout and support reflection. Further, the generated native code is only valid for a specific environment, and if configuration settings (such as the machine security policy) change, the Runtime will switch back to the normal JIT.

While PreJIT does eliminate the overhead of the JIT process, it also produces code that runs slightly slower because it requires a level of indirection that isn't required with the normal JIT.

So, the real benefit of PreJIT is to reduce the JIT overhead (and therefore the startup time) of a client application, and it isn't really terribly useful elsewhere.

At least that's the story for the first version of the runtime. In future versions, NGEN could perform more advanced optimizations than the normal JIT, since it could presumably spend more time in analysis.

CHAPTER 4

Exception Handling

In many programming books, exception handling warrants a chapter somewhat late in the book. In this book, however, it's very near the front, for a couple of reasons.

The first reason is that exception handling is deeply ingrained in the .NET Runtime, and is therefore very common in C# code. C++ code can be written without using exception handling, but that's not an option in C#.

The second reason is that it allows the code examples to be better. If exception handling is late in the book, early code samples can't use it, and that means the examples can't be written using good programming practices.

Unfortunately, this means that classes must be used without really introducing them. Read the following section for flavor; the classes will be covered in detail in the next chapter.

What's Wrong with Return Codes?

Most programmers have probably written code that looked like this:

```
bool success = CallFunction();
if (!success)
{
    // process the error
}
```

This works okay, but every return value has to be checked for an error. If the above was written as

```
CallFunction();
```

any error return would be thrown away. That's where bugs come from.

There are many different models for communicating status; some functions may return an `HRESULT`, some may return a Boolean value, and others may use some other mechanism.

In the .NET Runtime world, exceptions are the fundamental method of handling error conditions. Exceptions are nicer than return codes because they can't be silently ignored.

Trying and Catching

To deal with exceptions, code needs to be organized a bit differently. The sections of code that might throw exceptions are placed in a try block, and the code to handle exceptions in the try block is placed in a catch block. Here's an example:

```
using System;
class Test
{
    static int Zero = 0;
    public static void Main()
    {
            // watch for exceptions here
        try
        {
            int j = 22 / Zero;
        }
            // exceptions that occur in try are transferred here
        catch (Exception e)
        {
            Console.WriteLine("Exception " + e.Message);
        }
        Console.WriteLine("After catch");
    }
}
```

The try block encloses an expression that will generate an exception. In this case, it will generate an exception known as DivideByZeroException. When the division takes place, the .NET Runtime stops executing code and searches for a try block surrounding the code in which the exception took place. When it finds a try block, it then looks for associated catch blocks.

If it finds catch blocks, it picks the best one (more on how it determines which one is best in a minute), and executes the code within the catch block. The code in the catch block may process the event or rethrow it.

The example code catches the exception and writes out the message that is contained within the exception object.

The Exception Hierarchy

All C# exceptions derive from the class named Exception, which is part of the Common Language Runtime.[1] When an exception occurs, the proper catch block is

1. This is true of .NET classes in general, but there are some cases where this might not hold true.

determined by matching the type of the exception to the name of the exception mentioned. A `catch` block with an exact match wins out over a more general exception. Returning to the example:

```
using System;
class Test
{
    static int Zero = 0;
    public static void Main()
    {
        try
        {
            int j = 22 / Zero;
        }
            // catch a specific exception
        catch (DivideByZeroException e)
        {
            Console.WriteLine("DivideByZero {0}", e);
        }
            // catch any remaining exceptions
        catch (Exception e)
        {
            Console.WriteLine("Exception {0}", e);
        }
    }
}
```

The `catch` block that catches the `DivideByZeroException` is the more specific match, and is therefore the one that is executed. `catch` blocks always must be listed from most specific to least specific, so in this example, the two blocks couldn't be reversed. [2]

This example is a bit more complex:

```
using System;
class Test
{
    static int Zero = 0;
    static void AFunction()
    {
        int j = 22 / Zero;
            // the following line is never executed.
        Console.WriteLine("In AFunction()");
    }
```

2. More specifically, a clause catching a derived exception cannot be listed after a clause catching a base exception.

```
    public static void Main()
    {
        try
        {
            AFunction();
        }
        catch (DivideByZeroException e)
        {
            Console.WriteLine("DivideByZero {0}", e);
        }
    }
}
```

What happens here?

When the division is executed, an exception is generated. The runtime starts searching for a try block in `AFunction()`, but it doesn't find one, so it jumps out of `AFunction()`, and checks for a try in `Main()`. It finds one, and then looks for a `catch` that matches. The `catch` block then executes.

Sometimes, there won't be any `catch` clauses that match.

```
using System;
class Test
{
    static int Zero = 0;
    static void AFunction()
    {
        try
        {
            int j = 22 / Zero;
        }
            // this exception doesn't match
        catch (ArgumentOutOfRangeException e)
        {
            Console.WriteLine("OutOfRangeException: {0}", e);
        }
        Console.WriteLine("In AFunction()");
    }
    public static void Main()
    {
        try
```

```
        {
            AFunction();
        }
            // this exception doesn't match
        catch (ArgumentException e)
        {
            Console.WriteLine("ArgumentException {0}", e);
        }
    }
}
```

Neither the `catch` block in `AFunction()` nor the `catch` block in `Main()` matches the exception that's thrown. When this happens, the exception is caught by the "last chance" exception handler. The action taken by this handler depends on how the runtime is configured, but it will usually bring up a dialog box containing the exception information and halt the program.

Passing Exceptions on to the Caller

It's sometimes the case that there's not much that can be done when an exception occurs; it really has to be handled by the calling function. There are three basic ways to deal with this, which are named based on their result in the caller: Caller Beware, Caller Confuse, and Caller Inform.

Caller Beware

The first way is to merely not catch the exception. This is sometimes the right design decision, but it could leave the object in an incorrect state, causing problems when the caller tries to use it later. It may also give insufficient information to the caller.

Caller Confuse

The second way is to catch the exception, do some cleanup, and then rethrow the exception:

```
using System;
public class Summer
{
    int     sum = 0;
    int     count = 0;
    float   average;
    public void DoAverage()
```

```
    {
        try
        {
            average = sum / count;
        }
        catch (DivideByZeroException e)
        {
            // do some cleanup here
            throw;
        }
    }
}
class Test
{
    public static void Main()
    {
        Summer summer = new Summer();
        try
        {
            summer.DoAverage();
        }
        catch (Exception e)
        {
            Console.WriteLine("Exception {0}", e);
        }
    }
}
```

This is usually the minimal bar for handling exceptions; an object should always maintain a valid state after an exception.

This is called *Caller Confuse* because while the object is in a valid state after the exception occurs, the caller often has little information to go on. In this case, the exception information says that a `DivideByZeroException` occurred somewhere in the called function, without giving any insight into the details of the exception or how it might be fixed.

Sometimes this is okay if the exception passes back obvious information.

Caller Inform

In *Caller Inform*, additional information is returned for the user. The caught exception is wrapped in an exception that has additional information.

```
using System;
public class Summer
{
    int     sum = 0;
    int     count = 0;
    float   average;
    public void DoAverage()
    {
        try
        {
            average = sum / count;
        }
        catch (DivideByZeroException e)
        {
                // wrap exception in another one,
                // adding additional context.
                throw (new DivideByZeroException(
                    "Count is zero in DoAverage()", e));
        }
    }
}
public class Test
{
    public static void Main()
    {
        Summer summer = new Summer();
        try
        {
            summer.DoAverage();
        }
        catch (Exception e)
        {
            Console.WriteLine("Exception: {0}", e);
        }
    }
}
```

When the `DivideByZeroException` is caught in the `DoAverage()` function, it is wrapped in a new exception that gives the user additional information about what caused the exception. Usually the wrapper exception is the same type as the caught exception, but this might change depending on the model presented to the caller.

This program generates the following output:

```
Exception: System.DivideByZeroException: Count is zero in DoAverage() --->
System.DivideByZeroException
   at Summer.DoAverage()
   at Summer.DoAverage()
   at Test.Main()
```

Ideally, each function that wants to rethrow the exception will wrap it in an exception with additional contextual information.

User-Defined Exception Classes

One drawback of the last example is that the caller can't tell what exception happened in the call to `DoAverage()` by looking at the type of the exception. To know that the exception was because the count was zero, the expression message would have to be searched for the string "`Count is zero`".

That would be pretty bad, since the user wouldn't be able to trust that the text would remain the same in later versions of the class, and the class writer wouldn't be able to change the text. In this case, a new exception class can be created.

```
using System;
public class CountIsZeroException: ApplicationException
{
    public CountIsZeroException()
    {
    }
    public CountIsZeroException(string message)
    : base(message)
    {
    }
    public CountIsZeroException(string message, Exception inner)
    : base(message, inner)
    {
    }
}
public class Summer
{
    int     sum = 0;
    int     count = 0;
    float   average;
    public void DoAverage()
```

```
    {
        if (count == 0)
            throw(new CountIsZeroException("Zero count in DoAverage"));
        else
            average = sum / count;
    }
}
class Test
{
    public static void Main()
    {
        Summer summer = new Summer();
        try
        {
            summer.DoAverage();
        }
        catch (CountIsZeroException e)
        {
            Console.WriteLine("CountIsZeroException: {0}", e);
        }
    }
}
```

`DoAverage()` now determines whether there would be an exception (whether `count` is zero), and if so, creates a `CountIsZeroException` and throws it.

In this example, the `exception` class has three constructors, which is the recommended design pattern. It is important to follow this design pattern, because if the constructor that takes the inner exception is missing, it won't be possible to wrap the exception with the same exception type; it could only be wrapped in something more general. If, in the above example, our caller didn't have that constructor, a caught `CountIsZeroException` couldn't be wrapped in an exception of the same type, and the caller would have to choose between not catching the exception and wrapping it in a less-specific type.

Also notice that the `exception` class is derived from `ApplicationException`, which is the base of application-derived exceptions, and therefore should be used for all exceptions defined in an application.

Finally

Sometimes, when writing a function, there will be some cleanup that needs to be done before the function completes, such as closing a file. If an exception occurs, the cleanup could be skipped:

```
using System;
using System.IO;
class Processor
{
    int    count;
    int    sum;
    public int average;
    void CalculateAverage(int countAdd, int sumAdd)
    {
        count += countAdd;
        sum += sumAdd;
        average = sum / count;
    }
    public void ProcessFile()
    {
        FileStream f = new FileStream("data.txt", FileMode.Open);
        try
        {
            StreamReader t = new StreamReader(f);
            string    line;
            while ((line = t.ReadLine()) != null)
            {
                int count;
                int sum;
                count = Convert.ToInt32(line);
                line = t.ReadLine();
                sum = Convert.ToInt32(line);
                CalculateAverage(count, sum);
            }
                  }
            // always executed before function exit, even if an
            // exception was thrown in the try.
        finally
        {
            f.Close();
        }
    }
}
```

```
class Test
{
    public static void Main()
    {
        Processor processor = new Processor();
        try
        {
            processor.ProcessFile();
        }
        catch (Exception e)
        {
            Console.WriteLine("Exception: {0}", e);
        }
    }
}
```

This example walks through a file, reading a `count` and `sum` from a file and using it to accumulate an average. What happens, however, if the first `count` read from the file is a zero?

If this happens, the division in `CalculateAverage()` will throw a `DivideByZeroException`, which will interrupt the file-reading loop. If the programmer had written the function without thinking about exceptions, the call to `file.Close()` would have been skipped, and the file would have remained open.

The code inside the `finally` block is guaranteed to execute before the exit of the function, whether there is an exception or not. By placing the `file.Close()` call in the `finally` block, the file will always be closed.

Efficiency and Overhead

In languages without garbage collection, adding exception handling is expensive, since all objects within a function must be tracked to make sure that they are properly destroyed at any time that an exception could be thrown. The required tracking code both adds execution time and code size to a function.

In C#, however, objects are tracked by the garbage collector rather than the compiler, so exception handling is very inexpensive to implement and imposes little runtime overhead on the program when the exceptional case doesn't occur.

Design Guidelines

Exceptions should be used to communicate exceptional conditions. Don't use them to communicate events that are expected, such as reaching the end of a file. In normal operation of a class, there should be no exceptions thrown.

Conversely, don't use return values to communicate information that would be better contained in an exception.

If there's a good predefined exception in the `System` namespace that describes the exception condition—one that will make sense to the users of the class—use that one rather than defining a new exception class, and put specific information in the message. If the user might want to differentiate one case from others where that same exception might occur, then that would be a good place for a new exception class.

Finally, if code catches an exception that it isn't going to handle, consider whether it should wrap that exception with additional information before rethrowing it.

CHAPTER 5

Classes 101

CLASSES ARE THE HEART of any application in an object-oriented language. This chapter is broken into several sections. The first section describes the parts of C# that will be used often, and the later sections describe things that won't be used as often, depending on what kind of code is being written.

A Simple Class

A C# class can be very simple:

```
class VerySimple
{
    int    simpleValue = 0;
}
class Test
{
    public static void Main()
    {
        VerySimple vs = new VerySimple();
    }
}
```

This class is a container for a single integer. Because the integer is declared without specifying how accessible it is, it's private to the `VerySimple` class and can't be referenced outside the class. The `private` modifier could be specified to state this explicitly.

The integer `simpleValue` is a member of the class; there can be many different types of members.

In the `Main()` function, the system creates the instance in heap memory and returns a reference to the instance. A reference is simply a way to refer to an instance.[1]

There is no need to specify when an instance is no longer needed. In the preceding example, as soon as the `Main()` function completes, the reference to the instance will no longer exist. If the reference hasn't been stored elsewhere, the instance will

1. For those of you used to pointers, a reference is a pointer that you can only assign to and dereference.

then be available for reclamation by the garbage collector. The garbage collector will reclaim the memory that was allocated when necessary.[2]

This is all very nice, but this class doesn't do anything useful because the integer isn't accessible. Here's a more useful example:[3]

```
using System;
class Point
{
        // constructor
    public Point(int x, int y)
    {
        this.x = x;
        this.y = y;
    }

        // member fields
    public int x;
    public int y;
}

class Test
{
    public static void Main()
    {
        Point myPoint = new Point(10, 15);
        Console.WriteLine("myPoint.x {0}", myPoint.x);
        Console.WriteLine("myPoint.y {0}", myPoint.y);
    }
}
```

In this example, there is a class named `Point`, with two integers in the class named `x` and `y`. These members are public, which means that their values can be accessed by any code that uses the class.

In addition to the data members, there is a constructor for the class, which is a special function that is called to help construct an instance of the class. The constructor takes two integer parameters.

In this constructor, a special variable called `this` is used; the `this` variable is available within all member functions and always refers to the current instance.

In member functions, the compiler searches local variables and parameters for a name before searching instance members. When referring to an instance variable with the same name as a parameter, the `this.<name>` syntax must be used.

---

2. The garbage collector used in the .NET Runtime is discussed in Chapter 36, "Deeper into C#."
3. If you were really going to implement your own point class, you'd probably want it to be a value type (struct) rather than a reference type (class).

In this constructor, `x` by itself refers to the parameter named `x`, and `this.x` refers to the integer member named `x`.

In addition to the `Point` class, there is a `Test` class that contains a `Main` function that is called to start the program. The `Main` function creates an instance of the `Point` class, which will allocate memory for the object and then call the constructor for the class. The constructor will set the values for `x` and `y`.

The remainder of the lines of `Main()` print out the values of `x` and `y`.

In this example, the data fields are accessed directly. This is usually a bad idea, because it means that users of the class depend upon the names of fields, which constrains the modifications that can be made later.

In C#, rather than writing a member function to access a private value, a property would be used, which gives the benefits of a member function while retaining the user model of a field. See Chapter 18, "Properties," for more information.

Member Functions

The constructor in the previous example is an example of a member function; a piece of code that is called on an instance of the object. Constructors can only be called automatically when an instance of an object is created with `new`.

Other member functions can be declared as follows:

```
using System;
class Point
{
    public Point(int x, int y)
    {
        this.x = x;
        this.y = y;
    }

        // accessor functions
    public int GetX() {return(x);}
    public int GetY() {return(y);}

        // variables now private
    int x;
    int y;
}
```

```
class Test
{
    public static void Main()
    {
        Point myPoint = new Point(10, 15);
        Console.WriteLine("myPoint.X {0}", myPoint.GetX());
        Console.WriteLine("myPoint.Y {0}", myPoint.GetY());
    }
}
```

ref and out Parameters

Having to call two member functions to get the values may not always be convenient, so it would be nice to be able to get both values with a single function call. There's only one return value, however.

One solution is to use reference (or `ref`) parameters, so that the values of the parameters passed into the member function can be modified:

```
// error
using System;
class Point
{
    public Point(int x, int y)
    {
        this.x = x;
        this.y = y;
    }
        // get both values in one function call
    public void GetPoint(ref int x, ref int y)
    {
        x = this.x;
        y = this.y;
    }

    int x;
    int y;
}

class Test
{
    public static void Main()
    {
        Point myPoint = new Point(10, 15);
        int    x;
        int     y;
```

```
            // illegal
        myPoint.GetPoint(ref x, ref y);
        Console.WriteLine("myPoint({0}, {1})", x, y);
    }
}
```

In this code, the parameters have been declared using the `ref` keyword, as has the call to the function.

This code should work, but when compiled, it generates an error message that says that uninitialized values were used for the `ref` parameters `x` and `y`. This means that variables were passed into the function before having their values set, and the compiler won't allow the values of uninitialized variables to be exposed.

There are two ways around this. The first is to initialize the variables when they are declared:

```
using System;
class Point
{
    public Point(int x, int y)
    {
        this.x = x;
        this.y = y;
    }

    public void GetPoint(ref int x, ref int y)
    {
        x = this.x;
        y = this.y;
    }

    int x;
    int y;
}

class Test
{
    public static void Main()
    {
        Point myPoint = new Point(10, 15);
        int x = 0;
        int y = 0;

        myPoint.GetPoint(ref x, ref y);
        Console.WriteLine("myPoint({0}, {1})", x, y);
    }
}
```

The code now compiles, but the variables are initialized to zero only to be overwritten in the call to `GetPoint()`. For C#, another option is to change the definition of the function `GetPoint()` to use an `out` parameter rather than a `ref` parameter:

```
using System;
class Point
{
    public Point(int x, int y)
    {
        this.x = x;
        this.y = y;
    }

    public void GetPoint(out int x, out int y)
    {
        x = this.x;
        y = this.y;
    }

    int x;
    int y;
}

class Test
{
    public static void Main()
    {
        Point myPoint = new Point(10, 15);
        int    x;
        int     y;

        myPoint.GetPoint(out x, out y);
        Console.WriteLine("myPoint({0}, {1})", x, y);
    }
}
```

`Out` parameters are exactly like `ref` parameters except that an uninitialized variable can be passed to them, and the call is made with `out` rather than `ref`.[4]

---

4. From the perspective of other .NET languages, there is no difference between `ref` and `out` parameters. A C# program calling this function will see the parameters as `out` parameters, but other languages will see them as `ref` parameters.

Overloading

Sometimes it may be useful to have two functions that do the same thing but take different parameters. This is especially common for constructors, when there may be several ways to create a new instance.

```
class Point
{
        // create a new point from x and y values
    public Point(int x, int y)
    {
        this.x = x;
        this.y = y;
    }
        // create a point from an existing point
    public Point(Point p)
    {
        this.x = p.x;
        this.y = p.y;
    }

    int x;
    int y;
}

class Test
{
    public static void Main()
    {
        Point myPoint = new Point(10, 15);
        Point mySecondPoint = new Point(myPoint);
    }
}
```

The class has two constructors; one that can be called with `x` and `y` values, and one that can be called with another point. The `Main()` function uses both constructors; one to create an instance from an `x` and `y` value, and another to create an instance from an already-existing instance.[5]

When an overloaded function is called, the compiler chooses the proper function by matching the parameters in the call to the parameters declared for the function.

5. This function may look like a C++ copy constructor, but the C# language doesn't use such a concept. A constructor such as this must be called explicitly.

CHAPTER 6

Base Classes and Inheritance

AS DISCUSSED IN CHAPTER 1, "Object-Oriented Basics," it sometimes makes sense to derive one class from another, if the derived class is an example of the base class.

The Engineer Class

The following class implements an `Engineer` and methods to handle billing for that `Engineer`.

```
using System;
class Engineer
{
        // constructor
    public Engineer(string name, float billingRate)
    {
        this.name = name;
        this.billingRate = billingRate;
    }
        // figure out the charge based on engineer's rate
    public float CalculateCharge(float hours)
    {
        return(hours * billingRate);
    }
        // return the name of this type
    public string TypeName()
    {
        return("Engineer");
    }

    private string name;
    protected float billingRate;
}
```

```
class Test
{
    public static void Main()
    {
        Engineer engineer = new Engineer("Hank", 21.20F);
        Console.WriteLine("Name is: {0}", engineer.TypeName());
    }
}
```

`Engineer` will serve as a base class for this scenario. It contains the private field `name`, and the protected field `billingRate`. The `protected` modifier grants the same access as `private`, except that classes that are derived from this class also have access to the field. `Protected` is therefore used to give classes that derive from this class access to a field.

`Protected` access allows other classes to depend upon the internal implementation of the class, and therefore should be granted only when necessary. In the example, the `billingRate` member can't be renamed, since derived classes may access it. It is often a better design choice to use a protected property.

The `Engineer` class also has a member function that can be used to calculate the charge based on the number of hours of work done.

Simple Inheritance

A `CivilEngineer` is a type of engineer, and therefore can be derived from the `Engineer` class:

```
using System;
class Engineer
{
    public Engineer(string name, float billingRate)
    {
        this.name = name;
        this.billingRate = billingRate;
    }

    public float CalculateCharge(float hours)
    {
        return(hours * billingRate);
    }
```

```
    public string TypeName()
    {
        return("Engineer");
    }

    private string name;
    protected float billingRate;
}
class CivilEngineer: Engineer
{
    public CivilEngineer(string name, float billingRate) :
        base(name, billingRate)
    {
    }
        // new function, because it's different than the
        // base version
    public new float CalculateCharge(float hours)
    {
        if (hours < 1.0F)
            hours = 1.0F;        // minimum charge.
        return(hours * billingRate);
    }
        // new function, because it's different than the
        // base version
    public new string TypeName()
    {
        return("Civil Engineer");
    }
}
class Test
{
    public static void Main()
    {
        Engineer    e = new Engineer("George", 15.50F);
        CivilEngineer    c = new CivilEngineer("Sir John", 40F);

        Console.WriteLine("{0} charge = {1}",
                    e.TypeName(),
                    e.CalculateCharge(2F));
        Console.WriteLine("{0} charge = {1}",
                    c.TypeName(),
                    c.CalculateCharge(0.75F));
    }
}
```

Because the `CivilEngineer` class derives from `Engineer`, it inherits all the data members of the class (though the `name` member can't be accessed, because it's private), and it also inherits the `CalculateCharge()` member function.

Constructors can't be inherited, so a separate one is written for `CivilEngineer`. The constructor doesn't have anything special to do, so it calls the constructor for `Engineer`, using the `base` syntax. If the call to the `base` class constructor was omitted, the compiler would call the base class constructor with no parameters.

`CivilEngineer` has a different way to calculate charges; the minimum charge is for 1 hour of time, so there's a new version of `CalculateCharge()`.

The example, when run, yields the following output:

```
Engineer Charge = 31
Civil Engineer Charge = 40
```

Arrays of Engineers

This works fine in the early years, when there are only a few employees. As the company grows, it's easier to deal with an array of engineers.

Because `CivilEngineer` is derived from `Engineer`, an array of type `Engineer` can hold either type. This example has a different `Main()` function, putting the engineers into an array:

```
using System;
class Engineer
{
    public Engineer(string name, float billingRate)
    {
        this.name = name;
        this.billingRate = billingRate;
    }

    public float CalculateCharge(float hours)
    {
        return(hours * billingRate);
    }

    public string TypeName()
    {
        return("Engineer");
    }
```

```
    private string name;
    protected float billingRate;
}
class CivilEngineer: Engineer
{
    public CivilEngineer(string name, float billingRate) :
        base(name, billingRate)
    {
    }

    public new float CalculateCharge(float hours)
    {
        if (hours < 1.0F)
            hours = 1.0F;         // minimum charge.
        return(hours * billingRate);
    }

    public new string TypeName()
    {
        return("Civil Engineer");
    }
}
class Test
{
    public static void Main()
    {
            // create an array of engineers
        Engineer[] earray = new Engineer[2];
        earray[0] = new Engineer("George", 15.50F);
        earray[1] = new CivilEngineer("Sir John", 40F);

        Console.WriteLine("{0} charge = {1}",
                    earray[0].TypeName(),
                    earray[0].CalculateCharge(2F));
        Console.WriteLine("{0} charge = {1}",
                    earray[1].TypeName(),
                    earray[1].CalculateCharge(0.75F));
    }
}
```

This version yields the following output:

```
Engineer Charge = 31
Engineer Charge = 30
```

That's not right.

Because `CivilEngineer` is derived from Engineer, an instance of `CivilEngineer` can be used wherever an instance of Engineer is required.

When the engineers were placed into the array, the fact that the second engineer was really a `CivilEngineer` rather than an `Engineer` was lost. Because the array is an array of `Engineer`, when `CalculateCharge()` is called, the version from `Engineer` is called.

What is needed is a way to correctly identify the type of an engineer. This can be done by having a field in the `Engineer` class that denotes what type it is. Rewriting the classes with an `enum` field to denote the type of the engineer gives the following example:

```
using System;
enum EngineerTypeEnum
{
    Engineer,
    CivilEngineer
}
class Engineer
{
    public Engineer(string name, float billingRate)
    {
        this.name = name;
        this.billingRate = billingRate;
        type = EngineerTypeEnum.Engineer;
    }

    public float CalculateCharge(float hours)
    {
        if (type == EngineerTypeEnum.CivilEngineer)
        {
            CivilEngineer c = (CivilEngineer) this;
            return(c.CalculateCharge(hours));
        }
        else if (type == EngineerTypeEnum.Engineer)
            return(hours * billingRate);
        return(0F);
    }

    public string TypeName()
    {
        if (type == EngineerTypeEnum.CivilEngineer)
        {
            CivilEngineer c = (CivilEngineer) this;
            return(c.TypeName());
        }
```

```
        else if (type == EngineerTypeEnum.Engineer)
            return("Engineer");
        return("No Type Matched");
    }

    private string name;
    protected float billingRate;
    protected EngineerTypeEnum type;
}

class CivilEngineer: Engineer
{
    public CivilEngineer(string name, float billingRate) :
        base(name, billingRate)
    {
        type = EngineerTypeEnum.CivilEngineer;
    }

    public new float CalculateCharge(float hours)
    {
        if (hours < 1.0F)
            hours = 1.0F;        // minimum charge.
        return(hours * billingRate);
    }

    public new string TypeName()
    {
        return("Civil Engineer");
    }
}
class Test
{
    public static void Main()
    {
        Engineer[] earray = new Engineer[2];
        earray[0] = new Engineer("George", 15.50F);
        earray[1] = new CivilEngineer("Sir John", 40F);

        Console.WriteLine("{0} charge = {1}",
                    earray[0].TypeName(),
                    earray[0].CalculateCharge(2F));
        Console.WriteLine("{0} charge = {1}",
                    earray[1].TypeName(),
                    earray[1].CalculateCharge(0.75F));
    }
}
```

By looking at the `type` field, the functions in `Engineer` can determine the real type of the object and call the appropriate function.

The output of the code is as expected:

```
Engineer Charge = 31
Civil Engineer Charge = 40
```

Unfortunately, the base class has now become much more complicated; for every function that cares about the type of a class, there is code to check all the possible types and call the correct function. That's a lot of extra code, and it would be untenable if there were 50 kinds of engineers.

Worse is the fact that the base class needs to know the names of all the derived classes for it to work. If the owner of the code needs to add support for a new engineer, the base class must be modified. If a user who doesn't have access to the base class needs to add a new type of engineer, it won't work at all.

Virtual Functions

To make this work cleanly, object-oriented languages allow a function to be specified as virtual. Virtual means that when a call to a member function is made, the compiler should look at the real type of the object (not just the type of the reference), and call the appropriate function based on that type.

With that in mind, the example can be modified as follows:

```
using System;
class Engineer
{
    public Engineer(string name, float billingRate)
    {
        this.name = name;
        this.billingRate = billingRate;
    }
        // function now virtual
    virtual public float CalculateCharge(float hours)
    {
        return(hours * billingRate);
    }
        // function now virtual
    virtual public string TypeName()
    {
        return("Engineer");
    }
```

```
    private string name;
    protected float billingRate;
}

class CivilEngineer: Engineer
{
    public CivilEngineer(string name, float billingRate) :
        base(name, billingRate)
    {
    }
        // overrides function in Engineer
    override public float CalculateCharge(float hours)
    {
        if (hours < 1.0F)
            hours = 1.0F;        // minimum charge.
        return(hours * billingRate);
    }
        // overrides function in Engineer
    override public string TypeName()
    {
        return("Civil Engineer");
    }
}
class Test
{
    public static void Main()
    {
        Engineer[] earray = new Engineer[2];
        earray[0] = new Engineer("George", 15.50F);
        earray[1] = new CivilEngineer("Sir John", 40F);

        Console.WriteLine("{0} charge = {1}",
                    earray[0].TypeName(),
                    earray[0].CalculateCharge(2F));
        Console.WriteLine("{0} charge = {1}",
                    earray[1].TypeName(),
                    earray[1].CalculateCharge(0.75F));
    }
}
```

The `CalculateCharge()` and `TypeName()` functions are now declared with the virtual keyword in the base class, and that's all that the base class has to know. It needs no knowledge of the derived types, other than to know that each derived class can override `CalculateCharge()` and `TypeName()`, if desired. In the derived class, the functions are declared with the `override` keyword, which means that they are the same function that was declared in the base class. If the `override` keyword is missing, the compiler will assume that the function is unrelated to the base class's function, and virtual dispatching won't function.[1]

Running this example leads to the expected output:

```
Engineer Charge = 31
Civil Engineer Charge = 40
```

When the compiler encounters a call to `TypeName()` or `CalculateCharge()`, it goes to the definition of the function and notes that it is a virtual function. Instead of generating code to call the function directly, it writes a bit of dispatch code that at runtime will look at the real type of the object, and call the function associated with the real type, rather than just the type of the reference. This allows the correct function to be called even if the class wasn't implemented when the caller was compiled.

For example, if there was payroll processing code that stored an array of `Engineer`, a new class derived from `Engineer` could be added to the system without having to modify or recompile the payroll code.

There is a small amount of overhead with the virtual dispatch, so it shouldn't be used unless needed. A JIT could, however, notice that there were no derived classes from the class on which the function call was made, and convert the virtual dispatch to a straight call.

Abstract Classes

There is a small problem with the approach used so far. A new class doesn't have to implement the `TypeName()` function, since it can inherit the implementation from `Engineer`. This makes it easy for a new class of engineer to have the wrong name associated with it.

If the `ChemicalEngineer` class is added, for example:

```
using System;
class Engineer
{
    public Engineer(string name, float billingRate)
    {
        this.name = name;
        this.billingRate = billingRate;
    }
```

1. For a discussion of why this works this way, see Chapter 11, "Versioning."

```
    virtual public float CalculateCharge(float hours)
    {
        return(hours * billingRate);
    }

    virtual public string TypeName()
    {
        return("Engineer");
    }

    private string name;
    protected float billingRate;
}
class ChemicalEngineer: Engineer
{
    public ChemicalEngineer(string name, float billingRate) :
        base(name, billingRate)
    {
    }

    // overrides mistakenly omitted
}
class Test
{
    public static void Main()
    {
        Engineer[] earray = new Engineer[2];
        earray[0] = new Engineer("George", 15.50F);
        earray[1] = new ChemicalEngineer("Dr. Curie", 45.50F);

        Console.WriteLine("{0} charge = {1}",
                    earray[0].TypeName(),
                    earray[0].CalculateCharge(2F));
        Console.WriteLine("{0} charge = {1}",
                    earray[1].TypeName(),
                    earray[1].CalculateCharge(0.75F));
    }
}
```

The `ChemicalEngineer` class will inherit the `CalculateCharge()` function from `Engineer`, which might be correct, but it will also inherit `TypeName()`, which is definitely wrong. What is needed is a way to force `ChemicalEngineer` to implement `TypeName()`.

This can be done by changing `Engineer` from a normal class to an abstract class. In this abstract class, the `TypeName()` member function is marked as an abstract function, which means that all classes that derive from `Engineer` will be required to implement the `TypeName()` function.

An abstract class defines a contract that derived classes are expected to follow.[2] Because an abstract class is missing "required" functionality, it can't be instantiated, which for the example means that instances of the `Engineer class` cannot be created. So that there are still two distinct types of engineers, the `ChemicalEngineer class` has been added.

Abstract classes behave like normal classes except for one or more member functions that are marked as abstract.

```
using System;
abstract class Engineer
{
    public Engineer(string name, float billingRate)
    {
        this.name = name;
        this.billingRate = billingRate;
    }

    virtual public float CalculateCharge(float hours)
    {
        return(hours * billingRate);
    }

    abstract public string TypeName();

    private string name;
    protected float billingRate;
}

class CivilEngineer: Engineer
{
    public CivilEngineer(string name, float billingRate) :
        base(name, billingRate)
    {
    }
```

2. A similar effect can be achieved by using interfaces. See Chapter 10, "Interfaces," for a comparison of the two techniques.

```
    override public float CalculateCharge(float hours)
    {
        if (hours < 1.0F)
            hours = 1.0F;         // minimum charge.
        return(hours * billingRate);
    }
        // This override is required, or an error is generated.
    override public string TypeName()
    {
        return("Civil Engineer");
    }
}

class ChemicalEngineer: Engineer
{
    public ChemicalEngineer(string name, float billingRate) :
        base(name, billingRate)
    {
    }

    override public string TypeName()
    {
        return("Chemical Engineer");
    }
}
class Test
{
    public static void Main()
    {
        Engineer[] earray = new Engineer[2];
        earray[0] = new CivilEngineer("Sir John", 40.0F);
        earray[1] = new ChemicalEngineer("Dr. Curie", 45.0F);

        Console.WriteLine("{0} charge = {1}",
                    earray[0].TypeName(),
                    earray[0].CalculateCharge(2F));
        Console.WriteLine("{0} charge = {1}",
                    earray[1].TypeName(),
                    earray[1].CalculateCharge(0.75F));
    }
}
```

The `Engineer` class has changed by the addition of `abstract` before the class, which indicates that the class is abstract (i.e., has one or more abstract functions), and the addition of `abstract` before the `TypeName()` virtual function. The use of `abstract` on the virtual function is the important one; the one before the name of the class makes it clear that the class is abstract, since the abstract function could easily be buried amongst the other functions.

The implementation of `CivilEngineer` is identical, except that now the compiler will check to make sure that `TypeName()` is implemented by both `CivilEngineer` and `ChemicalEngineer`.

Sealed Classes and Methods

Sealed classes are used to prevent a class from being used as a base class. It is primarily useful to prevent unintended derivation.

```
// error
sealed class MyClass
{
    MyClass() {}
}
class MyNewClass : MyClass
{
}
```

This fails because `MyNewClass` can't use `MyClass` as a base class because `MyClass` is sealed.

Sealed classes are useful in cases where a class isn't designed with derivation in mind, or where derivation could cause the class to break. The `System.String` class is sealed because there are strict requirements that define how the internal structure must operate, and a derived class could easily break those rules.

A sealed method lets a class override a virtual function and prevents a derived class from overriding that same function. In other words, having sealed on a virtual method stops virtual dispatching. This is rarely useful, so sealed methods are rare.

CHAPTER 7

Member Accessibility and Overloading

ONE OF THE IMPORTANT DECISIONS to make when designing an object is how accessible to make the members. In C#, accessibility can be controlled in several ways.

Class Accessibility

The coarsest level at which accessibility can be controlled is at the class. In most cases, the only valid modifiers on a class are `public`, which means that everybody can see the class, and `internal`. The exception to this is nesting classes inside of other classes, which is a bit more complicated and is covered in Chapter 8, "Other Class Details."

`Internal` is a way of granting access to a wider set of classes without granting access to everybody, and it is most often used when writing helper classes that should be hidden from the ultimate user of the class. In the .NET Runtime world, `internal` equates to allowing access to all classes that are in the same assembly as this class.

> **NOTE** *In the C++ world, such accessibility is usually granted by the use of friends, which provide access to a specific class.* `Friend` *provides greater granularity in specifying who can access a class, but in practice the access provided by* `internal` *is sufficient.*

In general, all classes should be `internal` unless users need to be able to access them.

Using Internal on Members

The `internal` modifier can also be used on a member, which then allows that member to be accessible from classes in the same assembly as itself, but not from classes outside the assembly.

This is especially useful when several public classes need to cooperate, but some of the shared members shouldn't be exposed to the general public. Consider the following example:

```
public class DrawingObjectGroup
{
    public DrawingObjectGroup()
    {
        objects = new DrawingObject[10];
        objectCount = 0;
    }
    public void AddObject(DrawingObject obj)
    {
        if (objectCount < 10)
        {
            objects[objectCount] = obj;
            objectCount++;
        }
    }
    public void Render()
    {
        for (int i = 0; i < objectCount; i++)
        {
            objects[i].Render();
        }
    }

    DrawingObject[]    objects;
    int              objectCount;
}
public class DrawingObject
{
    internal void Render() {}
}
class Test
{
    public static void Main()
    {
        DrawingObjectGroup group = new DrawingObjectGroup();
        group.AddObject(new DrawingObject());
    }
}
```

Here, the `DrawingObjectGroup` object holds up to 10 drawing objects. It's valid for the user to have a reference to a `DrawingObject`, but it would be invalid for the user to call `Render()` for that object, so this is prevented by making the `Render()` function internal.

> **TIP** *This code doesn't make sense in a real program. The .NET Common Language Runtime has a number of collection classes that would make this sort of code much more straightforward and less error-prone.*

internal protected

To provide some extra flexibility in how a class is defined, the `internal protected` modifier can be used to indicate that a member can be accessed from either a class that could access it through the `internal` access path or a class that could access it through a `protected` access path. In other words, `internal protected` allows `internal` or `protected` access.

Note that there is no way to specify `internal` and `protected` in C#, though an internal class with a protected member will provide that level of access.

The Interaction of Class and Member Accessibility

Class and member accessibility modifiers must both be satisfied for a member to be accessible. The accessibility of members is limited by the class so that it does not exceed the accessibility of the class.

Consider the following situation:

```
internal class MyHelperClass
{
    public void PublicFunction() {}
    internal void InternalFunction() {}
    protected void ProtectedFunction() {}
}
```

If this class were declared as a public class, the accessibility of the members would be the same as the stated accessibility; i.e., `PublicFunction()` would be public, `InternalFunction()` would be internal, and `ProtectedFunction()` would be protected.

Because the class is internal, however, the `public` on `PublicFunction()` is reduced to `internal`.

Method Overloading

When there are several overloaded methods for a single named function, the C# compiler uses method overloading rules to determine which function to call.

In general, the rules are fairly straightforward, but the details can be somewhat complicated. Here's a simple example:

```
Console.WriteLine("Ummagumma");
```

To resolve this, the compiler will look at the `Console` class and find all methods that take a single parameter. It will then compare the type of the argument (`string` in this case) with the type of the parameter for each method, and if it finds a single match, that's the function to call. If it finds no matches, a compile-time error is generated. If it finds more than one match, things are a bit more complicated (see the "Better Conversions" section).

For an argument to match a parameter, it must fit one of the following cases:

- The argument type and the parameter type are the same type.
- An implicit conversion exists from the argument type to the parameter type *and* the argument is not passed using `ref` or `out`.

Note that in the previous description, the return type of a function is not mentioned. That's because for C#—and for the .NET Common Language Runtime—overloading based on return type is not allowed.[1] Additionally, because `out` is a C#-only construct (it looks like `ref` to other languages), there cannot be a `ref` overload and an `out` overload that differ only in their `ref` and `out`ness. There can, however, be a `ref` or `out` overload and a pass by value overload.

Method Hiding

When determining the set of methods to consider, the compiler will walk up the inheritance tree until it finds a method that is applicable and then perform overload resolution at that level in the inheritance hierarchy only; it will not consider functions declared at different levels of the hierarchy. Consider the following example:

1. In other words, C++ covariant return types are not supported.

```
using System;
public class Base
{
    public void Process(short value)
    {
        Console.WriteLine("Base.Process(short): {0}", value);
    }
}
public class Derived: Base
{
    public void Process(int value)
    {
        Console.WriteLine("Derived.Process(int): {0}", value);
    }

    public void Process(string value)
    {
        Console.WriteLine("Derived.Process(string): {0}", value);
    }
}
class Test
{
    public static void Main()
    {
        Derived d = new Derived();
        short i = 12;
        d.Process(i);
        ((Base) d).Process(i);
    }
}
```

This example generates the following output:

```
Derived.Process(int): 12
Base.Process(short): 12
```

A quick look at this code might lead one to suspect that the `d.Process(i)` call would call the base class function because that version takes a `short`, which matches exactly. But according to the rules, once the compiler has determined that `Derived.Process(int)` is a match, it doesn't look any further up the hierarchy; therefore, `Derived.Process(int)` is the function called.

To call the base class function requires an explicit cast to the base class because the derived function hides the base class version.

Better Conversions

In some situations there are multiple matches based on the simple rule mentioned previously. When this happens, a few rules determine which situation is considered better, and if there is a single one that is better than all the others, it is the one called.[2]

The three rules are as follows:

1. An exact match of type is preferred over one that requires a conversion.

2. If an implicit conversion exists from one type to another, and there is no implicit conversion the other direction, the type that has the implicit conversion is preferred.

3. If the argument is a signed integer type, a conversion to another signed integer type is preferred over one to an unsigned integer type.

Rules 1 and 3 don't require a lot of explanation. Rule 2, however, seems a bit more complex. An example should make it clearer:

```
using System;
public class MyClass
{
    public void Process(long value)
    {
        Console.WriteLine("Process(long): {0}", value);
    }
    public void Process(short value)
    {
        Console.WriteLine("Process(short): {0}", value);
    }
}

class Test
{
    public static void Main()
    {
        MyClass myClass = new MyClass();

        int i = 12;
        myClass.Process(i);
```

2. The rules for this are detailed in section 7.4.2.3 of the C# Language Reference.

```
        sbyte s = 12;
        myClass.Process(s);
    }
}
```

This example generates the following output:

```
Process(long): 12
Process(short): 12
```

In the first call to `Process()`, an `int` is passed as an argument. This matches the `long` version of the function because there's an implicit conversion from `int` to `long` and no implicit conversion from `int` to `short`.

In the second call, however, there are implicit conversions from `sbyte` to `short` or `long`. In this case, the second rule applies. There is an implicit conversion from `short` to `long`, and there isn't one from `long` to `short`; therefore, the version that takes a `short` is preferred.

Variable-Length Parameter Lists

It is sometimes useful to define a parameter to take a variable number of parameters (`Console.WriteLine()` is a good example). C# allows such support to be easily added:

```
using System;
class Port
{
        // version with a single object parameter
    public void Write(string label, object arg)
    {
        WriteString(label);
        WriteString(arg.ToString());
    }
        // version with an array of object parameters
    public void Write(string label, params object[] args)
    {
        WriteString(label);
        foreach (object o in args)
        {
            WriteString(o.ToString());
        }
    }
    void WriteString(string str)
    {
```

```
            // writes string to the port here
            Console.WriteLine("Port debug: {0}", str);
        }
    }

    class Test
    {
        public static void Main()
        {
            Port    port = new Port();
            port.Write("Single Test", "Port ok");
            port.Write("Port Test: ", "a", "b", 12, 14.2);
            object[] arr = new object[4];
            arr[0] = "The";
            arr[1] = "answer";
            arr[2] = "is";
            arr[3] = 42;
            port.Write("What is the answer?", arr);
        }
    }
```

The `params` keyword on the last parameter changes the way the compiler looks up functions. When it encounters a call to that function, it first checks to see if there is an exact match for the function. The first function call matches:

```
public void Write(string, object arg)
```

Similarly, the third function passes an object array, and it matches:

```
public void Write(string label, params object[] args)
```

Things get interesting for the second call. The definition with the object parameter doesn't match, but neither does the one with the object array.

When both of these matches fail, the compiler notices that the `params` keyword is present, and it then tries to match the parameter list by removing the array part of the `params` parameter and duplicating that parameter until there are the same number of parameters.

If this results in a function that matches, it then writes the code to create the object array. In other words, the line

```
port.Write("Port Test: ", "a", "b", 12, 14.2);
```

is rewritten as

```
object[] temp = new object[4];
temp[0] = "a";
temp[1] = "b";
temp[2] = 12;
temp[3] = 14.2;
port.Write("Port Test: ", temp);
```

In this example, the `params` parameter was an `object` array, but it can be an array of any type.

In addition to the version that takes the array, it usually makes sense to provide one or more specific versions of the function. This is useful both for efficiency (so the object array doesn't have to be created) and so languages that don't support the params syntax don't have to use the object array for all calls. Overloading a function with versions that take one, two, and three parameters, plus a version that takes an array, is a good rule of thumb.

CHAPTER 8

Other Class Details

THIS CHAPTER DISCUSSES some of the miscellaneous issues of classes, including constructors, nesting, and overloading rules.

Nested Classes

Sometimes, it is convenient to nest classes within other classes, such as when a helper class is used by only one other class. The accessibility of the nested class follows similar rules to the ones outlined for the interaction of class and member modifiers. As with members, the accessibility modifier on a nested class defines what accessibility the nested class has outside of the nested class. Just as a private field is visible only within a class, a private nested class is also visible only from within the class that contains it.

In the following example, the `Parser` class has a `Token` class that it uses internally. Without using a nested class, it might be written as follows:

```
public class Parser
{
    Token[]    tokens;
}
public class Token
{
    string name;
}
```

In this example, both the `Parser` and `Token` classes are publicly accessible, which isn't optimal. Not only is the `Token` class one more class taking up space in the designers that list classes, but it isn't designed to be generally useful. It's therefore helpful to make `Token` a nested class, which will allow it to be declared with `private` accessibility, hiding it from all classes except `Parser`.

Here's the revised code:

```
public class Parser
{
    Token[]    tokens;
    private class Token
    {
        string name;
    }
}
```

Now, nobody else can see Token. Another option would be to make Token an internal class so that it wouldn't be visible outside the assembly, but with that solution, it would still be visible inside the assembly.

Making Token an internal class also misses out on an important benefit of using a nested class. A nested class makes it very clear to those reading the source code that the Token class can safely be ignored unless the internals for Parser are important. If this organization is applied across an entire assembly, it can help simplify the code considerably.

Nesting can also be used as an organizational feature. If the Parser class were within a namespace named Language, you might require a separate namespace named Parser to nicely organize the classes for Parser. The Parser namespace would contain the Token class and a renamed Parser class. By using nested classes, the Parser class could be left in the Language namespace and contain the Token class.

Other Nesting

Classes aren't the only types that can be nested; interfaces, structs, delegates, and enums can also be nested within a class.

Creation, Initialization, Destruction

In any object-oriented system, dealing with the creation, initialization, and destruction of objects is very important. In the .NET Runtime, the programmer can't control the destruction of objects, but it's helpful to know the other areas that can be controlled.

Constructors

If there is no default constructor, the C# compiler will create a public parameterless constructor.

A constructor can invoke a constructor of the base type by using the `base` syntax, like this:

```
using System;
public class BaseClass
{
    public BaseClass(int x)
    {
        this.x = x;
    }
    public int X
    {
        get
        {
            return(x);
        }
    }
    int    x;
}
public class Derived: BaseClass
{
    public Derived(int x): base(x)
    {
    }
}
class Test
{
    public static void Main()
    {
        Derived d = new Derived(15);
        Console.WriteLine("X = {0}", d.X);
    }
}
```

In this example, the constructor for the `Derived` class merely forwards the construction of the object to the `BaseClass` constructor.

Sometimes it's useful for a constructor to forward to another constructor in the same object, as in the following example:

```
using System;
class MyObject
{
    public MyObject(int x)
    {
        this.x = x;
    }
    public MyObject(int x, int y): this(x)
    {
        this.y = y;
    }
    public int X
    {
        get
        {
            return(x);
        }
    }
    public int Y
    {
        get
        {
            return(y);
        }
    }
    int x;
    int y;
}
class Test
{
    public static void Main()
    {
        MyObject my = new MyObject(10, 20);
        Console.WriteLine("x = {0}, y = {1}", my.X, my.Y);
    }
}
```

Private Constructors

Private constructors are—not surprisingly—only usable from within the class on which they're declared. If the only constructor on the class is private, this prevents any user from instantiating an instance of the class, which is useful for classes that are merely containers of static functions (such as `System.Math`, for example).

Private constructors are also used to implement the singleton pattern, when there should only be a single instance of a class within a program. This is usually done as follows:

```
public class SystemInfo
{
    static SystemInfo cache = null;
    static object cacheLock = new object();
    private SystemInfo()
    {
        // useful stuff here...
    }

    public static SystemInfo GetSystemInfo()
    {
        lock(cacheLock)
        {
            if (cache == null)
                cache = new SystemInfo();

            return(cache);
        }
    }
}
```

This example uses locking to make sure the code works correctly in a multi-threaded environment. For more information on locking, see Chapter 29, "Threading and Asynchronous Operations."

Initialization

If the default value of the field isn't what is desired, it can be set in the constructor. If there are multiple constructors for the object, it may be more convenient—and less error-prone—to set the value through an initializer rather than setting it in every constructor.

Here's an example of how initialization works:

```
public class Parser        // Support class
{
    public Parser(int number)
    {
        this.number = number;
    }
    int number;
}
class MyClass
{
    public int counter = 100;
    public string heading = "Top";
    private Parser parser = new Parser(100);
}
```

This is pretty convenient; the initial values can be set when a member is declared. It also makes class maintenance easier since it's clearer what the initial value of a member is.

To implement this, the compiler adds code to initialize these functions to the beginning of every constructor.

> **TIP** *As a general rule, if a member has differing values depending on the constructor used, the field value should be set in the constructor. If the value is set in the initializer, it may not be clear that the member may have a different value after a constructor call.*

Destructors

Strictly speaking, C# doesn't have destructors, at least not in the way that most developers think of destructors, where the destructor is called when the object is deleted.

What is known as a "destructor" in C# is known as a "finalizer" in some other languages and is called by the garbage collector when an object is collected. The programmer doesn't have direct control over when the destructor is called, and it is therefore less useful than in languages such as C++. If cleanup is done in a destructor, there should also be another method that performs the same operation so that the user can control the process directly.

When a destructor is written in C#, the compiler will automatically add a call to the base class's finalizer (if present).

For more information on this, see the section on garbage collection in Chapter 36, "Deeper into C#." If garbage collection is new to you, you'll probably want to read that chapter before delving into the following section.

Managing Non-Memory Resources

The garbage collector does a good job of managing memory resources, but it doesn't know anything about other resources, such as database handles, graphics handles, and so on. Because of this, classes that hold such resources will have to do the management themselves.

In many cases, this isn't a real problem; all that it takes is writing a destructor for the class that cleans up the resource:

```
using System;
using System.Runtime.InteropServices;

class ResourceWrapper
{
    int handle = 0;

    public ResourceWrapper()
    {
        handle = GetWindowsResource();
    }

    ~ResourceWrapper()
    {
        FreeWindowsResource(handle);
        handle = 0;
    }

    [DllImport("dll.dll")]
    static extern int GetWindowsResource();

    [DllImport("dll.dll")]
    static extern void FreeWindowsResource(int handle);
}
```

Some resources, however, are scarce and need to be cleaned up in a more timely manner than the next time a garbage collection occurs. Since there's no way to call finalizers automatically when an object is no longer needed,[1] it needs to be done manually.

In the .NET Frameworks, objects can indicate that they hold on to such resources by implementing the `IDisposable` interface, which has a single member named `Dispose()`. This member does the same cleanup as the finalizer, but it also needs to do some additional work. If either its base class or any of the other resources it holds implement `IDisposable`, it needs to call `Dispose()` on them so that they also get cleaned up at this time.[2] After it does this, it calls `GC.SuppressFinalize()` so that the garbage collector won't bother to finalize this object. Here's the modified code:

```
using System;
using System.Runtime.InteropServices;

class ResourceWrapper: IDisposable
{
    int handle = 0;

    public ResourceWrapper()
    {
        handle = GetWindowsResource();
    }

        // does cleanup for this object only
    void DoDispose()
    {
        FreeWindowsResource(handle);
        handle = 0;
    }

    ~ResourceWrapper()
    {
        DoDispose();
    }
```

1. The discussion why this isn't possible is long and involved. In summary, lots of really smart people tried to make it work and couldn't.
2. This is different from the finalizer. Finalizers are only responsible for their own resources, while dispose also deals with referenced resources.

```
        // dispose cleans up its object, and any objects it holds
        // that also implement IDisposable.
    public void Dispose()
    {
        DoDispose();
        // call Dispose() on our base class (if necessary), and
        // on any other resources we hold that implement IDisposable

        GC.SuppressFinalize(this);
    }

    [DllImport("dll.dll")]
    static extern int GetWindowsResource();

    [DllImport("dll.dll")]
    static extern void FreeWindowsResource(int handle);
}
```

If your object has semantics where another name is more appropriate than `Dispose()` (a file would have `Close()`, for example), then you should implement `IDisposable` using explicit interface implementation. You would then have the better-named function forward to `Dispose()`.

IDisposable and the Using Statement

When using classes that implement `IDisposable`, it's important to make sure `Dispose()` gets called at the appropriate time. When a class is used locally, this is easily done by wrapping the usage in `try-finally`, like in this example:

```
ResourceWrapper rw = new ResourceWrapper();
try
{
    // use rw here
}
finally
{
    if (rw != null)
        ((IDisposable) rw).Dispose();
}
```

The cast of the rw to IDisposable is required because ResourceWrapper could have implemented Dispose() with explicit interface implementation.[3] The try-finally is a bit ugly to write and remember, so C# provides the using statement to simplify the code, like this:

```
using (ResourceWrapper rw = new ResourceWrapper())
{
    // use rw here
}
```

If two or more instances of a single class are used, the using statement can be written as:

```
using (ResourceWrapper rw = new ResourceWrapper(), rw2 = new ResourceWrapper())
```

For different classes, two using statements can be placed next to each other:

```
using (ResourceWrapper rw = new ResourceWrapper())
using (FileWrapper fw = new FileWrapper())
```

In either case, the compiler will generate the appropriate nested try-finally blocks.

IDisposable and Longer-Lived Objects

The using statement provides a nice way to deal with objects that are only around for a single function. For longer-lived objects, however, there's no automatic way to make sure Dispose() is called.

It's fairly easy to track this through the finalizer, however. If it's important that Dispose() is always called, it's possible to add some error checking to the finalizer to track any such cases. This could be done with a few changes to the ResourceWrapper class:

```
    static int finalizeCount = 0;
    ~ResourceWrapper()
    {
        finalizeCount++;
        DoDispose();
    }

    [Conditional("DEBUG")]
```

3. See Chapter 10, "Interfaces."

```
static void CheckDisposeUsage(string location)
{
    GC.Collect();
    GC.WaitForPendingFinalizers();
    if (finalizeCount != 0)
    {
        finalizeCount = 0;
        throw new Exception("ResourceWrapper(" + location +
        ": Dispose()=" + finalizeCount);
    }
}
```

The finalizer increments a counter whenever it is called, and the `CheckDebugUsage()` routine first makes sure that all objects are finalized and then checks to see if there were any finalizations since the last check. If so, it throws an exception.[4]

Static Fields

It is sometimes useful to define members of an object that aren't associated with a specific instance of the class but rather with the class as a whole. Such members are known as `static` members.

A static field is the simplest type of static member; to declare a static field, simply place the `static` modifier in front of the variable declaration. For example, the following could be used to track the number of instances of a class that were created:

```
using System;
class MyClass
{
    public MyClass()
    {
        instanceCount++;
    }
    public static int instanceCount = 0;
}
```

4. It might make more sense to log this to a file, depending on the application.

```
class Test
{
    public static void Main()
    {
        MyClass my = new MyClass();
        Console.WriteLine(MyClass.instanceCount);
        MyClass my2 = new MyClass();
        Console.WriteLine(MyClass.instanceCount);
    }
}
```

The constructor for the object increments the instance count, and the instance count can be referenced to determine how many instances of the object have been created. A static field is accessed through the name of the class rather than through the instance of the class; this is true for all static members.

> **NOTE** *This is unlike the C++ behavior where a static member can be accessed through either the class name or the instance name. In C++, this leads to some readability problems, as it's sometimes not clear from the code whether an access is static or through an instance.*

Static Member Functions

The previous example exposes an internal field, which is usually something to be avoided. It can be restructured to use a static member function instead of a static field, like in the following example:

```
using System;
class MyClass
{
    public MyClass()
    {
        instanceCount++;
    }
    public static int GetInstanceCount()
    {
        return(instanceCount);
    }
    static int instanceCount = 0;
}
```

```
class Test
{
    public static void Main()
    {
        MyClass my = new MyClass();
        Console.WriteLine(MyClass.GetInstanceCount());
    }
}
```

This now uses a static member function and no longer exposes the field to users of the class, which increases future flexibility. Because it is a static member function, it is called using the name of the class rather than the name of an instance of the class.

In the real world, this example would probably be better written using a static property, which is discussed Chapter 18, "Properties."

Static Constructors

Just as there can be other static members, there can also be static constructors. A static constructor will be called before the first instance of an object is created. It is useful to do setup work that needs to be done only once.

> **NOTE** *Like a lot of other things in the .NET Runtime world, the user has no control over when the static constructor is called; the runtime only guarantees it is called sometime after the start of the program and before the first instance of an object is created. Therefore, it can't be determined in the static constructor that an instance is about to be created.*

A static constructor is declared simply by adding the `static` modifier in front of the constructor definition. A static constructor cannot have any parameters:

```
using System;
class MyClass
{
    static MyClass()
    {
        Console.WriteLine("MyClass is initializing");
    }
}
```

There is no static analog of a destructor.

Constants

C# allows values to be defined as constants. For a value to be a constant, its value must be something that can be written as a constant. This limits the types of constants to the built-in types that can be written as literal values.

Not surprisingly, putting `const` in front of a variable means that its value cannot be changed. Here's an example of some constants:

```
using System;
enum MyEnum
{
    Jet
}
class LotsOLiterals
{
        // const items can't be changed.
        // const implies static.
    public const int value1 = 33;
    public const string value2 = "Hello";
    public const MyEnum value3 = MyEnum.Jet;
}
class Test
{
    public static void Main()
    {
        Console.WriteLine("{0} {1} {2}",
                LotsOLiterals.value1,
                LotsOLiterals.value2,
                LotsOLiterals.value3);
    }
}
```

Read-Only Fields

Because of the restriction on constant types being knowable at compile time, `const` cannot be used in many situations.

In a `Color` class, it can be useful to have constants as part of the class for the common colors. If there were no restrictions on `const`, the following would work:

```
// error
class Color
{
    public Color(int red, int green, int blue)
    {
        this.red = red;
        this.green = green;
        this.blue = blue;
    }

    int red;
    int green;
    int blue;
        // call to new can't be used with static
    public const Color Red = new Color(255, 0, 0);
    public const Color Green = new Color(0, 255, 0);
    public const Color Blue = new Color(0, 0, 255);
}
class Test
{
    static void Main()
    {
        Color background = Color.Red;
    }
}
```

This clearly doesn't work because the static members `Red`, `Green`, and `Blue` can't be calculated at compile time. But making them normal public members doesn't work either; anybody could change the red value to olive drab or puce.

The `readonly` modifier is designed for exactly that situation. By applying `readonly`, the value can be set in the constructor or in an initializer, but it can't be modified later.

Because the color values belong to the class and not a specific instance of the class, they'll be initialized in the static constructor, like so:

```
class Color
{
    public Color(int red, int green, int blue)
    {
        this.red = red;
        this.green = green;
        this.blue = blue;
    }
```

```
    int red;
    int green;
    int blue;

    public static readonly Color Red;
    public static readonly Color Green;
    public static readonly Color Blue;

        // static constructor
    static Color()
    {
        Red = new Color(255, 0, 0);
        Green = new Color(0, 255, 0);
        Blue = new Color(0, 0, 255);
    }
}
class Test
{
    static void Main()
    {
        Color background = Color.Red;
    }
}
```

This provides the correct behavior.

If the number of static members was high or creating them was expensive (either in time or memory), it might make more sense to declare them as `readonly` properties so that members could be constructed on the fly as needed.

On the other hand, it might be easier to define an enumeration with the different color names and return instances of the values as needed:

```
class Color
{
    public Color(int red, int green, int blue)
    {
        this.red = red;
        this.green = green;
        this.blue = blue;
    }
```

```
    public enum PredefinedEnum
    {
        Red,
        Blue,
        Green
    }
    public static Color GetPredefinedColor(
    PredefinedEnum pre)
    {
        switch (pre)
        {
            case PredefinedEnum.Red:
                return(new Color(255, 0, 0));

            case PredefinedEnum.Green:
                return(new Color(0, 255, 0));

            case PredefinedEnum.Blue:
                return(new Color(0, 0, 255));

            default:
                return(new Color(0, 0, 0));
        }
    }
    int red;
    int blue;
    int green;
}
class Test
{
    static void Main()
    {
        Color background =
            Color.GetPredefinedColor(Color.PredefinedEnum.Blue);
    }
}
```

This requires a little more typing, but there isn't a startup penalty or lots of objects taking up space. It also keeps the class interface simple; if there were 30 members for predefined colors, the class would be much harder to understand.[5]

NOTE *Experienced C++ programmers are probably cringing at the last code example. It embodies one of the classic problems with the way C++ deals with memory management. Passing back an allocated object means the caller has to free it. It's pretty easy for the user of the class to either forget to free the object or lose the pointer to the object, which leads to a memory leak.*

In C#, however, this isn't an issue, because the runtime handles memory allocation. In the preceding example, the object created in the `Color.GetPredefinedColor()` *function gets copied immediately to the* `background` *variable and then is available for collection when* `background` *goes out of scope.*

5. For an explanation on why a `default` case is required, see Chapter 20, "Enumerations."

CHAPTER 9

Structs (Value Types)

CLASSES WILL BE USED to implement most objects. Sometimes, however, it may be desirable to create an object that behaves like one of the built-in types; one that is cheap and fast to allocate and doesn't have the overhead of references. In that case, a value type is used, which is done by declaring a `struct` in C#.

Structs act similarly to classes, but with a few added restrictions. They can't inherit from any other type (though they implicitly inherit from `object`), and other classes can't inherit from them.[1]

A Point Struct

In a graphics system, a value class could be used to encapsulate a point. Here's how it would be declared:

```
using System;
struct Point
{
    public Point(int x, int y)
    {
        this.x = x;
        this.y = y;
    }
    public override string ToString()
    {
        return(String.Format("({0}, {1})", x, y));
    }

    public int x;
    public int y;
}
```

1. Technically, structs are derived from `System.ValueType`, but that's only an implementation detail. From a language perspective, they act as if they're derived from `System.Object`.

```
class Test
{
    public static void Main()
    {
        Point    start = new Point(5, 5);
        Console.WriteLine("Start: {0}", start);
    }
}
```

The x and y components of the Point can be accessed. In the Main() function, a Point is created using the new keyword. For value types, new creates an object on the stack and then calls the appropriate constructor.

The call to Console.WriteLine() is a bit mysterious. If Point is allocated on the stack, how does that call work?

Boxing and Unboxing

In C# and the .NET Runtime world, there's a little bit of magic that goes on to make value types look like reference types, and that magic is called boxing. As magic goes, it's pretty simple. In the call to Console.WriteLine(), the compiler is looking for a way to convert start to an object, because the type of the second parameter to WriteLine() is object. For a reference type (i.e., class), this is easy, because object is the base class of all classes. The compiler merely passes an object reference that refers to the class instance.

There's no reference-based instance for a value class, however, so the C# compiler allocates a reference type "box" for the Point, marks the box as containing a Point, and copies the value of the Point into the box. It is now a reference type, and we can treat it as if it were an object.

This reference is then passed to the WriteLine() function, which calls the ToString() function on the boxed Point, which gets dispatched to the ToString() function, and the code writes:

```
Start: (5, 5)
```

Boxing happens automatically whenever a value type is used in a location that requires (or could use) an object.

The boxed value is retrieved into a value type by unboxing it:

```
int v = 123;
object o = v;        // box the int 123
int v2 = (int) o;    // unbox it back to an integer
```

Assigning the object `o` the value `123` boxes the integer, which is then extracted back on the next line. That cast to `int` is required, because the object `o` could be any type of object, and the cast could fail.

This code can be represented by Figure 9.1. Assigning the `int` to the `object` variable results in the box being allocated on the heap and the value being copied into the box. The box is then labeled with the type it contains so the runtime knows the type of the boxed object.

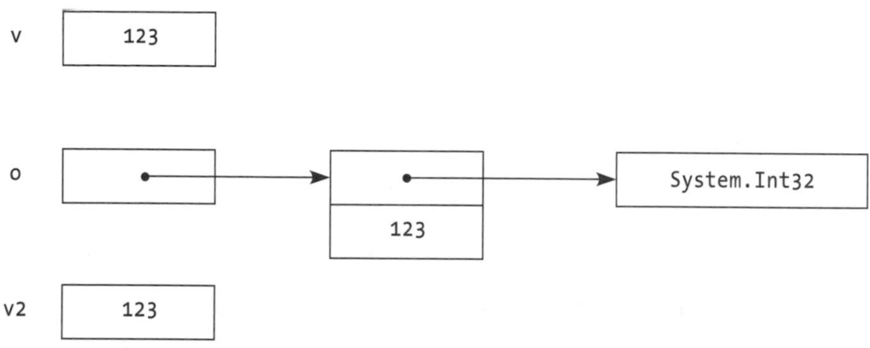

Figure 9-1. Boxing and unboxing a value type

During the unboxing conversion, the type must match exactly; a boxed value type can't be unboxed to a compatible type:

```
object o = 15;
short s = (short) o;        // fails, o doesn't contain a short
short t = (short)(int) o;   // this works
```

It's fairly rare to write code that does boxing explicitly. It's much more common to write code where the boxing happens because the value type is passed to a function that expects a parameter of type `object`, like the following code:

```
int value = 15;
DateTime date = new DateTime();
Console.WriteLine("Value, Date: {0} {1}", value, date);
```

In this case, both `value` and `date` will be boxed when `WriteLine()` is called.

Structs and Constructors

Structs and constructors behave a bit differently from classes. In classes, an instance must be created by calling `new` before the object is used; if `new` isn't called, there will be no created instance, and the reference will be null.

There is no reference associated with a struct, however. If `new` isn't called on the struct, an instance that has all of its fields zeroed is created. In some cases, a user can then use the instance without further initialization. For example:

```
using System;
struct Point
{
    int x;
    int y;

    Point(int x, int y)
    {
        this.x = x;
        this.y = y;
    }
    public override string ToString()
    {
        return(String.Format("({0}, {1})", x, y));
    }
}
class Test
{
    public static void Main()
    {
        Point[] points = new Point[5];
        Console.WriteLine("[2] = {0}", points[2]);
    }
}
```

Although this struct has no default constructor, it's still easy to get an instance that didn't come through the right constructor.

It is therefore important to make sure that the all-zeroed state is a valid initial state for all value types.

A default (parameterless) constructor for a struct could set different values than the all-zeroed state, which would be unexpected behavior. The .NET Runtime therefore prohibits default constructors for structs.

Design Guidelines

Structs should only be used for types that are really just a piece of data—for types that could be used in a similar way to the built-in types. A type, for example, like the built-in type `decimal`, which is implemented as a value type.

Even if more complex types *can* be implemented as value types, they probably shouldn't be, since the value type semantics will probably not be expected by the user. The user will expect that a variable of the type could be `null`, which is not possible with value types.

Immutable Classes

Value types nicely result in value semantics, which is great for types that "feel like data." But what if it's a type that needs to be a class type for implementation reasons but is still a data type, such as the `string` type?

To get a class to behave as if it was a value type, the class needs to be written as an immutable type. Basically, an immutable type is one designed so that it's not possible to tell that it has reference semantics for assignment.

Consider the following example, with `string` written as a normal class:

```
string s = "Hello There";
string s2 = s;
s.Replace("Hello", "Goodbye");
```

Because `string` is a reference type, both `s` and `s2` will end up referring to the same string instance. When that instance is modified through `s`, the views through both variables will be changed.

The way to get around this problem is simply to prohibit any member functions that change the value of the class instance. In the case of `string`, member functions that look like they would change the value of the string instead return a new string with the modified value.

A class where there are no member functions that can change—or mutate—the value of an instance is called an immutable class. The revised example looks like this:

```
string s = "Hello There";
string s2 = s;
s = s.Replace("Hello", "Goodbye");
```

After the third line has been executed, `s2` still points to the original instance of the string, and `s` now points to a new instance containing the modified value.

CHAPTER 10

Interfaces

INTERFACES ARE CLOSELY RELATED to abstract classes that have all members abstract.

A Simple Example

The following code defines the interface `IScalable` and the class `TextObject`, which implements the interface, meaning that it contains implementations of all the functions defined in the interface.

```
public class DiagramObject
{
    public DiagramObject() {}
}

interface IScalable
{
    void ScaleX(float factor);
    void ScaleY(float factor);
}
    // A diagram object that also implements IScalable
public class TextObject: DiagramObject, IScalable
{
    public TextObject(string text)
    {
        this.text = text;
    }
        // implementing IScalable.ScaleX()
    public void ScaleX(float factor)
    {
        // scale the object here.
    }
```

```
        // implementing IScalable.ScaleY()
    public void ScaleY(float factor)
    {
        // scale the object here.
    }

    private string text;
}

class Test
{
    public static void Main()
    {
        TextObject text = new TextObject("Hello");

        IScalable scalable = (IScalable) text;
        scalable.ScaleX(0.5F);
        scalable.ScaleY(0.5F);
    }
}
```

This code implements a system for drawing diagrams. All of the objects derive from `DiagramObject`, so that they can implement common virtual functions (not shown in this example). Some of the objects can be scaled, and this is expressed by the presence of an implementation of the `IScalable` interface.

Listing the interface name with the base class name for `TextObject` indicates that `TextObject` implements the interface. This means that `TextObject` must have functions that match every function in the interface. Interface members have no access modifiers, and the class members that implement the interface members must be publicly accessible.

When an object implements an interface, a reference to the interface can be obtained by casting to the interface. This can then be used to call the functions on the interface.

This example could have been done with abstract methods, by moving the `ScaleX()` and `ScaleY()` methods to `DiagramObject` and making them virtual. The "Design Guidelines" section later in this chapter will discuss when to use an abstract method and when to use an interface.

Working with Interfaces

Typically, code doesn't know whether an object supports an interface, so it needs to check whether the object implements the interface before doing the cast.

```
using System;
interface IScalable
{
    void ScaleX(float factor);
    void ScaleY(float factor);
}
public class DiagramObject
{
    public DiagramObject() {}
}
public class TextObject: DiagramObject, IScalable
{
    public TextObject(string text)
    {
        this.text = text;
    }
        // implementing ISclalable.ScaleX()
    public void ScaleX(float factor)
    {
        Console.WriteLine("ScaleX: {0} {1}", text, factor);
        // scale the object here.
    }

        // implementing IScalable.ScaleY()
    public void ScaleY(float factor)
    {
        Console.WriteLine("ScaleY: {0} {1}", text, factor);
        // scale the object here.
    }

    private string text;
}
class Test
{
    public static void Main()
    {
        DiagramObject[] dArray = new DiagramObject[100];

        dArray[0] = new DiagramObject();
        dArray[1] = new TextObject("Text Dude");
        dArray[2] = new TextObject("Text Backup");
```

```
        // array gets initialized here, with classes that
        // derive from DiagramObject. Some of them implement
        // IScalable.

        foreach (DiagramObject d in dArray)
        {
            if (d is IScalable)
            {
                IScalable scalable = (IScalable) d;
                scalable.ScaleX(0.1F);
                scalable.ScaleY(10.0F);
            }
        }
    }
}
```

Before the cast is done, it is checked to make sure that the cast will succeed. If it will succeed, the object is cast to the interface, and the scale functions are called.

This construct unfortunately checks the type of the object twice; once as part of the `is` operator, and once as part of the cast. This is wasteful, since the cast can never fail.

One way around this would be to restructure the code with exception handling, but that's not a great idea, because it would make the code more complex, and exception handling should generally be reserved for exceptional conditions. It's also not clear whether it would be faster, since exception handling has some overhead.

The `as` Operator

C# provides a special operator for this situation, the `as` operator. Using the `as` operator, the loop can be rewritten as follows:

```
using System;
interface IScalable
{
    void ScaleX(float factor);
    void ScaleY(float factor);
}
public class DiagramObject
{
    public DiagramObject() {}
}
public class TextObject: DiagramObject, IScalable
{
```

```
    public TextObject(string text)
    {
        this.text = text;
    }
        // implementing IScalable.ScaleX()
    public void ScaleX(float factor)
    {
        Console.WriteLine("ScaleX: {0} {1}", text, factor);
        // scale the object here.
    }

        // implementing IScalable.ScaleY()
    public void ScaleY(float factor)
    {
        Console.WriteLine("ScaleY: {0} {1}", text, factor);
        // scale the object here.
    }

    private string text;
}
class Test
{
    public static void Main()
    {
        DiagramObject[] dArray = new DiagramObject[100];

        dArray[0] = new DiagramObject();
        dArray[1] = new TextObject("Text Dude");
        dArray[2] = new TextObject("Text Backup");

        // array gets initialized here, with classes that
        // derive from DiagramObject. Some of them implement
        // IScalable.

        foreach (DiagramObject d in dArray)
        {
            IScalable scalable = d as IScalable;
            if (scalable != null)
            {
                scalable.ScaleX(0.1F);
                scalable.ScaleY(10.0F);
            }
        }
    }
}
```

The `as` operator checks the type of the left operand, and if it can be converted explicitly to the right operand, the result of the operator is the object converted to the right operand. If the conversion would fail, the operator returns null.

Both the `is` and `as` operators can also be used with classes.

Interfaces and Inheritance

When converting from an object to an interface, the inheritance hierarchy is searched until it finds a class that lists the interface on its base list. Having the right functions alone is not enough:

```
using System;
interface IHelper
{
    void HelpMeNow();
}
public class Base: IHelper
{
    public void HelpMeNow()
    {
        Console.WriteLine("Base.HelpMeNow()");
    }
}
    // Does not implement IHelper, though it has the right
    // form.
public class Derived: Base
{
    public new void HelpMeNow()
    {
        Console.WriteLine("Derived.HelpMeNow()");
    }
}
class Test
{
    public static void Main()
    {
        Derived der = new Derived();
        der.HelpMeNow();
        IHelper helper = (IHelper) der;
        helper.HelpMeNow();
    }
}
```

This code gives the following output:

```
Derived.HelpMeNow()
Base.HelpMeNow()
```

It doesn't call the `Derived` version of `HelpMeNow()` when calling through the interface, even though `Derived` does have a function of the correct form, because `Derived` doesn't implement the interface.

Design Guidelines

Both interfaces and abstract classes have similar behaviors and can be used in similar situations. Because of how they work, however, interfaces make sense in some situations, and abstract classes in others. Here are a few guidelines to determine whether a capability should be expressed as an interface or an abstract class.

The first thing to check is whether the object would be properly expressed using the "is-a" relationship. In other words, is the capability an object, and would the derived classes be examples of that object?

Another way of looking at this is to list what kind of objects would want to use this capability. If the capability would be useful across a range of different objects that aren't really related to each other, an interface is the proper choice.

> **CAUTION** *Because there can be only one base class in the .NET Runtime world, this decision is pretty important. If a base class is required, users will be very disappointed if they already have a base class and are unable to use the feature.*

When using interfaces, remember that there is no versioning support for an interface. If a function is added to an interface after users are already using it, their code will break at runtime and their classes will not properly implement the interface until the appropriate modifications are made.

Multiple Implementation

Unlike object inheritance, a class can implement more than one interface.

```
interface IFoo
{
    void ExecuteFoo();
}
```

```
interface IBar
{
    void ExecuteBar();
}

class Tester: IFoo, IBar
{
    public void ExecuteFoo() {}
    public void ExecuteBar() {}
}
```

That works fine if there are no name collisions between the functions in the interfaces. But if the example was just a bit different, there might be a problem:

```
// error
interface IFoo
{
    void Execute();
}

interface IBar
{
    void Execute();
}

class Tester: IFoo, IBar
{
        // IFoo or IBar implementation?
    public void Execute() {}
}
```

Does `Tester.Execute()` implement `IFoo.Execute()`, or `IBar.Execute()`?

In this example, `IFoo.Execute()` and `IBar.Execute()` are implemented by the same function. If they are supposed to be separate, one of the member names could be changed, but that's not a very good solution in most cases.

More seriously, if `IFoo` and `IBar` came from different vendors, they couldn't be changed.

The .NET Runtime and C# support a technique known as explicit interface implementation, which allows a function to specify which interface member it's implementing.

Explicit Interface Implementation

To specify which interface a member function is implementing, qualify the member function by putting the interface name in front of the member name.

Here's the previous example, revised to use explicit interface implementation:

```
using System;
interface IFoo
{
    void Execute();
}

interface IBar
{
    void Execute();
}

class Tester: IFoo, IBar
{
    void IFoo.Execute()
    {
        Console.WriteLine("IFoo.Execute implementation");
    }
    void IBar.Execute()
    {
        Console.WriteLine("IBar.Execute implementation");
    }
}

class Test
{
    public static void Main()
    {
        Tester tester = new Tester();

        IFoo iFoo = (IFoo) tester;
        iFoo.Execute();

        IBar iBar = (IBar) tester;
        iBar.Execute();
    }
}
```

This prints:

```
IFoo.Execute implementation
IBar.Execute implementation
```

This is what we expected. But what does the following test class do?

```
// error
using System;
interface IFoo
{
    void Execute();
}

interface IBar
{
    void Execute();
}

class Tester: IFoo, IBar
{
    void IFoo.Execute()
    {
        Console.WriteLine("IFoo.Execute implementation");
    }
    void IBar.Execute()
    {
        Console.WriteLine("IBar.Execute implementation");
    }
}
class Test
{
    public static void Main()
    {
        Tester tester = new Tester();

        tester.Execute();
    }
}
```

Is `IFoo.Execute()` called, or is `IBar.Execute()` called?

The answer is that neither is called. There is no access modifier on the implementations of `IFoo.Execute()` and `IBar.Execute()` in the `Tester` class, and therefore the functions are private and can't be called.

In this case, this behavior isn't because the public modifier wasn't used on the function, it's because access modifiers are prohibited on explicit interface implementations, so that the only way the interface can be accessed is by casting the object to the appropriate interface.

To expose one of the functions, a forwarding function is added to `Tester`:

```
using System;
interface IFoo
{
    void Execute();
}

interface IBar
{
    void Execute();
}
class Tester: IFoo, IBar
{
    void IFoo.Execute()
    {
        Console.WriteLine("IFoo.Execute implementation");
    }
    void IBar.Execute()
    {
        Console.WriteLine("IBar.Execute implementation");
    }

    public void Execute()
    {
        ((IFoo) this).Execute();
    }
}
class Test
{
    public static void Main()
    {
        Tester tester = new Tester();

        tester.Execute();
    }
}
```

Now, calling the `Execute()` function on an instance of `Tester` will forward to `Tester.IFoo.Execute()`.

This hiding can be used for other purposes, as detailed in the next section.

Implementation Hiding

There may be cases where it makes sense to hide the implementation of an interface from the users of a class, either because it's not generally useful, or just to reduce the member clutter. Doing so can make an object much easier to use. For example:

```
using System;
class DrawingSurface
{

}
interface IRenderIcon
{
    void DrawIcon(DrawingSurface surface, int x, int y);
    void DragIcon(DrawingSurface surface, int x, int y, int x2, int y2);
    void ResizeIcon(DrawingSurface surface, int xsize, int ysize);
}
class Employee: IRenderIcon
{
    public Employee(int id, string name)
    {
        this.id = id;
        this.name = name;
    }
    void IRenderIcon.DrawIcon(DrawingSurface surface, int x, int y)
    {
    }
    void IRenderIcon.DragIcon(DrawingSurface surface, int x, int y,
                                                      int x2, int y2)
    {
    }
    void IRenderIcon.ResizeIcon(DrawingSurface surface, int xsize, int ysize)
    {
    }
    int id;
    string name;
}
```

If the interface had been implemented normally, the `DrawIcon()`, `DragIcon()`, and `ResizeIcon()` member functions would be visible as part of `Employee`, which might be confusing to users of the class. By implementing them through explicit implementation, they can only be accessed through the interface.

Interfaces Based on Interfaces

Interfaces can also be combined together to form new interfaces. The `ISortable` and `ISerializable` interfaces can be combined together, and new interface members can be added.

```
using System.Runtime.Serialization;
using System;
interface IComparableSerializable :
    IComparable, ISerializable
{
    string GetStatusString();
}
```

A class that implements `IComparableSerializable` would need to implement all the members in `IComparable`, `ISerializable`, and the `GetStatusString()` function introduced in `IComparableSerializable`.

Interfaces and Structs

Like classes, structs can also implement interfaces. Here's a short example:

```
using System;
struct Number: IComparable
{
    int value;

    public Number(int value)
    {
        this.value = value;
    }
```

```
    public int CompareTo(object obj2)
    {
        Number num2 = (Number) obj2;
        if (value < num2.value)
            return(-1);
        else if (value > num2.value)
            return(1);
        else
            return(0);
    }
}
class Test
{
    public static void Main()
    {
        Number x = new Number(33);
        Number y = new Number(34);

        IComparable Ic = (IComparable) x;
        Console.WriteLine("x compared to y = {0}", Ic.CompareTo(y));
    }
}
```

This struct implements the `IComparable` interface, which is used to compare the values of two elements for sorting or searching operations.

Like classes, interfaces are reference types, so there's a boxing operation involved here. When a value type is cast to an interface, the value type is boxed and the interface pointer is to the boxed value type.

CHAPTER 11

Versioning

SOFTWARE PROJECTS RARELY EXIST as a single version of code that is never revised, unless the software never sees the light of day. In most cases, the software library writer is going to want to change some things, and the client will need to adapt to such changes.

Dealing with such issues is known as versioning, and it's one of the harder things to do in software. One reason why it's tough is that it requires a bit of planning and foresight; the areas that might change have to be determined, and the design must be modified to allow change.

Another reason why versioning is tough is that most execution environments don't provide much help to the programmer. In C++, compiled code has internal knowledge of the size and layout of all classes burned into it. With care, some revisions can be made to the class without forcing all users to recompile, but the restrictions are fairly severe. When compatibility is broken, all users need to recompile to use the new version. This may not be that bad, though installing a new version of a library may cause other applications that use an older version of the library to cease functioning.

Managed environments that don't expose class member or layout information in the metadata fare better at versioning but it's still possible to write code that versions poorly.

A Versioning Example

The following code presents a simple versioning scenario and explains why C# has `new` and `override` keywords. The program uses a class named `Control`, which is provided by another company.

```
public class Control
{
}
public class MyControl: Control
{
}
```

During implementation of `MyControl`, the virtual function `Foo()` is added:

```
public class Control
{

}
public class MyControl: Control
{
    public virtual void Foo() {}
}
```

This works well, until an upgrade notice arrives from the suppliers of the `Control` object. The new library includes a virtual `Foo()` function on the `Control` object.

```
public class Control
{
        // newly added virtual
    public virtual void Foo() {}
}
public class MyControl: Control
{
    public virtual void Foo() {}
}
```

That `Control` uses `Foo()` as the name of the function is only a coincidence. In the C++ world, the compiler will assume that the version of `Foo()` in `MyControl` does what a virtual override of the `Foo()` in `Control` should do, and will blindly call the version in `MyControl`.

Which is bad.

In the Java world, this will also happen, but things can be a fair bit worse; if the virtual function doesn't have the same return type, the class loader will consider the `Foo()` in `MyControl` to be an invalid override of the `Foo()` in `Control`, and the class will fail to load at runtime.

In C# and the .NET Runtime, a function defined with `virtual` is always considered to be the root of a virtual dispatch. If a function is introduced into a base class that could be considered a base virtual function of an existing function, the runtime behavior is unchanged.

When the class is next compiled, however, the compiler will generate a warning, requesting that the programmer specify their versioning intent. Returning to the example, to specify that the default behavior of not considering the function an override continue, the `new` modifier is added in front of the function:

```
class Control
{
    public virtual void Foo() {}
}
class MyControl: Control
{
        // not an override
    public new virtual void Foo() {}
}
```

The presence of `new` will suppress the warning.

If, on the other hand, the derived version is an override of the function in the base class, the `override` modifier is used.

```
class Control
{
    public virtual void Foo() {}
}
class MyControl: Control
{
        // an override for Control.Foo()
    public override void Foo() {}
}
```

This tells the compiler that the function really is an override.

> **CAUTION** *About this time, you may be thinking, "I'll just put* `new` *on all of my virtual functions, and then I'll never have to deal with the situation again." However, doing so reduces the value that the* `new` *annotation has to somebody reading the code. If* `new` *is only used when it is required, the reader can find the base class and understand what function isn't being overridden. If* `new` *is used indiscriminately, the user will have to refer to the base class every time to see if* `new` *has meaning.*

Designed for Versioning

The C# language provides some assistance in writing code that versions well.

Methods, for example, aren't virtual by default. This helps limits the areas where versioning is constrained to those areas that were intended by the designer of the class and prevents "stray virtuals" that constrain future changes to the class.

C# also has lookup rules designed to aid in versioning. Adding a new function with a more specific overload (in other words, one that matches a parameter better) to a base class won't prevent a less specific function in a derived class from being called,[1] so a change to the base class won't break existing behavior.

A language can only do so much. That's why versioning is something to keep in mind when doing class design.

Designing for Versioning

One specific area that has some versioning tradeoffs is the choice between classes and interfaces.

The choice between class and interface should be fairly straightforward. Classes are only appropriate for "is-a" relationships (where the derived class is really an instance of the base class), and interfaces are appropriate for all others.

If an interface is chosen, however, good design becomes more important because interfaces simply don't version; when a class implements an interface, it needs to implement the interface *exactly*, and adding another method at a later time will mean that classes that thought they implemented the interface no longer do.

1. See Chapter 7, "Member Accessibility and Overloading," for just such an example.

CHAPTER 12
Statements and Flow of Execution

THE FOLLOWING SECTIONS DETAIL the different statements that are available within the C# language.

Selection Statements

The selection statements are used to perform operations based on the value of an expression.

If

The `if` statement in C# requires that the condition inside the `if` statement evaluate to an expression of type `bool`. In other words, the following is illegal:

```
// error
using System;
class Test
{
    public static void Main()
    {
        int    value;

        if (value)        // invalid
            System.Console.WriteLine("true");

        if (value == 0)    // must use this
            System.Console.WriteLine("true");
    }
}
```

Switch

`Switch` statements have often been error-prone; it is just too easy to inadvertently omit a `break` statement at the end of a `case`, or , more likely, not to notice that there is fall-through when reading code.

C# gets rid of this possibility by requiring that there be either a `break` at the end of every `case` block, or a `goto` another `case` label in the `switch`.

```
using System;
class Test
{
    public void Process(int i)
    {
        switch (i)
        {
            case 1:
            case 2:
                // code here handles both 1 and 2
                Console.WriteLine("Low Number");
                break;

            case 3:
                Console.WriteLine("3");
                goto case 4;

            case 4:
                Console.WriteLine("Middle Number");
                break;

            default:
                Console.WriteLine("Default Number");
                break;
        }
    }
}
```

C# also allows the switch statement to be used with string variables:

```
using System;
class Test
{
    public void Process(string htmlTag)
    {
        switch (htmlTag)
        {
            case "P":
                Console.WriteLine("Paragraph start");
                break;
            case "DIV":
                Console.WriteLine("Division");
                break;
            case "FORM":
                Console.WriteLine("Form Tag");
                break;
            default:
                Console.WriteLine("Unrecognized tag");
                break;
        }
    }
}
```

Not only is it easier to write a switch statement than a series of if statements, but it's also more efficient, as the compiler uses an efficient algorithm to perform the comparison.

For small numbers of entries[1] in the switch, the compiler uses a feature in the .NET Runtime known as string interning. The runtime maintains an internal table of all constant strings so that all occurrences of that string in a single program will have the same object. In the switch, the compiler looks up the switch string in the runtime table. If it isn't there, the string can't be one of the cases, so the default case is called. If it is found, a sequential search is done of the interned case strings to find a match.

For larger numbers of entries in the case, the compiler generates a hash function and hash table and uses the hash table to efficiently look up the string.[2]

1. The actual number is determined based upon the performance tradeoffs of each method.
2. If you're unfamiliar with hashing, consider looking at the System.Collections.HashTable class or a good algorithms book.

Iteration Statements

Iteration statements are often known as looping statements, and they are used to perform operations while a specific condition is true.

While

The `while` loop functions as expected: while the condition is true, the loop is executed. Like the `if` statement, the `while` requires a Boolean condition:

```
using System;
class Test
{
    public static void Main()
    {
        int n = 0;
        while (n < 10)
        {
            Console.WriteLine("Number is {0}", n);
            n++;
        }
    }
}
```

The `break` statement may be used to exit the `while` loop, and the `continue` statement may be used to skip to the closing brace of the `while` block for this iteration, and then continue with the next iteration.

```
using System;
class Test
{
    public static void Main()
    {
        int n = 0;
        while (n < 10)
        {
            if (n == 3)
            {
                n++;
                continue;
            }
```

```
            if (n == 8)
                break;
            Console.WriteLine("Number is {0}", n);
            n++;
        }
    }
}
```

This code will generate the following output:

```
0
1
2
4
5
6
7
```

Do

A `do` loop functions just like a `while` loop, except the condition is evaluated at the end of the loop rather than the beginning of the loop:

```
using System;
class Test
{
    public static void Main()
    {
        int n = 0;
        do
        {
            Console.WriteLine("Number is {0}", n);
            n++;
        } while (n < 10);
    }
}
```

Like the `while` loop, the `break` and `continue` statements may be used to control the flow of execution in the loop.

For

A `for` loop is used to iterate over several values. The loop variable may be declared as part of the `for` statement:

```
using System;
class Test
{
    public static void Main()
    {
        for (int n = 0; n < 10; n++)
            Console.WriteLine("Number is {0}", n);
    }
}
```

The scope of the loop variable in a `for` loop is the scope of the statement or statement block that follows the `for`. It cannot be accessed outside of the loop structure:

```
// error
using System;
class Test
{
    public static void Main()
    {
        for (int n = 0; n < 10; n++)
        {
            if (n == 8)
                break;
            Console.WriteLine("Number is {0}", n);
        }
            // error; n is out of scope
        Console.WriteLine("Last Number is {0}", n);
    }
}
```

As with the `while` loop, the `break` and `continue` statements may be used to control the flow of execution in the loop.

Foreach

This is a very common looping idiom:

```
using System;
using System.Collections;
class MyObject
{
}
class Test
{
    public static void Process(ArrayList arr)
    {
        for (int nIndex = 0; nIndex < arr.Count; nIndex++)
        {
                // cast is required by ArrayList stores
                // object references
            MyObject current = (MyObject) arr[nIndex];
            Console.WriteLine("Item: {0}", current);
        }
    }
}
```

This works fine, but it requires the programmer to ensure that the array in the `for` statement matches the array that is used in the indexing operation. If they don't match, it can sometimes be difficult to track down the bug. It also requires declaring a separate index variable, which could accidentally be used elsewhere.

It's also a lot of typing.

Some languages[3] provide a different construct for dealing with this problem, and C# also provides such a construct. The preceding example can be rewritten as follows:

```
using System;
using System.Collections;
class MyObject
{
}
```

3. Depending on your language background, this might be Perl or Visual Basic.

```
class Test
{
    public static void Process(ArrayList arr)
    {
        foreach (MyObject current in arr)
        {
            Console.WriteLine("Item: {0}", current);
        }
    }
}
```

This is a lot simpler, and it doesn't have the same opportunities for mistakes. The type returned by the index operation on `arr` is explicitly converted to the type declared in the `foreach`. This is nice, because collection types such as `ArrayList` can only store values of type `object`.

`Foreach` also works for objects other than arrays. In fact, it works for any object that implements the proper interfaces. It can, for example, be used to iterate over the keys of a hash table:

```
using System;
using System.Collections;
class Test
{
    public static void Main()
    {
        Hashtable    hash = new Hashtable();
        hash.Add("Fred", "Flintstone");
        hash.Add("Barney", "Rubble");
        hash.Add("Mr.", "Slate");
        hash.Add("Wilma", "Flintstone");
        hash.Add("Betty", "Rubble");

        foreach (string firstName in hash.Keys)
        {
            Console.WriteLine("{0} {1}", firstName, hash[firstName]);
        }
    }
}
```

User-defined objects can be implemented so that they can be iterated over using `foreach`; see the "Indexers and Foreach" section in Chapter 19, "Indexers," for more information.

The one thing that can't be done in a `foreach` loop is changing the contents of the container. In other words, in the previous example, the `firstName` variable can't be modified. If the container supports indexing, the contents could be changed through that route, though many containers that enable use by `foreach` don't provide indexing. Another thing to watch is to make sure the container isn't modified during the `foreach`; the behavior in such situations is undefined.[4]

As with other looping constructs, `break` and `continue` can be used with the `foreach` statement.

Jump Statements

Jump statements are used to do just that—jump from one statement to another.

Break

The `break` statement is used to break out of the current iteration or `switch` statement, and continue execution after that statement.

Continue

The `continue` statement skips all of the later lines in the current iteration statement, and then continues executing the iteration statement.

Goto

The `goto` statement can be used to jump directly to a label. Because the use of `goto` statements is widely considered to be harmful,[5] C# prohibits some of their worst abuses. A goto cannot be used to jump into a statement block, for example. The only place where their use is recommended is in switch statements or to transfer control to outside of a nested loop, though they can be used elsewhere.

Return

The `return` statement returns to the calling function, and optionally returns a value as well.

---

4. A container could throw an exception in this case, though that may be expensive to detect the condition.

5. See "GO TO considered harmful," by Edsger W. Dijkstra, at `http://www.net.org/html/history/detail/1968-goto.html`

Other Statements

The following statements are covered in other chapters.

lock

The `lock` statement is used to provide exclusive access to a thread. See the section on threads in Chapter 29, "Threading and Asynchronous Operations."

using

The `using` statement is used in two ways. The first is to specify namespaces, which is covered in Chapter 3, "C# QuickStart and Developing in C#." The second use is to ensure that `Dispose()` is called at the end of a block, which is covered in detail in Chapter 8, "Other Class Details."

try/catch/finally

The `try`, `catch`, and `finally` statements are used to control exception handling and are covered in Chapter 4, "Exception Handling."

checked/unchecked

The `checked` and `unchecked` statements control whether exceptions are thrown if conversions or expressions overflow and are covered in Chapter 14, "Operators and Expressions."

CHAPTER 13

Variable Scoping and Definite Assignment

In C#, local variables can only be given names that allow them to be uniquely identified in a given scope. If a name has more than one meaning in a scope and there is no way to disambiguate the name, the innermost declaration of the name is an error and must be changed. Consider the following:

```
using System;
class MyObject
{
    public MyObject(int x, int y)
    {
        this.x = x;
        this.y = y;
    }
    int x;
    int y;
}
```

In the constructor, `x` refers to the parameter named `x` because parameters take precedence over member variables. To access the instance variable named `x`, it must be prefixed with `this.`, which indicates that it must be an instance variable.

The preceding construct is preferred to renaming the constructor parameters or member variables to avoid the name conflict.[1]

In the following situation, there is no way to name both variables, and the inner declaration is therefore an error:

1. This is really a style thing, but in general it is considered to be cleaner.

```
// error
using System;
class MyObject
{
    public void Process()
    {
        int    x = 12;
        for (int y = 1; y < 10; y++)
        {
                // no way to name outer x here.
            int x = 14;
            Console.WriteLine("x = {0}", x);
        }
    }
}
```

Because the inner declaration of `x` would hide the outer declaration of `x`, it isn't allowed.

C# has this restriction to improve code readability and maintainability. If this restriction wasn't in place, it might be difficult to determine which version of the variable was being used—or even that there *were* multiple versions—inside a nested scope.

Definite Assignment

Definite assignment rules prevent the value of an unassigned variable from being observed. Suppose the following is written:

```
// error
using System;
class Test
{
    public static void Main()
    {
        int n;
        Console.WriteLine("Value of n is {0}", n);
    }
}
```

When this is compiled, the compiler will report an error because the value of `n` is used before it has been initialized.

Similarly, operations cannot be done with a class variable before it is initialized:

```
// error
using System;
class MyClass
{
    public MyClass(int value)
    {
        this.value = value;
    }
    public int Calculate()
    {
        return(value * 10);
    }
    public int    value;
}
class Test
{
    public static void Main()
    {
        MyClass mine;

        Console.WriteLine("{0}", mine.value);            // error
        Console.WriteLine("{0}", mine.Calculate());        // error
        mine = new MyClass(12);
        Console.WriteLine("{0}", mine.value);        // okay now…
    }
}
```

Structs work slightly differently when definite assignment is considered. The runtime will always make sure they're zeroed out, but the compiler will still check to make sure they're initialized to a value before they're used.

A struct is initialized either through a call to a constructor or by setting all the members of an instance before it is used:

```
using System;
struct Complex
{
    public Complex(float real, float imaginary)
    {
        this.real = real;
        this.imaginary = imaginary;
    }
```

```
    public override string ToString()
    {
        return(String.Format("({0}, {1})", real, imaginary));
    }

    public float    real;
    public float    imaginary;
}

class Test
{
    public static void Main()
    {
        Complex    myNumber1;
        Complex    myNumber2;
        Complex    myNumber3;

        myNumber1 = new Complex();
        Console.WriteLine("Number 1: {0}", myNumber1);

        myNumber2 = new Complex(5.0F, 4.0F);
        Console.WriteLine("Number 2: {0}", myNumber2);

        myNumber3.real = 1.5F;
        myNumber3.imaginary = 15F;
        Console.WriteLine("Number 3: {0}", myNumber3);
    }
}
```

In the first section, `myNumber1` is initialized by the call to `new`. Remember that for structs, there is no default constructor, so this call doesn't do anything; it merely has the side effect of marking the instance as initialized.

In the second section, `myNumber2` is initialized by a normal call to a constructor.

In the third section, `myNumber3` is initialized by assigning values to all members of the instance. Obviously, this can be done only if the members are public.

Definite Assignment and Arrays

Arrays work a bit differently for definite assignment. For arrays of both reference and value types (classes and structs), an element of an array *can* be accessed, even if it hasn't been initialized to a non-zero value.

For example, suppose there is an array of `Complex`:

```
using System;
struct Complex
{
    public Complex(float real, float imaginary)
    {
        this.real = real;
        this.imaginary = imaginary;
    }
    public override string ToString()
    {
        return(String.Format("({0}, {0})", real, imaginary));
    }

    public float    real;
    public float    imaginary;
}

class Test
{
    public static void Main()
    {
        Complex[]    arr = new Complex[10];
        Console.WriteLine("Element 5: {0}", arr[5]);        // legal
    }
}
```

Because of the operations that might be performed on an array—such as `Reverse()`–the compiler can't track definite assignment in all situations, and it could lead to spurious errors. It therefore doesn't try.

CHAPTER 14

Operators and Expressions

THE C# EXPRESSION SYNTAX is based upon the C++ expression syntax.

Operator Precedence

When an expression contains multiple operators, the precedence of the operators controls the order in which the elements of the expression are evaluated. The default precedence can be changed by grouping elements with parentheses.

```
int     value = 1 + 2 * 3;          // 1 + (2 * 3) = 7
        value = (1 + 2) * 3;        // (1 + 2) * 3 = 9
```

In C#, all binary operators are left-associative, which means that operations are performed left to right, except for the assignment and conditional (?:) operators, which are performed right to left.

The following table summarizes all operators in precedence from highest to lowest.

CATEGORY	OPERATORS
Primary	(x) x.y f(x) a[x] x++ x-- new typeof sizeof checked unchecked
Unary	+ - ! ~ ++x --x (T)x
Multiplicative	* / %
Additive	+ -
Shift	<< >>
Relational	< > <= >= is
Equality	== !=
Logical AND	&
Logical XOR	^

(Continued)

CATEGORY	OPERATORS
Logical OR	|
Conditional AND	&&
Conditional OR	||
Conditional	?:
Assignment	= *= /= %= += -= <<= >>= &= ^= |=

Built-In Operators

For numeric operations in C#, there are typically built-in operators for the `int`, `uint`, `long`, `ulong`, `float`, `double`, and `decimal` types. Because there aren't built-in operators for other types, expressions must first be converted to one of the types for which there is an operator before the operation is performed.

A good way to think about this is to consider that an operator (| in this case)[1] has the following built-in overloads:

```
int operator +(Int x, Int y);
uint operator +(uint x, Int y);
long operator +(long x, long y);
ulong operator +(ulong x, ulong y);
float operator +(float x, float y);
double operator +(double x, double y);
```

Notice that these operations all take two parameters of the same type, and return that type. For the compiler to perform an addition, it can use only one of these functions. This means that smaller sizes (such as two | values) cannot be added without them being converted to |, and such an operation will return an |.

The result of this is that when operations are done with numeric types that can be converted implicitly to | those types that are "smaller" than | the result will have to be cast to store it in the smaller type.[2]

1. There's also the overload for strings, but that's outside the scope of this example.
2. You may object to this, but you really wouldn't like the type system of C# if it didn't work this way.

```
// error
class Test
{
    public static void Main()
    {
        short   s1 = 15;
        short   s2 = 16;
        short ssum = (short) (s1 + s2);   // cast is required

        int i1 = 15;
        int i2 = 16;
        int isum = i1 + i2;               // no cast required
    }
}
```

User-Defined Operators

User-defined operators may be declared for classes or structs, and they function in the same manner in which the built-in operators function. In other words, the + operator can be defined on a class or struct so that an expression like `a + b` is valid. In the following sections, the operators that can be overloaded are marked with "over" in subscript. See Chapter 25, "Operator Overloading," for more information.

Numeric Promotions

See Chapter 15, "Conversions," for information on the rules for numeric promotion.

Arithmetic Operators

The following sections summarize the arithmetic operations that can be performed in C#. The floating-point types have very specific rules that they follow;[3] for full details, see the CLR. If executed in a checked context, arithmetic expressions on non-floating types may throw exceptions.

Unary Plus (+) $_{over}$

For unary plus, the result is simply the value of the operand.

3. They conform to IEEE 754 arithmetic.

Unary Minus (-) over

Unary minus only works on types for which there is a valid negative representation, and it returns the value of the operand subtracted from zero.

Bitwise Complement (~) over

The ~ operator is used to return the bitwise complement of a value.

Addition (+) over

In C#, the + sign is used both for addition and for string concatenation.

Numeric Addition

The two operands are added together. If the expression is evaluated in a checked context and the sum is outside the range of the result type, an `OverflowException` is thrown. This is demonstrated by the following code:

```
using System;
class Test
{
    public static void Main()
    {
        byte val1 = 200;
        byte val2 = 201;
        byte sum = (byte) (val1 + val2);            // no exception
        checked
        {
            byte sum2 = (byte) (val1 + val2);      // exception
        }
    }
}
```

String Concatenation

String concatenation can be performed between two strings, or between a string and an operand of type `object`.[4] If either operand is null, an empty string is substituted for that operand.

4. Since any type can convert to object, this means any type.

Operands that are not of type `string` will be automatically be converted to a string by calling the virtual `ToString()` method on the object.

Subtraction (-) over

The second operand is subtracted from the first operand. If the expression is evaluated in a checked context and the difference is outside the range of the result type, an `OverflowException` is thrown.

Multiplication (*) over

The two operands are multiplied together. If the expression is evaluated in a checked context and the result is outside the range of the result type, an `OverflowException` is thrown.

Division (/) over

The first operand is divided by the second operand. If the second operand is zero, a `DivideByZero` exception is thrown.

Remainder (%) over

The result `x % y` is computed as `x - (x / y) * y` using integer operations. If y is zero, a `DivideByZero` exception is thrown.

Shift (<< and >>) over

For left shifts, the high-order bits are discarded and the low-order empty bit positions are set to zero.

For right shifts with `uint` or `ulong`, the low-order bits are discarded and the high-order empty bit positions are set to zero.

For right shifts with `int` or `long`, the low-order bits are discarded, and the high-order empty bit positions are set to zero if `x` is non-negative, and 1 if `x` is negative.

Increment and Decrement (++ and --) over

The increment operator increases the value of a variable by 1, and the decrement operator decreases the value of the variable by 1.[5]

Increment and decrement can either be used as a prefix operator, where the variable is modified before it is read, or as a postfix operator, where the value is returned before it is modified.

For example:

```
int    k = 5;
int    value = k++;    // value is 5
       value = --k;    // value is still 5
       value = ++k;    // value is 6
```

Note that increment and decrement are exceptions to the rule about smaller types requiring casts to function. A cast is required when adding two shorts and assigning them to another short:

```
short s = (short) a + b;
```

Such a cast is not required for an increment of a short:[6]

```
s++;
```

Relational and Logical Operators

Relational operators are used to compare two values, and logical operators are used to perform bitwise operations on values.

Logical Negation (!) over

The ! operator is used to return the negation of a Boolean value.

5. In unsafe mode, pointers increment and decrement by the size of the pointed-to object.

6. In other words, there are predefined increment and decrement functions for the types smaller than int and uint.

Relational Operators over

C# defines the following relational operations:

OPERATION	DESCRIPTION
`a == b`	Returns true if `a` is equal to `b`
`a != b`	Returns true if `a` is not equal to `b`
`a < b`	Returns true if `a` is less than `b`
`a <= b`	Returns true if `a` is less than or equal to `b`
`a > b`	Returns true if `a` is greater than `b`
`a >= b`	Returns true if `a` is greater than or equal to `b`

These operators return a result of type `bool`.

When performing a comparison between two reference-type objects, the compiler will first look for relational operators defined on the objects (or base classes of the objects). If it finds no applicable operator, and the relational is `==` or `!=`, the appropriate relational operator will be called from the `object` class. This operator compares whether the two operands reference the same instance, not whether they have the same value.

For value types, the process is the same if `==` and `!=` are overloaded. If they aren't overloaded, there is no default implementation for value types, and an error is generated.

The overloaded versions of `==` and `!=` are closely related to the `Object.Equals()` member. See Chapter 27, "Making Friends with the .NET Frameworks," for more information.

For the `string` type, the relational operators are overloaded so that `==` and `!=` compare the values of the strings, not the references.

Logical Operators over

C# defines the following logical operators:

<table>
<tr><th>OPERATOR</th><th>DESCRIPTION</th></tr>
<tr><td>&</td><td>Bitwise AND of the two operands</td></tr>
<tr><td>|</td><td>Bitwise OR of the two operands</td></tr>
<tr><td>^</td><td>Bitwise exclusive OR (XOR) of the two operands</td></tr>
<tr><td>&&</td><td>Logical AND of the two operands</td></tr>
<tr><td>||</td><td>Logical OR of the two operands</td></tr>
</table>

The operators `&`, `|`, and `^` are usually used on integer data types, though they can also be applied to the `bool` type.

The operators `&&` and `||` differ from the single-character versions in that they perform short-circuit evaluation. In the expression

```
a && b
```

`b` is only evaluated if `a` is true. In the expression

```
a || b
```

`b` is only evaluated if `a` is false.

Conditional Operator (?:)

Sometimes called the ternary or question operator, the conditional operator selects from two expressions based on a Boolean expression.

```
int    value = (x < 10) ? 15 : 5;
```

In this example, the control expression `(x < 10)` is evaluated. If it is true, the value of the operator is the first expression following the question mark, or `15` in this case. If the control expression is false, the value of the operator is the expression following the colon, or `5`.

Assignment Operators

Assignment operators are used to assign a value to a variable. There are two forms: the simple assignment and the compound assignment.

Simple Assignment

Simple assignment is done in C# using the single equals "=". For the assignment to succeed, the right side of the assignment must be a type that can be implicitly converted to the type of the variable on the left side of the assignment.

Compound Assignment

Compound assignment operators perform some operation in addition to simple assignment. The compound operators are the following:

```
+=  -=  *=  /=  %=  &=  |=  ^=  <<=  >>=
```

The compound operator

```
x <op>= y
```

is evaluated exactly as if it were written as

```
x = x <op> y
```

with two exceptions:

- x is only evaluated once, and that evaluation is used for both the operation and the assignment.
- If x contains a function call or array reference, it is only performed once.

Under normal conversion rules, if x and y are both short integers, evaluating

```
x = x + 3;
```

would produce a compile-time error, because addition is performed on int values, and the int result is not implicitly converted to a short. In this case however, because short can be implicitly converted to int, and it is possible to write

```
x = 3;
```

the operation is permitted.

Type Operators

Rather than dealing with the values of an object, the type operators are used to deal with the type of an object.

typeof

The `typeof` operator returns the type of the object, which is an instance of the `System.Type` class. `Typeof` is useful to avoid having to create an instance of an object just to obtain the `type` object. If an instance already exists, a `type` object can be obtained by calling the `GetType()` function on the instance.

Once the `type` object is obtained for a type, it can be queried using reflection to obtain information about the type. See the section titled "Deeper Reflection" in Chapter 36, "Deeper into C#," for more information.

is

The `is` operator is used to determine whether an object reference can be converted to a specific type or interface. The most common use of this operator is to determine whether an object supports a specific interface:

```
using System;
interface IAnnoy
{
    void PokeSister(string name);
}
class Brother: IAnnoy
{
    public void PokeSister(string name)
    {
        Console.WriteLine("Poking {0}", name);
    }
}
class BabyBrother
{
}
```

```
class Test
{
    public static void AnnoyHer(string sister, params object[] annoyers)
    {
        foreach (object o in annoyers)
        {
            if (o is IAnnoy)
            {
                IAnnoy annoyer = (IAnnoy) o;
                annoyer.PokeSister(sister);
            }
        }
    }
    public static void Main()
    {
        Test.AnnoyHer("Jane", new Brother(), new BabyBrother());
    }
}
```

This code produces the following output:

```
Poking: Jane
```

In this example, the `Brother` class implements the `IAnnoy` interface, and the `BabyBrother` class doesn't. The `AnnoyHer()` function walks through all the objects that are passed to it, checks to see if an object supports `IAnnoy`, and then calls the `PokeSister()` function if the object supports the interface.

as

The `as` operator is very similar to the `is` operator, but instead of just determining whether an object is a specific type or interface, it also performs the explicit conversion to that type. If the object can't be converted to that type, the operator returns null. Using `as` is more efficient than the `is` operator, since the `as` operator only needs to check the type of the object once, while the example using `is` checks the type when the operator is used, and again when the conversion is performed.

In the previous example, these lines

```
if (o is IAnnoy)
{
    IAnnoy annoyer = (IAnnoy) o;
    annoyer.PokeSister(sister);
}
```

could be replaced with these:

```
IAnnoy annoyer = o as IAnnoy;
if (annoyer != null)
    annoyer.PokeSister(sister);
```

Note that the as operator can't be used with boxed value types:

```
int value = o as int;
```

doesn't work, because there's no way to get a null value as a reference type.

Checked and Unchecked Expressions

When dealing with expressions, it's often difficult to strike the right balance between the performance of expression evaluation and the detection of overflow in expressions or conversions. Some languages choose performance and can't detect overflow, and other languages put up with reduced performance and always detect overflow.

In C#, the programmer is able to choose the appropriate behavior for a specific situation. This is done using the checked and unchecked keywords.

Code that depends upon the detection of overflow can be wrapped in a checked block:

```
using System;

class Test
{
    public static void Main()
    {
        checked
        {
            byte a = 55;
            byte b = 210;
            byte c = (byte) (a + b);
        }
    }
}
```

When this code is compiled and executed, it will generate an OverflowException.

Similarly, if the code depends on the truncation behavior, the code can be wrapped in an unchecked block:

```
using System;

class Test
{
    public static void Main()
    {
        unchecked
        {
            byte a = 55;
            byte b = 210;
            byte c = (byte) (a + b);
        }
    }
}
```

For the remainder of the code, the behavior can be controlled with the `/checked+` compiler switch. Usually, `/checked+` is turned on for debug builds to catch possible problems and then turned off in retail builds to improve performance.

CHAPTER 15

Conversions

In C#, conversions are divided into implicit and explicit conversions. Implicit conversions are those that will always succeed; the conversion can always be performed without data loss.[1] For numeric types, this means that the destination type can fully represent the range of the source type. For example, a short can be converted implicitly to an int, because the short range is a subset of the int range.

Numeric Types

For the numeric types, there are widening implicit conversions for all the signed and unsigned numeric types. Figure 15-1 shows the conversion hierarchy. If a path of arrows can be followed from a source type to a destination type, there is an implicit conversion from the source to the destination. For example, there are implicit conversions from sbyte to short, from byte to decimal, and from ushort to long.

Note that the path taken from a source type to a destination type in the figure does not represent how the conversion is done; it merely indicates that it can be done. In other words, the conversion from byte to long is done in a single operation, not by converting through ushort and uint.

```
class Test
{
    public static void Main()
    {
            // all implicit
        sbyte v = 55;
        short v2 = v;
        int v3 = v2;
        long v4 = v3;

            // explicit to "smaller" types
        v3 = (int) v4;
        v2 = (short) v3;
        v = (sbyte) v2;
    }
}
```

1. Conversions from int, uint, or long to float and from long to double may result in a loss of precision, but will not result in a loss of magnitude.

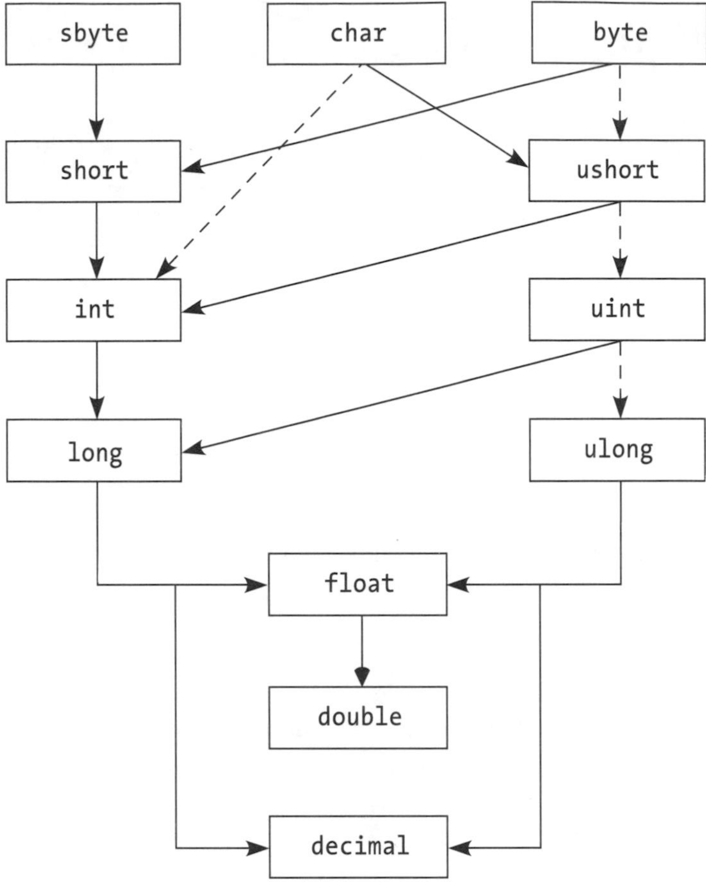

Figure 15-1. C# conversion hierarchy

Conversions and Member Lookup

When considering overloaded members, the compiler may have to choose between several functions. Consider the following:

```
using System;
class Conv
{
    public static void Process(sbyte value)
    {
        Console.WriteLine("sbyte {0}", value);
    }
```

```
    public static void Process(short value)
    {
        Console.WriteLine("short {0}", value);
    }
    public static void Process(int value)
    {
        Console.WriteLine("int {0}", value);
    }
}
class Test
{
    public static void Main()
    {
        int     value1 = 2;
        sbyte    value2 = 1;
        Conv.Process(value1);
        Conv.Process(value2);
    }
}
```

The preceding code produces the following output:

```
int 2
sbyte 1
```

In the first call to `Process()`, the compiler could only match the `int` parameter to one of the functions, the one that took an `int` parameter.

In the second call, however, the compiler had three versions to choose from, taking `sbyte`, `short`, or `int`. To select one version, it first tries to match the type exactly. In this case, it can match `sbyte`, so that's the version that gets called. If the `sbyte` version wasn't there, it would select the `short` version, because a `short` can be converted implicitly to an `int`. In other words, `short` is "closer to" `sbyte` in the conversion hierarchy, and is therefore preferred.

The preceding rule handles many cases, but it doesn't handle the following one:

```
using System;
class Conv
{
    public static void Process(short value)
    {
        Console.WriteLine("short {0}", value);
    }
```

```
    public static void Process(ushort value)
    {
        Console.WriteLine("ushort {0}", value);
    }
}
class Test
{
    public static void Main()
    {
        byte    value = 3;
        Conv.Process(value);
    }
}
```

Here, the earlier rule doesn't allow the compiler to choose one function over the other, because there are no implicit conversions in either direction between `ushort` and `short`.

In this case, there's another rule that kicks in, which says that if there is a single-arrow implicit conversion to a signed type, it will be preferred over all conversions to unsigned types. This is graphically represented in Figure 15-1 by the dotted arrows; the compiler will choose a single solid arrow over any number of dotted arrows.

Explicit Numeric Conversions

Explicit conversions—those using the cast syntax—are the conversions that operate in the opposite direction from the implicit conversions. Converting from `short` to `long` is implicit, and therefore converting from `long` to `short` is an explicit conversion.

Viewed another way, an explicit numeric conversion may result in a value that is different than the original:

```
using System;
class Test
{
    public static void Main()
    {
        uint value1 = 312;
        byte value2 = (byte) value1;
        Console.WriteLine("Value2: {0}", value2);
    }
}
```

The preceding code results in the following output:

```
56
```

In the conversion to byte, the least-significant (lowest-valued) part of the uint is put into the byte value. In many cases, the programmer either knows that the conversion will succeed, or is depending on this behavior.

Checked Conversions

In other cases, it may be useful to check whether the conversion succeeded. This is done by executing the conversion in a checked context:

```
using System;
class Test
{
    public static void Main()
    {
        checked
        {
            uint value1 = 312;
            byte value2 = (byte) value1;
            Console.WriteLine("Value: {0}", value2);
        }
    }
}
```

When an explicit numeric conversion is done in a checked context, if the source value will not fit in the destination data type, an exception will be thrown.

The checked statement creates a block in which conversions are checked for success. Whether a conversion is checked or not is determined at compile time, and the checked state does not apply to code in functions called from within the checked block.

Checking conversions for success does have a small performance penalty, and therefore may not be appropriate for released software. It can, however, be useful to check all explicit numeric conversions when developing software. The C# compiler provides a /checked compiler option that will generate checked conversions for all explicit numeric conversions. This option can be used while developing software, and then can be turned off to improve performance for released software.

If the programmer is depending upon the unchecked behavior, turning on /checked could cause problems. In this case, the unchecked statement can be used to indicate that none of the conversions in a block should ever be checked for conversions.

It is sometimes useful to be able to specify the checked state for a single statement; in this case, the checked or unchecked operator can be specified at the beginning of an expression:

```
using System;
class Test
{
    public static void Main()
    {
        uint value1 = 312;
        byte value2;

        value2 = unchecked((byte) value1);    // never checked
        value2 = (byte) value1;               // checked if /checked
        value2 = checked((byte) value1);      // always checked
    }
}
```

In this example, the first conversion will never be checked, the second conversion will be checked if the /checked statement is present, and the third conversion will always be checked.

Conversions of Classes (Reference Types)

Conversions involving classes are similar to those involving numeric values, except that object conversions deal with casts up and down the object inheritance hierarchy instead of conversions up and down the numeric type hierarchy.

C# also allows conversion between unrelated classes (or structs) to be overloaded. This is discussed later in this chapter.

As with numeric conversions, implicit conversions are those that will always succeed, and explicit conversions are those that may fail.

To the Base Class of an Object

A reference to an object can be converted implicitly to a reference to the base class of an object. Note that this does *not* convert the object to the type of the base class; only the reference is to the base class type. The following example illustrates this:

```
using System;
public class Base
{
    public virtual void WhoAmI()
    {
        Console.WriteLine("Base");
    }
}
public class Derived: Base
{
    public override void WhoAmI()
    {
        Console.WriteLine("Derived");
    }
}
public class Test
{
    public static void Main()
    {
        Derived d = new Derived();
        Base b = d;

        b.WhoAmI();
        Derived d2 = (Derived) b;

        object o = d;
        Derived d3 = (Derived) o;
    }
}
```

This code produces the following output:

```
Derived
```

Initially, a new instance of `Derived` is created, and the variable `d` contains a reference to that object. The reference `d` is then converted to a reference to the base type `Base`. The object referenced by both variables, however, is still a `Derived`; this is shown because when the virtual function `WhoAmI()` is called, the version from `Derived` is called.[2] It is also possible to convert the `Base` reference `b` back to a reference of type `Derived`, or to convert the `Derived` reference to an `object` reference and back.

Converting to the base type is an implicit conversion because, as discussed in Chapter 1, "Object-Oriented Basics," a derived class *is* always an example of the base class. In other words, `Derived` is-a `Base`.

2. Similarly, `Type.GetType`, `is`, and `as` would also show it to be a derived instance.

Explicit conversions are possible between classes when there is a "could-be" relationship. Because `Derived` is derived from `Base`, any reference to `Base` could really be a `Base` reference to a `Derived` object, and therefore the conversion can be attempted. At runtime, the actual type of the object referenced by the `Base` reference (`b` in the previous example) will be checked to see if it is really a reference to `Derived`. If it isn't, an exception will be thrown on the conversion.

Because `object` is the ultimate base type, any reference to a class can be implicitly converted to a reference to `object`, and a reference to `object` may be explicitly converted to a reference to any class type.

Figure 15-2 shows the previous example pictorially.

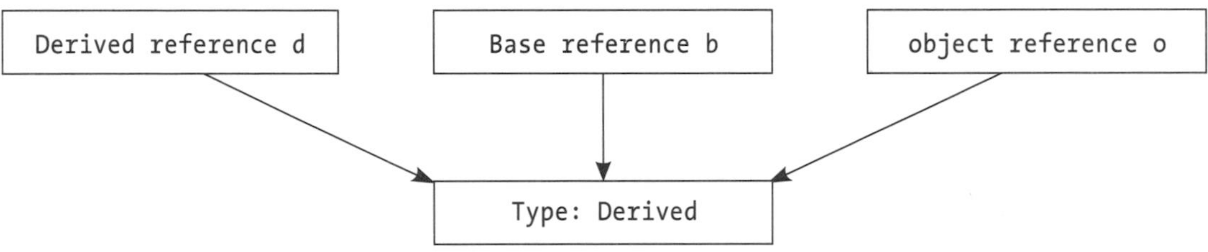

Figure 15-2. Different references to the same instance

To an Interface the Object Implements

Interface implementation is somewhat like class inheritance. If a class implements an interface, an implicit conversion can be used to convert from a reference to an instance of the class to the interface. This conversion is implicit because it is known at compile time that it works.

Once again, the conversion to an interface does not change the underlying type of an object. A reference to an interface can therefore be converted explicitly back to a reference to an object that implements the interface, since the interface reference "could-be" referencing an instance of the specified object.

In practice, converting back from the interface to an object is an operation that is rarely, if ever, used.

To an Interface the Object Might Implement

The implicit conversion from an object reference to an interface reference discussed in the previous section isn't the common case. An interface is especially useful in situations where it isn't known whether an object implements an interface.

The following example implements a debug trace routine that uses an interface if it's available:

```
using System;
interface IDebugDump
{
    string DumpObject();
}
class Simple
{
    public Simple(int value)
    {
        this.value = value;
    }
    public override string ToString()
    {
        return(value.ToString());
    }
    int value;
}
class Complicated: IDebugDump
{
    public Complicated(string name)
    {
        this.name = name;
    }
    public override string ToString()
    {
        return(name);
    }
    string IDebugDump.DumpObject()
    {
        return(String.Format(
            "{0}\nLatency: {1}\nRequests: {2}\nFailures: {3}\n",
            new object[] {name,    latency, requestCount, failedCount} ));
    }
    string name;
    int latency = 0;
    int requestCount = 0;
    int failedCount = 0;
}
```

```
class Test
{
    public static void DoConsoleDump(params object[] arr)
    {
        foreach (object o in arr)
        {
            IDebugDump dumper = o as IDebugDump;
            if (dumper != null)
                Console.WriteLine("{0}", dumper.DumpObject());
            else
                Console.WriteLine("{0}", o);
        }
    }
    public static void Main()
    {
        Simple s = new Simple(13);
        Complicated c = new Complicated("Tracking Test");
        DoConsoleDump(s, c);
    }
}
```

This produces the following output:

```
13
Tracking Test
Latency: 0
Requests: 0
Failures: 0
```

In this example, there are dumping functions that can list objects and their internal state. Some objects have a complicated internal state and need to pass back some rich information, while others can get by with the information returned by their `ToString()` functions.

This is nicely expressed by the `IDebugDump` interface, which is used to generate the output if an implementation of the interface is present.

This example uses the `as` operator, which will return the interface if the object implements it, and null if it doesn't.

From One Interface Type to Another

A reference to an interface can be converted implicitly to a reference to an interface that it is based upon. It can be converted explicitly to a reference to any interface that it isn't based upon. This would be successful only if the interface reference was a reference to an object that implemented the other interface as well.

Conversions of Structs (Value Types)

The only built-in conversion dealing with structs is an implicit conversion from a struct to an interface that it implements. The instance of the struct will be boxed to a reference, and then converted to the appropriate interface reference. There are no implicit or explicit conversions from an interface to a struct.

CHAPTER 16

Arrays

ARRAYS IN C# ARE reference objects; they are allocated out of heap space rather than on the stack. The elements of an array are stored as dictated by the element type; if the element type is a reference type (such as `string`), the array will store references to strings. If the element is a value type (such as a numeric type, or a `struct` type), the elements are stored directly within the array. In other words, an array of a value type does not contain boxed instances.

Arrays are declared using the following syntax:

```
<type>[] identifier;
```

The initial value of an array is null. An array object is created using `new`:

```
int[] store = new int[50];
string[] names = new string[50];
```

When an array is created, it initially contains the default values for the types that are in the array. For the `store` array, each element is an `int` with the value 0. For the `names` array, each element is a `string` reference with the value `null`.

Array Initialization

Arrays can be initialized at the same time as they are created. During initialization, the `new int[x]` can be omitted, and the compiler will determine the size of the array to allocate from the number of items in the initialization list:

```
int[] store = {0, 1, 2, 3, 10, 12};
```

The preceding line is equivalent to this:

```
int[] store = new int[6] {0, 1, 2, 3, 10, 12};
```

Multidimensional and Jagged Arrays

To index elements in more than one dimension, either a multidimensional or jagged array can be used.

Multidimensional Arrays

Multidimensional arrays have more than one dimension:

```
int[,] matrix = new int[4,int[5, 2];
matrix[0, 0] = 5;
matrix[5, 5] = 10;
```

The `matrix` array has a first dimension of 5, and a second dimension of 2. This array could be initialized using the following statement:

```
int[,] matrix = { {1, 1}, {2, 2}, {3, 5}, {4, 5}, {134, 44} };
```

The `matrix` array has a first dimension of 5, and a second dimension of 2.

Multidimensional arrays are sometimes called rectangular arrays because the elements can be written in a rectangular table (for dimensions <= 2). When the matrix array is allocated, a single chunk is obtained from the heap to store the entire array. It can be represented by Figure 16-1.

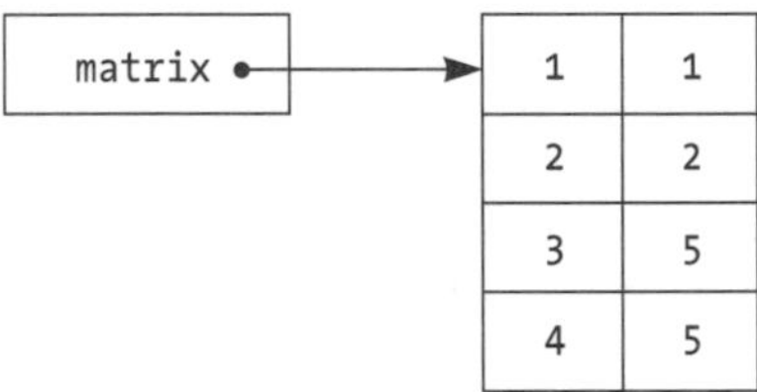

Figure 16-1. Storage in a multidimensional array

The following is an example of using a multidimensional array:

```
using System;
class Test
{
    public static void Main()
    {
        int[,] matrix = { {1, 1}, {2, 2}, {3, 5}, {4, 5}, {134, 44} };
```

```
        for (int i = 0; i < matrix.GetLength(0); i++)
        {
            for (int j = 0; j < matrix.GetLength(1); j++)
            {
                Console.WriteLine("matrix[{0}, {1}] = {2}", i, j, matrix[i, j]);
            }
        }
    }
}
```

The `GetLength()` member of an array will return the length of that dimension. This example produces the following output:

```
matrix[0, 0] = 1
matrix[0, 1] = 1
matrix[1, 0] = 2
matrix[1, 1] = 2
matrix[2, 0] = 3
matrix[2, 1] = 5
matrix[3, 0] = 4
matrix[3, 1] = 5
matrix[4, 0] = 134
matrix[4, 1] = 44
```

Jagged Arrays

A jagged array is merely an array of arrays and is called a "jagged" array because it doesn't have to be rectangular. For example:

```
int[][] matrix = new int[3][];
matrix[0] = new int[5];
matrix[1] = new int[4];
matrix[2] = new int[2];
matrix[0][3] = 4;
matrix[1][1] = 8;
matrix[2][0] = 5;
```

The `matrix` array here has only a single dimension of 3 elements. Its elements are integer arrays. The first element is an array of 5 integers, the second is an array of 4 integers, and the third is an array of 2 integers.

This array could be represented by Figure 16-2. The `matrix` variable is a reference to an array of 3 references to arrays of integers. Four heap allocations were required for this array.

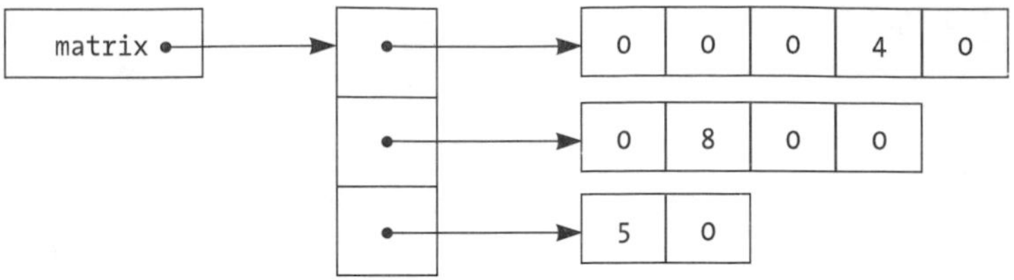

Figure 16-2. Storage in a jagged array

Using the initialization syntax for arrays, a full example can be written as follows:

```
using System;
class Test
{
    public static void Main()
    {
        int[][] matrix = {new int[5], new int[4], new int[2] };
        matrix[0][3] = 4;
        matrix[1][1] = 8;
        matrix[2][0] = 5;

        for (int i = 0; i < matrix.Length; i++)
        {
            for (int j = 0; j < matrix[i].Length; j++)
            {
                Console.WriteLine("matrix[{0}, {1}] = {2}", i, j, matrix[i][j]);
            }
        }
    }
}
```

Note that the traversal code is different than the multidimensional case. Because `matrix` is an array of arrays, a nested single-dimensional traverse is used.

Arrays of Reference Types

Arrays of reference types can be somewhat confusing, because the elements of the array are initialized to null rather than to the element type. For example:

```
class Employee
{
    public void LoadFromDatabase(int employeeID)
    {
        // load code here
    }
}
class Test
{
    public static void Main()
    {
        Employee[] emps = new Employee[3];
        emps[0].LoadFromDatabase(15);
        emps[1].LoadFromDatabase(35);
        emps[2].LoadFromDatabase(255);
    }
}
```

When `LoadFromDatabase()` is called, a null exception will be generated because the elements referenced have never been set and are therefore still null.

The class can be rewritten as follows:

```
class Employee
{
    public static Employee LoadFromDatabase(int employeeID)
    {
        Employee emp = new Employee();
        // load code here
        return(emp);
    }
}
class Test
{
    public static void Main()
    {
        Employee[] emps = new Employee[3];
        emps[0] = Employee.LoadFromDatabase(15);
        emps[1] = Employee.LoadFromDatabase(35);
        emps[2] = Employee.LoadFromDatabase(255);
    }
}
```

This allows us to create an instance and load it, and then save it into the array.

The reason that arrays aren't initialized is for performance. If the compiler did do the initialization, it would need to do the same initialization for each element, and if that wasn't the right initialization, all of those allocations would be wasted.

Array Conversions

Conversions are allowed between arrays based on the number of dimensions and the conversions available between the element types.

An implicit conversion is permitted from array S to array T if the arrays have the same number of dimensions, the elements of S have an implicit reference conversion to the element type of T, and both S and T are reference types. In other words, if there is an array of class references, it can be converted to an array of a base type of the class.

Explicit conversions have the same requirements, except that the elements of S must be explicitly convertible to the element type of T.

```
using System;
class Test
{
    public static void PrintArray(object[] arr)
    {
        foreach (object obj in arr)
            Console.WriteLine("Word: {0}", obj);
    }
    public static void Main()
    {
        string s = "I will not buy this record, it is scratched.";
        char[] separators = {' '};
        string[] words = s.Split(separators);
        PrintArray(words);
    }
}
```

In this example, the `string` array of words can be passed as an `object` array, because each `string` element can be converted to `object` through a reference conversion. This is not possible, for example, if there is a user-defined implicit conversion..

The `System.Array` **Type**

Because arrays in C# are based on the .NET Runtime `System.Array` type, there are several operations that can be done with them that aren't traditionally supported by array types.

Sorting and Searching

The ability to do sorting and searching is built into the `System.Array` type. The `Sort()` function will sort the items of an array, and the `IndexOf()`, `LastIndexOf()`, and `BinarySearch()` functions are used to search for items in the array. For more information, see Chapter 28, "`System.Array` and the Collection Classes."

Reverse

Calling `Reverse()` simply reverses all the elements of the array:

```
using System;
class Test
{
    public static void Main()
    {
        int[] arr = {5, 6, 7};
        Array.Reverse(arr);
        foreach (int value in arr)
        {
            Console.WriteLine("Value: {0}", value);
        }
    }
}
```

This produces the following output:

```
7
6
5
```

CHAPTER 17

Strings

ALL STRINGS IN C# are instances of the `System.String` type in the Common Language Runtime. Because of this, there are many built-in operations available that work with strings. For example, the `String` class defines an indexer function that can be used to iterate over the characters of the string:

```
using System;
class Test
{
    public static void Main()
    {
        string s = "Test String";

        for (int index = 0; index < s.Length; index++)
            Console.WriteLine("Char: {0}", s[index]);
    }
}
```

See Chapter 26, "Other Language Details," for information about string literals.

Operations

The `string` class is an example of an immutable type, which means that the characters contained in the string cannot be modified by users of the string. All operations that are performed by the `string` class return a modified version of the string rather than modifying the instance on which the method is called.

Immutable types are used to make reference types that have value semantics (in other words, act like value types).

The `String` class supports the following comparison and searching methods:

ITEM	DESCRIPTION
`Compare()`	Compares two strings
`CompareOrdinal()`	Compares two string regions using an ordinal comparison
`CompareTo()`	Compares the current instance with another instance
`EndsWith()`	Determines whether a substring exists at the end of a string
`StartsWith()`	Determines whether a substring exists at the beginning of a string
`IndexOf()`	Returns the position of the first occurrence of a substring
`LastIndexOf()`	Returns the position of the last occurrence of a substring

The `String` class supports the following modification methods , which all return a new string instance:

ITEM	DESCRIPTION
`Concat()`	Concatenates two or more strings or objects together. If objects are passed, the `ToString()` function is called on them.
`CopyTo()`	Copies a specified number of characters from a location in this string into an array
`Insert()`	Returns a new string with a substring inserted at a specific location
`Join()`	Joins an array of strings together with a separator between each array element
`PadLeft()`	Right aligns a string in a field
`PadRight()`	Left aligns a string in a field
`Remove()`	Deletes characters from a string
`Replace()`	Replaces all instances of a character with a different character
`Split()`	Creates an array of strings by splitting a string at any occurrence of one or more characters
`Substrng()`	Extracts a substring from a string
`ToLower()`	Returns a lowercase version of a string
`ToUpper()`	Returns an uppercase version of a string
`Trim()`	Removes whitespace from a string
`TrimEnd()`	Removes a string of characters from the end of a string
`TrimStart()`	Removes a string of characters from the beginning of a string

String Encodings and Conversions

From the C# perspective, strings are always Unicode strings. When dealing only in the .NET world, this greatly simplifies working with strings.

Unfortunately, it's sometimes necessary to deal with the messy details of other kinds of strings. The `System.Text` namespace contains classes that can be used to convert between an array of bytes and a character encoding such as ASCII, Unicode, UTF7, or UTF8. Each coding is encapsulated in a class such as `ASCIIEncoding`.

To convert from a string to a block of bytes, the `GetEncoder()` method on the encoding class is called to obtain an `Encoder`, which is then used to do the encoding.

Similarly, to convert from a block of bytes to a specific encoding, `GetDecoder()` is called to obtain a decoder.

Converting Objects to Strings

The function `object.ToString()` is overridden by the built-in types to provide an easy way of converting from a value to a string representation of that value. Calling `ToString()` produces the default representation of a value; a different representation may be obtained by calling `String.Format()`. See the section on formatting in Chapter 32, ".NET Frameworks Overview," for more information.

An Example

The split function can be used to break a string into substrings at separators.

```
using System;
class Test
{
    public static void Main()
    {
        string s = "Oh, I hadn't thought of that";
        char[] separators = new char[] {' ', ','};
        foreach (string sub in s.Split(separators))
        {
            Console.WriteLine("Word: {0}", sub);
        }
    }
}
```

This example produces the following output:

```
Word: Oh
Word:
Word: I
Word: hadn't
Word: thought
Word: of
Word: that
```

The `separators` character array defines what characters the string will be broken on. The `Split()` function returns an array of strings, and the `foreach` statement iterates over the array and prints it out.

In this case, the output isn't particularly useful because the "`,` " string gets broken twice. This can be fixed by using the regular expression classes.

String Interning

It is common to use a string more than once within a single program. To avoid storing duplicate copies of the same literal string, the runtime has a feature known as string interning.

Simply put, string interning means that all usages of the same string in a program refer to a single instance of a `string` object. This optimization is usually transparent but sometimes can be visible when writing test programs that deal with equality. For example, the following program appears to test the difference between string equality and reference equality:

```
using System;
class Test
{
    public static void Main()
    {
        string s1 = "Hello";
        string s2 = "Hello";
        string s3 = "Hello".Substring(0, 4) + "o";

        Console.WriteLine("Str == : {0}", s1 == s2);
        Console.WriteLine("Ref == : {0}", (object) s1 == (object) s2);

        Console.WriteLine("Str == : {0}", s1 == s3);
        Console.WriteLine("Ref == : {0}", (object) s1 == (object) s3);
    }
}
```

This program produces the following output:

```
Str == : True
Ref == : True
Str == : True
Ref == : False
```

The first comparison compares the strings directly, which calls the overloaded `operator==` function, which in turn compares the contents and produces the expected `true` as output.

The second comparison, however, casts both strings to `object`, which means the overloaded `operator==` for `object` will be called and the two references will be compared to see if they point to the same object. Because of string interning, this comparison also returns `true`.

The third and fourth comparisons are done using `s3`, which is constructed at runtime, and therefore is not the same instance as `s1` and `s2`. The test therefore produces the expected results.

StringBuilder

Though the `String.Format()` function can be used to create a string based on the values of other strings, it isn't the most efficient way to assemble strings. The runtime provides the `StringBuilder` class to make this process easier.

The `StringBuilder` class supports the following properties and methods:

PROPERTY	DESCRIPTION
`Capacity`	Retrieves or sets the number of characters the `StringBuilder` can hold
`[]`	The `StringBuilder` indexer is used to get or set a character at a specific position
`Length`	Retrieves or sets the length
`MaxCapacity`	Retrieves the maximum capacity of the `StringBuilder`

METHOD	DESCRIPTION
`Append()`	Appends the string representation of an object
`AppendFormat()`	Appends a string representation of an object, using a specific format string for the object
`EnsureCapacity()`	Ensures the `StringBuilder` has enough room for a specific number of characters
`Insert()`	Inserts the string representation of a specified object at a specified position
`Remove()`	Removes the specified characters
`Replace()`	Replaces all instances of a character with a new character

The following example demonstrates how the `StringBuilder` class can be used to create a string from separate strings.

```
using System;
using System.Text;
class Test
{
    public static void Main()
    {
        string s = "I will not buy this record, it is scratched";
        char[] separators = new char[] {' ', ','};
        StringBuilder sb = new StringBuilder();
        int number = 1;
        foreach (string sub in s.Split(separators))
        {
            sb.AppendFormat("{0}: {1} ", number++, sub);
        }
        Console.WriteLine("{0}", sb);
    }
}
```

This code will create a string with numbered words, and will produce the following output:

```
1: I 2: will 3: not 4: buy 5: this 6: record 7:  8: it 9: is 10: scratched
```

Because the call to `split()` specified both the space and the comma as separators, it considers there to be a word between the comma and the following space, which results in an empty entry.

Regular Expressions

If the searching functions found in the `String` class aren't powerful enough, the `System.Text` namespace contains a regular expression class named `Regex`. Regular expressions provide a very powerful method for doing search and/or replace functions.

While this section has a few examples of using regular expressions, a detailed description of them is beyond the scope of the book. There are several regular expression books available, and the subject is also covered in most books about Perl.

The regular expression class uses a rather interesting technique to get maximum performance. Rather than interpret the regular expression for each match, it writes a short program on the fly to implement the regular expression match, and that code is then run.[1]

The previous example using `Split()` can be revised to use a regular expression, rather than single characters, to specify how the split should occur. This will remove the blank word that was found in the preceding example.

```
// file: regex.cs
using System;
using System.Text.RegularExpressions;
class Test
{
    public static void Main()
    {
        string s = "Oh, I hadn't thought of that";
        Regex regex = new Regex(@"( |, ");
        char[] separators = new char[] {' ', ','};
        foreach (string sub in regex.Split(s))
        {
            Console.WriteLine("Word: {0}", sub);
        }
    }
}
```

This example produces the following output:

```
Word: Oh
Word: I
Word: hadn't
Word: thought
Word: of
Word: that
```

1. The program is written using the .NET intermediate language—the same one that C# produces as output from a compilation. See Chapter 30, "Execution-Time Code Generation,", for information on how this works.

In the regular expression, the string is split either on a space or on a comma followed by a space.

Regular Expression Options

When creating a regular expression, there are several options that can be specified to control how the matches are performed. `Compiled` is especially useful to speed up searches.

OPTION	DESCRIPTION
`Compiled`	Compiles the regular expression into a custom implementation so that matches are faster
`ExplicitCapture`	Specifies that the only valid captures are named
`IgnoreCase`	Performs case-insensitive matching
`IgnorePatternWhitespace`	Removes unescaped whitespace from the pattern, to allow # comments
`Multiline`	Changes the meaning of "^" and "$" so they match at the beginning or end of any line, not the beginning or end of the whole string
`RightToLeft`	Performs searches from right to left rather than from left to right
`Singleline`	Single-line mode, where "." matches any character including "\n"

More Complex Parsing

Using regular expressions to improve the function of `Split()` doesn't really demonstrate their power. The following example uses regular expressions to parse an IIS log file. That log file looks something like this:

```
#Software: Microsoft Internet Information Server 4.0
#Version: 1.0
#Date: 1999-12-31 00:01:22
#Fields: time c-ip cs-method cs-uri-stem sc-status
00:01:31 157.56.214.169 GET /Default.htm 304
00:02:55 157.56.214.169 GET /docs/project/overview.htm 200
```

The following code will parse this into a more useful form.

```
// file=logparse.cs
// compile with: csc logparse.cs
using System;
using System.Net;
using System.IO;
using System.Text.RegularExpressions;
using System.Collections;

class Test
{
    public static void Main(string[] args)
    {
        if (args.Length  == 0) //we need a file to parse
        {
            Console.WriteLine("No log file specified.");
        }
        else
            ParseLogFile(args[0]);
    }
    public static void ParseLogFile(string    filename)
    {
        if (!System.IO.File.Exists(filename))
        {
            Console.WriteLine ("The file specified does not exist.");
        }
        else
        {
            FileStream f = new FileStream(filename, FileMode.Open);
            StreamReader stream = new StreamReader(f);

            string line;
            line = stream.ReadLine();     // header line
            line = stream.ReadLine();     // version line
            line = stream.ReadLine();     // Date line

            Regex    regexDate= new Regex(@"\:\s(?<date>[^\s]+)\s");
            Match    match = regexDate.Match(line);
            string    date = "";
            if (match.Length != 0)
                date = match.Groups["date"].ToString();
```

```
                line = stream.ReadLine();    // Fields line

                Regex    regexLine =
                    new Regex(        // match digit or :
                            @"(?<time>(\d|\:)+)\s" +
                                // match digit or .
                            @"(?<ip>(\d|\.)+)\s" +
                                // match any non-white
                            @"(?<method>\S+)\s" +
                                // match any non-white
                            @"(?<uri>\S+)\s" +
                                // match any non-white
                            @"(?<status>\d+)");

                    // read through the lines, add an
                    // IISLogRow for each line
                while ((line = stream.ReadLine()) != null)
                {
                    //Console.WriteLine(line);
                    match = regexLine.Match(line);
                    if (match.Length != 0)
                    {
                        Console.WriteLine("date: {0} {1}", date,
                                          match.Groups["time"]);
                        Console.WriteLine("IP Address: {0}",
                                         match.Groups["ip"]);
                        Console.WriteLine("Method: {0}",
                                          match.Groups["method"]);
                        Console.WriteLine("Status: {0}",
                                          match.Groups["status"]);
                        Console.WriteLine("URI: {0}\n",
                                          match.Groups["uri"]);
                    }
                }
                f.Close();
            }
        }
    }
```

The general structure of this code should be familiar. There are two regular expressions used in this example. The date string and the regular expression used to match it are the following:

```
#Date: 1999-12-31 00:01:22
\:\s(?<date>[^\s]+)\s
```

In the code, regular expressions are usually written using the verbatim string syntax, since the regular expression syntax also uses the backslash character. Regular expressions are most easily read if they are broken down into separate elements. This

```
\:
```

matches the colon (:). The backslash (\) is required because the colon by itself means something else. This

```
\s
```

matches a single character of whitespace (tab or space). In this next part

```
(?<date>[^\s]+)
```

the ?<date> names the value that will be matched, so it can be extracted later. The [^\s] is called a character group, with the ^ character meaning "none of the following characters." This group therefore matches any non-whitespace character. Finally, the + character means to match one or more occurrences of the previous description (non-whitespace). The parentheses are used to delimit how to match the extracted string. In the preceding example, this part of the expression matches 1999-12-31.

To match more carefully, the /d (digit) specifier could have been used, with the whole expression written as:

```
\:\s(?<date>\d\d\d\d-\d\d-\d\d)\s
```

That covers the simple regular expression. A more complex regular expression is used to match each line of the log file. Because of the regularity of the line, Split() could also have been used, but that wouldn't have been as illustrative. The clauses of the regular expression are as follows:

```
(?<time>(\d|\:)+)\s       // match digit or : to extract time
(?<ip>(\d|\.)+)\s         // match digit or . to get IP address
(?<method>\S+)\s          // any non-whitespace for method
(?<uri>\S+)\s             // any non-whitespace for uri
(?<status>\d+)            // any digit for status
```

CHAPTER 18

Properties

A FEW MONTHS AGO, I was writing some code, and I came up with a situation where one of the fields in a class (`Filename`) could be derived from another (`Name`). I therefore decided to use the property idiom (or design pattern) in C++, and wrote a `getFilename()` function for the field that was derived from the other. I then had to walk through all the code and replace the reference to the field with calls to `getFilename()`. This took a while, since the project was fairly big.

I also had to remember that when I wanted to get the filename, I had to call the `getFilename()` member function to get it, rather than merely referring to the `Filename` member of the class. This makes the model a bit tougher to grasp; instead of `Filename` just being a field, I have to remember that I'm really calling a function whenever I need to access it. Similarly, I need to call a `setFilename()` function to set the value of filename.

That `getFilename()` and `setFilename()` are logically related to a single "virtual field" isn't obvious when looking at a class, especially when class members are listed alphabetically, as they usually are. The property pattern is good for the author of a class but a bit clunky for the user of the class.

C# adds properties as first-class citizens of the language. Properties appear to be fields to the user of a class, but they use a block of code (known as an accessor) to get the current value and set a new value. You can separate the user model (a field) from the implementation model (a member function), which reduces the amount of coupling between a class and the users of a class, leaving more flexibility in design and maintenance.

In the .NET Runtime, properties are implemented using a naming pattern and a little bit of extra metadata linking the member functions to the property name. This allows properties to appear as properties in some languages, and merely as member functions in other languages.

Properties are used heavily throughout the .NET Frameworks; in fact, there are few (if any) public fields.

Accessors

A property consists of a property declaration and either one or two blocks of code—known as accessors[1]—that handle getting or setting the property. Here's a simple example:

```
class Test
{
    private string name;

    public string Name
    {
        get
        {
            return name;
        }
        set
        {
            name = value;
        }
    }
}
```

This class declares a property called `Name`, and defines both a getter and a setter for that property. The getter merely returns the value of the private variable, and the setter updates the internal variable through a special parameter named `value`. Whenever the setter is called, the variable `value` contains the value that the property should be set to. The type of `value` is the same as the type of the property.

Properties can have a getter, a setter, or both. A property that only has a getter is called a read-only property, and a property that only has a setter is called a write-only property.

Properties and Inheritance

Like member functions, properties can also be declared using the `virtual`, `override`, or `abstract` modifiers. These modifiers are placed on the property and affect both accessors.

When a derived class declares a property with the same name as in the base class, it hides the entire property; it is not possible to hide only a getter or setter.

---

1. In some languages/idioms, a set accessor is also known as a mutator.

Use of Properties

Properties separate the interface of a class from the implementation of a class. This is useful in cases where the property is derived from other fields, and also to do lazy initialization and only fetch a value if the user really needs it.

Suppose that a car maker wanted to be able to produce a report that listed some current information about the production of cars.

```
using System;
class Auto
{
    public Auto(int id, string name)
    {
        this.id = id;
        this.name = name;
    }

        // query to find # produced
    public int ProductionCount
    {
        get
        {
            if (productionCount == -1)
            {
                // fetch count from database here.
            }
            return(productionCount);
        }
    }
    public int SalesCount
    {
        get
        {
            if (salesCount == -1)
            {
                // query each dealership for data
            }
            return(salesCount);
        }
    }
    string name;
    int id;
    int productionCount = -1;
    int salesCount = -1;
}
```

Both the `ProductionCount` and `SalesCount` properties are initialized to `-1`, and the expensive operation of calculating them is deferred until it is actually needed.

Side Effects When Setting Values

Properties are also very useful to do something beyond merely setting a value when the setter is called. A shopping basket could update the total when the user changed an item count, for example:

```
using System;
using System.Collections;
class Basket
{
    internal void UpdateTotal()
    {
        total = 0;
        foreach (BasketItem item in items)
        {
            total += item.Total;
        }
    }

    ArrayList    items = new ArrayList();
    Decimal    total;
}
class BasketItem
{
    BasketItem(Basket basket)
    {
        this.basket = basket;
    }
    public int Quantity
    {
        get
        {
            return(quantity);
        }
        set
        {
            quantity = value;
            basket.UpdateTotal();
        }
    }
```

```
    public Decimal Price
    {
        get
        {
            return(price);
        }
        set
        {
            price = value;
            basket.UpdateTotal();
        }
    }
    public Decimal Total
    {
        get
        {
                // volume discount; 10% if 10 or more are purchased
            if (quantity >= 10)
                return(quantity * price * 0.90m);
            else
                return(quantity * price);
        }
    }

    int        quantity;      // count of the item
    Decimal    price;         // price of the item
    Basket     basket;        // reference back to the basket
}
```

In this example, the `Basket` class contains an array of `BasketItem`. When the price or quantity of an item is updated, an update is fired back to the `Basket` class, and the basket walks through all the items to update the total for the basket.

This interaction could also be implemented more generally using events, which are covered in Chapter 23, "Events."

Static Properties

In addition to member properties, C# also allows the definition of static properties, which belong to the whole class rather than to a specific instance of the class. Like static member functions, static properties cannot be declared with the `virtual`, `abstract`, or `override` modifiers.

When `readonly` fields were discussed Chapter 8, "Other Class Details," there was a case that initialized some static readonly fields. The same thing can be done with static properties without having to initialize the fields until necessary. The value can also be fabricated when needed, and not stored. If creating the field is costly and it will likely be used again, then the value should be cached in a private field. If it is cheap to create or it is unlikely to be used again, it can be created as needed.

```
class Color
{
    public Color(int red, int green, int blue)
    {
        this.red = red;
        this.green = green;
        this.blue = blue;
    }

    int    red;
    int    green;
    int    blue;

    public static Color Red
    {
        get
        {
            return(new Color(255, 0, 0));
        }
    }
    public static Color Green
    {
        get
        {
            return(new Color(0, 255, 0));
        }
    }
    public static Color Blue
    {
        get
        {
            return(new Color(0, 0, 255));
        }
    }
}
```

```
class Test
{
    static void Main()
    {
        Color background = Color.Red;
    }
}
```

When the user wants one of the predefined color values, the getter in the property creates an instance with the proper color on the fly, and returns that instance.

Property Efficiency

Returning to the first example in this chapter, let's consider the efficiency of the code when executed:

```
class Test
{
    private string    name;

    public string Name
    {
        get
        {
            return name;
        }
        set
        {
            name = value;
        }
    }
}
```

This may seem to be an inefficient design, because a member function call is added where there would normally be a field access. However, there is no reason that the underlying runtime environment can't inline the accessors as it would any other simple function, so there is often[2] no performance penalty in choosing a property instead of a simple field. The opportunity to be able to revise the implementation at a later time without changing the interface can be invaluable, so properties are usually a better choice than fields for public members.

---

2. The Win32 version of the .NET Runtime does perform the inlining of trivial accessors, though other environments wouldn't have to.

There does remain a small downside of using properties; they aren't supported natively by all .NET languages, so other languages may have to call the accessor functions directly, which is a bit more complicated than using fields.

Property Accessibility

In C#, a property is modeled after a "virtual field," which constrains the author of the property a bit. It is not possible to set the accessibility separately for the `get` and `set` accessors (to have a public `get` and a protected `set`, for example) because this couldn't be done for a field.[3]

To allow a derived class to set the value of a read-only property can be done through two different approaches. The first is simply to add this:

```
protected void SetValue(int value);
```

function to the class. The second is to add a protected read-write property to the class:

```
protected int ValueProt
```

This may seem like unnecessary work, but the simplification on the user side is considerable, and a property can be treated as if it was a field. Since this user case is much more prevalent than the derived class case, it makes sense to leave the complexity on the authoring side.

Virtual Properties

If a property makes sense as part of base class, it may make sense to make the property virtual. Virtual properties follow the same rules as other virtual entities. Here's a quick example of a virtual property:

```
using System;

public abstract class DrawingObject
{
    public abstract string Name
    {
        get;
    }
}
```

3. Properties could support a more complicated model, and they do in the Managed Extensions to C++. The simplification this gives for the property author is more than offset by the added complexity of the model for the user, so C# doesn't do this.

```
class Circle: DrawingObject
{
    string name = "Circle";

    public override string Name
    {
        get
        {
            return(name);
        }
    }
}
class Test
{
    public static void Main()
    {
        DrawingObject d = new Circle();
        Console.WriteLine("Name: {0}", d.Name);
    }
}
```

The abstract property `Name` is declared in the `DrawingObject` class, with an abstract `get` accessor. This accessor must then be overridden in the derived class.

When the `Name` property is accessed through a reference to the base class, the overridden property in the derived class is called.

CHAPTER 19

Indexers and Enumerators

IT SOMETIMES MAKES SENSE to be able to index an object as if it were an array. This can be done by writing an indexer for the object, which can be thought of as a smart array. As a property looks like a field but has accessors to perform get and set operations, an indexer looks like an array, but has accessors to perform array indexing operations.

Indexing with an Integer Index

A class that contains a database row might implement an indexer to access the columns in the row:

```
using System;
using System.Collections;
class DataValue
{
    public DataValue(string name, object data)
    {
        this.name = name;
        this.data = data;
    }
    public string Name
    {
        get
        {
            return(name);
        }
        set
        {
            name = value;
        }
    }
```

```
    public object Data
    {
        get
        {
            return(data);
        }
        set
        {
            data = value;
        }
    }
    string    name;
    object data;
}
class DataRow
{
    public DataRow()
    {
        row = new ArrayList();
    }

    public void Load()
    {
        /* load code here */
        row.Add(new DataValue("Id", 5551212));
        row.Add(new DataValue("Name", "Fred"));
        row.Add(new DataValue("Salary", 2355.23m));
    }

        // the indexer
    public DataValue this[int column]
    {
        get
        {
            return((DataValue) row[column - 1]);
        }
        set
        {
            row[column - 1] = value;
        }
    }
    ArrayList    row;
}
```

```
class Test
{
    public static void Main()
    {
        DataRow row = new DataRow();
        row.Load();
        Console.WriteLine("Column 0: {0}", row[1].Data);
        row[1].Data = 12;    // set the ID
    }
}
```

The `DataRow` class has functions to load in a row of data, functions to save the data, and an indexer function to provide access to the data. In a real class, the `Load()` function would load data from a database.

The indexer function is written the same way that a property is written, except that it takes an indexing parameter. The indexer is declared using the name `this` since it has no name.

Indexing with a String Index

A class can have more than one indexer. For the `DataRow` class, it might be useful to be able to use the name of the column for indexing:

```
using System;
using System.Collections;
class DataValue
{
    public DataValue(string name, object data)
    {
        this.name = name;
        this.data = data;
    }
    public string Name
    {
        get
        {
            return(name);
        }
        set
        {
            name = value;
        }
    }
```

```
    public object Data
    {
        get
        {
            return(data);
        }
        set
        {
            data = value;
        }
    }
    string   name;
    object data;
}
class DataRow
{
    public DataRow()
    {
        row = new ArrayList();
    }

    public void Load()
    {
        /* load code here */
        row.Add(new DataValue("Id", 5551212));
        row.Add(new DataValue("Name", "Fred"));
        row.Add(new DataValue("Salary", 2355.23m));
    }

    public DataValue this[int column]
    {
        get
        {
            return( (DataValue) row[column - 1]);
        }
        set
        {
            row[column - 1] = value;
        }
    }
```

```
    int FindColumn(string name)
    {
        for (int index = 0; index < row.Count; index++)
        {
            DataValue dataValue = (DataValue) row[index];
            if (dataValue.Name == name)
                return(index);
        }
        return(-1);
    }
    public DataValue this[string name]
    {
        get
        {
            return( (DataValue) this[FindColumn(name)]);
        }
        set
        {
            this[FindColumn(name)] = value;
        }
    }
    ArrayList    row;
}
class Test
{
    public static void Main()
    {
        DataRow row = new DataRow();
        row.Load();
        DataValue val = row["Id"];
        Console.WriteLine("Id: {0}", val.Data);
        Console.WriteLine("Salary: {0}", row["Salary"].Data);
        row["Name"].Data = "Barney";    // set the name
        Console.WriteLine("Name: {0}", row["Name"].Data);
    }
}
```

The string indexer uses the `FindColumn()` function to find the index of the name, and then uses the `int` indexer to do the proper thing.

Indexing with Multiple Parameters

Indexers can have more than one parameter, to simulate a multidimensional virtual array. The following example illustrates such a use:

```
using System;

public class Player
{
    string name;

    public Player(string name)
    {
        this.name = name;
    }

    public override string ToString()
    {
        return(name);
    }
}

public class Board
{
    Player[,] board = new Player[8, 8];

    int RowToIndex(string row)
    {
        string temp = row.ToUpper();
        return((int) temp[0] - (int) 'A');
    }

    int PositionToColumn(string pos)
    {
        return(pos[1] - '0' - 1);
    }

    public Player this[string row, int column]
    {
        get
        {
            return(board[RowToIndex(row), column - 1]);
        }
```

```
        set
        {
            board[RowToIndex(row), column - 1] = value;
        }
    }

    public Player this[string position]
    {
        get
        {
            return(board[RowToIndex(position),
                       PositionToColumn(position)]);
        }
        set
        {
            board[RowToIndex(position),
                      PositionToColumn(position)] = value;
        }
    }
}
class Test
{
    public static void Main()
    {
        Board board = new Board();

        board["A", 4] = new Player("White King");
        board["H", 4] = new Player("Black King");

        Console.WriteLine("A4 = {0}", board["A", 4]);
        Console.WriteLine("H4 = {0}", board["H4"]);
    }
}
```

The example implements a chessboard that can be accessed using standard chess notation (a letter from A to H followed by a number from 1 to 8). The first indexer is used to access the board using string and integer indices, and the second indexer uses a single string like "C5."

Enumerators and Foreach

If an object can be treated as an array, it is often convenient to iterate through it using the `foreach` statement. To understand what is required to enable `foreach`, it helps to know what goes on behind the scenes.

When the compiler sees the following `foreach` block:

```
foreach (string s in myCollection)
{
    Console.WriteLine("String is {0}", s);
}
```

it transforms this code into the following:

```
IEnumerator enumerator = ((IEnumerable) myCollection).GetEnumerator();
while (enumerator.GetNext())
{
    string s = (string) enumerator.Current();
    Console.WriteLine("String is {0}", s);
}
```

The first step of the process is to cast the collection class to `IEnumerable`. If that succeeds, the class supports enumeration, and an `IEnumerator` interface reference to perform the enumeration is returned. The `GetNext()` and `Current` members of the class are then called to perform the iteration.

The `IEnumerator` interface can be implemented directly by the container class, or it can be implemented by a separate private class. Private implementation is preferable since it simplifies the collection class and allows multiple users to iterate over the same instance at the same time.

The following example shows an integer collection class that enables `foreach` usage (note that this is not intended to be a full implementation of such a class):

```
using System;
using System.Collections;

// Note: This class is not thread-safe
public class IntList: IEnumerable
{
    int[] values = new int[10];
    int allocated = 10;
    int count = 0;
    int revision = 0;

    public void Add(int value)
```

```
{
        // reallocate if necessary...
    if (count + 1 == allocated)
    {
        int[] newValues = new int[allocated * 2];
        for (int index = 0; index < count; index++)
        {
            newValues[index] = values[index];
        }
        allocated *= 2;
    }
    values[count] = value;
    count++;
    revision++;
}

public int Count
{
    get
    {
        return(count);
    }
}

void CheckIndex(int index)
{
    if (index >= count)
        throw new ArgumentOutOfRangeException("Index value out of range");
}

public int this[int index]
{
    get
    {
        CheckIndex(index);
        return(values[index]);
    }
    set
    {
        CheckIndex(index);
        values[index] = value;
        revision++;
    }
}

public IEnumerator GetEnumerator()
```

```
    {
        return(new IntListEnumerator(this));
    }

    internal int Revision
    {
        get
        {
            return(revision);
        }
    }
}

class IntListEnumerator: IEnumerator
{
    IntList    intList;
    int revision;
    int index;

    internal IntListEnumerator(IntList intList)
    {
        this.intList = intList;
        Reset();
    }

    public bool MoveNext()
    {
        index++;
        if (index >= intList.Count)
            return(false);
        else
            return(true);
    }
```

```
    public object Current
    {
        get
        {
            if (revision != intList.Revision)
                throw new InvalidOperationException
                ("Collection modified while enumerating.");
            return(intList[index]);
        }
    }

    public void Reset()
    {
        index = -1;
        revision = intList.Revision;
    }
}

class Test
{
    public static void Main()
    {
        IntList list = new IntList();

        list.Add(1);
        list.Add(55);
        list.Add(43);

        foreach (int value in list)
        {
            Console.WriteLine("Value = {0}", value);
        }

        foreach (int value in list)
        {
            Console.WriteLine("Value = {0}", value);
            list.Add(124);
        }
    }
}
```

The collection class itself only needs a couple of modifications. It implements `IEnumerable` and therefore has a `GetEnumerator()` method that returns an `IEnumerator` reference to an instance of our enumerator class that points to the current list.

The IntListEnumerator implements enumeration on the IntList that its passed using the IEnumerator interface and therefore implements the members of that interface.

Having a collection change as it is being iterated over is a bad thing, so these classes detect that condition (as illustrated in the second foreach in Main()). The IntList class has a revision number that it updates when the list contents change. The current revision number for the list is stored when the enumeration is started and then checked in the Current property to ensure that the list is unchanged.

Improving the Enumerator

The enumerator in the previous section has two deficiencies that should be addressed.

The first is that the enumerator isn't compile-time typesafe, but only runtime typesafe. If the following code is written:

```
IntList intList = new IntList();
intList.Add(55);
//...
foreach (string s in intList)
{
}
```

The error can't be identified at compile time, but an exception will be generated when then code is executed. The reason that this can't be identified at compile time is that IEnumerator.Current is of type object, and in the above example, converting from object to int is a legal operation.

A second problem with Current being of type object is that returning a value type (such as int) requires that the value type be boxed. This is wasteful, since IntListEnumerator.Current boxes the int, only to have it immediately unboxed after the property is accessed.

To address this situation, the C# compiler implements a pattern-matching approach instead of a strict interface-based approach when dealing with enumerators. Instead of requiring the collection class implement IEnumerable, it has to have a GetEnumerator() method. This method doesn't have to return IEnumerator but can return a real class instance for the enumerator. This enumerator, in turn, needs to have the usual enumerator functions (GetNext(), Reset(), Current), but the type of Current doesn't have to be object.

With this modification, a strongly typed collection class can now get compile-time type checking, and classes that store value types can avoid boxing overhead. The modifications to the classes are fairly simple. First, the interface names are removed. IntList.GetEnumerator()is modified as follows:

```
public IntListEnumerator GetEnumerator()
{
    return(new IntListEnumerator(this));
}
```

The modification to `IntListEnumerator.Current` is also minimal:

```
public int Current
{
    get
    {
        if (revision != intList.Revision)
            throw new InvalidOperationException
            ("Collection modified while
            enumerating.");
        return(intList[index]);
    }
}
```

That was easy.

Unfortunately, there's a problem. The standard method of enabling enumeration is to implement `IEnumerable` and `IEnumerator`, so any language that looks for those isn't going to be able to iterate over the `IntList` collection.

The solution is to add back explicit implementations of those interfaces.[1] This means adding an explicit implementation of `IEnumerable.GetEnumerator() to IntList:`

```
public IEnumerator IEnumerable.GetEnumerator()
{
    return(GetEnumerator());
}
```

`and an explicit implementation of IEnumerator.Current` to `IntListEnumerator`:

```
public object IEnumerator.Current
{
    get
    {
            return(Current);
    }
}
```

1. For more information, see Chapter 10, "Interfaces."

That now enables the standard method of iteration, and the resulting class can be used either with a compiler that supports the strongly typed pattern-matching approach or a compiler that supports `IEnumerable`/`IEnumerator`.

Disposable Enumerators

Sometimes, an enumerator holds a valuable resource, such as a database connection. The resources will be released when the enumerator is finalized, but it would be useful if the resource could be released when the enumerator was no longer needed. Because of this, the expansion of a foreach isn't quite as simple as was implied previously.

The C# compiler does this by relying on the `IDisposable` interface, in a similar manner to the `using` statement. It's a bit more complicated in this case, however. For the `using` statement, it's easy for the compiler to determine whether the class implements `IDisposable`, but that's not true in this case. There are three cases the compiler must handle when it expands:

```
foreach (Resource r in container) …
```

GetEnumerator() Returns IEnumerator

In this case, the compiler must determine dynamically whether the class implements `IDisposable`. The `foreach` expands to:

```
IEnumerator e = container.GetEnumerator();
try {
    while (e.MoveNext()) {
        Resource r = e.Current;
        ...;
    }
}
finally {
    IDisposable d = e as IDisposable;
    if (d != null) d.Dispose();
}
```

GetEnumerator() Returns a Class That Implements IDisposable

If the compiler can statically know that a class implements `IDisposable`, the compiler will call `Dispose()` without the dynamic test:

```
IEnumerator e = container.GetEnumerator();
try {
    while (e.MoveNext()) {
        Resource r = e.Current;
        ...;
    }
}
finally {
    ((IDisposable) e).Dispose();
}
```

GetEnumerator() Returns a Class That Doesn't Implement IDisposable

In this case, the normal expansion is used:

```
IEnumerator e = container.GetEnumerator();
while (e.MoveNext()) {
    Resource r = e.Current;
    ...;
}
```

Design Guidelines

Indexers should be used only in situations where the abstraction makes sense. This usually depends on whether the object is a container for some other object.

VB.NET views what C# terms an indexer as a default property, and a class can have more than one indexed property in a VB.NET program. Since C# views an indexer as an indication that an object is composed of the indexed type, the VB.NET view doesn't map into the C# perspective (how can an object be an array of two different types?). C# therefore only allows access to the default indexed property directly.[2]

2. If you have to access other ones, you can call the `get` and `set` functions directly.

C# gives its indexer the name `Item`, which is fine from the C# perspective because the name is never used. Languages such as VB.NET, however, do see the name, and it may therefore be helpful to set the name to something other than `Item`. This is done by placing the `IndexerNameAttribute` on the indexer (this attribute is found in the `System.Runtime.CompilerServices` namespace).

CHAPTER 20

Enumerations

ENUMERATIONS ARE USEFUL WHEN a value in the program can only have a specific set of values. A control that could only be one of four colors, or a network package that supports only two protocols, are situations where an enumeration can improve code.

A Line Style Enumeration

In the following example, a line drawing class uses an enumeration to declare the styles of lines it can draw:

```
using System;
public class Draw
{
    public enum LineStyle
    {
        Solid,
        Dotted,
        DotDash,        // trailing comma is optional
    }

    public void DrawLine(int x1, int y1, int x2, int y2, LineStyle lineStyle)
    {
        switch (lineStyle)
        {
            case LineStyle.Solid:
                // draw solid
                break;

            case LineStyle.Dotted:
                // draw dotted
                break;

            case LineStyle.DotDash:
                // draw dotdash
                break;
```

```
            default:
                throw(new ArgumentException("Invalid line style"));
        }
    }
}
class Test
{
    public static void Main()
    {
        Draw draw = new Draw();
        draw.DrawLine(0, 0, 10, 10, Draw.LineStyle.Solid);
        draw.DrawLine(5, 6, 23, 3, (Draw.LineStyle) 35);
    }
}
```

The `LineStyle` enum defines the values that can be specified for the enum, and then that same enum is used in the function call to specify the type of line to draw.

While enums do prevent the accidental specification of values outside of the enum range, the values that can be specified for an enum are not limited to the identifiers specified in the enum declaration. The second call to `DrawLine()` is legal, so an enum value passed into a function must still be validated to ensure that it is in the range of valid values. The `Draw` class throws an invalid argument exception if the argument is invalid.

Enumeration Base Types

Each enumeration has an underlying type that specifies how much storage is allocated for that enumeration. The valid base types for enumeration are `byte`, `sbyte`, `short`, `ushort`, `int`, `uint`, `long`, and `ulong`. If the base type is not specified, the base type defaults to `int`. The base type is specified by listing the base type after the enum name:

```
enum SmallEnum : byte
{
    A,
    B,
    C,
    D
}
```

Specifying the base type can be useful if size is a concern, or if the number of entries would exceed the number of possible values for `int`.

Initialization

By default, the value of the first enum member is set to 0, and incremented for each subsequent member. Specific values may be specified along with the member name:

```
enum Values
{
    A = 1,
    B = 5,
    C = 3,
    D = 42
}
```

Computed values can also be used, as long as they only depend on values already defined in the enum:

```
enum Values
{
    A = 1,
    B = 2,
    C = A + B,
    D = A * C + 33
}
```

If an enum is declared without a 0 value, this can lead to problems, since 0 is the default initialized value for the enum:

```
enum Values
{
    A = 1,
    B = 2,
    C = A + B,
    D = A * C + 33
}
class Test
{
    public static void Member(Values value)
    {
        // do some processing here
    }
```

```
    public static void Main()
    {
        Values value = 0;
        Member(value);
    }
}
```

A member with the value 0 should always be defined as part of an enum.

Bit Flag Enums

Enums may also be used as bit flags by specifying a different bit value for each bit. Here's a typical definition:

```
using System;
[Flags]
enum BitValues : uint
{
    NoBits = 0,
    Bit1 = 0x00000001,
    Bit2 = 0x00000002,
    Bit3 = 0x00000004,
    Bit4 = 0x00000008,
    Bit5 = 0x00000010,
    AllBits = 0xFFFFFFFF
}
class Test
{
    public static void Member(BitValues value)
    {
        // do some processing here
    }
    public static void Main()
    {
        Member(BitValues.Bit1 | BitValues.Bit2);
    }
}
```

The `[Flags]` attribute before the enum definition is used so that designers and browsers can present a different interface for enums that are flag enums. In such enums, it would make sense to allow the user to `OR` several bits together, which wouldn't make sense for non-flag enums.

The `Main()` function `OR`s two bit values together, and then passes the value to the member function.

Conversions

Enum types can be converted to their underlying type and back again with an explicit conversion:

```
enum Values
{
    A = 1,
    B = 5,
    C = 3,
    D = 42
}
class Test
{
    public static void Main()
    {
        Values v = (Values) 2;
        int ival = (int) v;
    }
}
```

The sole exception to this is that the literal `0` can be converted to an enum type without a cast. This is allowed so that the following code can be written:

```
public void DoSomething(BitValues bv)
{
    if (bv == 0)
    {

    }
}
```

The `if` statement would have to be written as

```
    if (bv == (BitValues) 0)
```

if this exception wasn't present. That's not bad for this example, but it could be quite cumbersome in actual use if the enum is nested deeply in the hierarchy:

```
    if (bv == (CornSoft.PlotLibrary.Drawing.LineStyle.BitValues) 0)
```

That's a lot of typing.

The System.Enum Type

Like the other predefined type, the `Enum` type has some methods that make enums in C# a fair bit more useful that enums in C++.

The first of these is that the `ToString()` function is overridden to return the textual name for an enum value, so that the following can be done:

```
using System;

enum Color
{
    red,
    green,
    yellow
}

public class Test
{
    public static void Main()
    {
        Color c = Color.red;

        Console.WriteLine("c is {0}", c);
    }
}
```

The example produces:

```
c is red
```

rather than merely giving the numeric equivalent of `Color.red`.

Other operations can be done as well:

```
using System;

enum Color
{
    red,
    green,
    yellow
}
```

```
public class Test
{
    public static void Main()
    {
        Color c = Color.red;

            // enum values and names
        foreach (int i in Enum.GetValues(c.GetType()))
        {
           Console.WriteLine("Value: {0} ({1})", i, Enum.GetName(c.GetType(), i));
        }

            // or just the names
        foreach (string s in Enum.GetNames(c.GetType()))
        {
            Console.WriteLine("Name: {0}", s);
        }

            // enum value from a string, ignore case
        c = (Color) Enum.Parse(typeof(Color), "Red", true);
        Console.WriteLine("string value is: {0}", c);

            // see if a specific value is a defined enum member
        bool defined = Enum.IsDefined(typeof(Color), 5);
        Console.WriteLine("5 is a defined value for Color: {0}", defined);    }
}
```

The output from this example is:

```
Value: 0 (red)
Value: 1 (green)
Value: 2 (yellow)
Name: red
Name: green
Name: yellow
string value is: red
5 is a defined value for Color: False
```

In this example, the values and/or names of the enum constants can be fetched from the enum, and the string name for a value can be converted to an enum value. Finally, a value is checked to see if it is the same as one of the defined constants.

CHAPTER 21

Attributes

IN MOST PROGRAMMING LANGUAGES, some information is expressed through declaration, and other information is expressed through code. For example, in the following class member declaration

```
public int Test;
```

the compiler and runtime will reserve space for an integer variable and set its protection so that it is visible everywhere. This is an example of declarative information; it's nice because of the economy of expression and because the compiler handles the details for us.

Typically, the types of declarative information are predefined by the language designer and can't be extended by users of the language. A user who wants to associate a specific database field with a field of a class, for example, must invent a way of expressing that relationship in the language, a way of storing the relationship, and a way of accessing the information at runtime. In a language like C++, a macro might be defined that stores the information in a field that is part of the object. Such schemes work, but they're error-prone and not generalized. They're also ugly.

The .NET Runtime supports attributes, which are merely annotations that are placed on elements of source code, such as classes, members, parameters, etc. Attributes can be used to change the behavior of the runtime, provide transaction information about an object, or convey organizational information to a designer. The attribute information is stored with the metadata of the element and can be easily retrieved at runtime through a process known as reflection.

C# uses a conditional attribute to control when member functions are called. A use for the conditional attribute would look like this:

```
using System.Diagnostics;
class Test
{
    [Conditional("DEBUG")]
    public void Validate()
    {
    }
}
```

Most programmers will use predefined attributes much more often than writing an attribute class.

Using Attributes

Suppose that for a project that a group was doing, it was important to keep track of the code reviews that had been performed on the classes so that it could be determined when code reviews were finished. The code review information could be stored in a database, which would allow easy queries about status, or it could be stored in comments, which would make it easy to look at the code and the information at the same time.

Or an attribute could be used, which would enable both kinds of access.

To do that, an attribute class is needed. An attribute class defines the name of an attribute, how it can be created, and the information that will be stored. The gritty details of defining attribute classes will be covered in the section entitled "An Attribute of Your Own."

The attribute class will look like this:

```
using System;
[AttributeUsage(AttributeTargets.Class)]
public class CodeReviewAttribute: System.Attribute
{
    public CodeReviewAttribute(string reviewer, string date)
    {
        this.reviewer = reviewer;
        this.date = date;
    }
    public string Comment
    {
        get
        {
            return(comment);
        }
        set
        {
            comment = value;
        }
    }
    public string Date
    {
        get
        {
            return(date);
        }
    }
```

```
    public string Reviewer
    {
        get
        {
            return(reviewer);
        }
    }
    string reviewer;
    string date;
    string comment;
}
[CodeReview("Eric", "01-12-2000", Comment="Bitchin' Code")]
class Complex
{
}
```

The `AttributeUsage` attribute before the class specifies that this attribute can only be placed on classes. When an attribute is used on a program element, the compiler checks to see whether the use of that attribute on that program element is allowed.

The naming convention for attributes is to append `Attribute` to the end of the class name. This makes it easier to tell which classes are attribute classes and which classes are normal classes. All attributes must derive from `System.Attribute`.

The class defines a single constructor that takes a reviewer and a date as parameters, and it also has the public string property `Comment`.

When the compiler comes to the attribute use on class `Complex`, it first looks for a class derived from `Attribute` named `CodeReview`. It doesn't find one, so it next looks for a class named `CodeReviewAttribute`, which it finds.

Next, it checks to see whether the attribute is allowed for this usage (on a class).

Then, it checks to see if there is a constructor that matches the parameters we've specified in the attribute use. If it finds one, an instance of the object is created—the constructor is called with the specified values.

If there are named parameters, it matches the name of the parameter with a field or property in the attribute class, and then it sets the field or property to the specified value.

After this is done, the current state of the attribute class is saved to the metadata for the program element for which it was specified.

At least, that's what happens *logically*. In actuality, it only *looks* like it happens that way; see the "Attribute Pickling" sidebar for a description of how it is implemented.

Attribute Pickling

There are a few reasons why it doesn't really work the way it's described, and they're related to performance. For the compiler to actually create the attribute object, the .NET Runtime environment would have to be running, so every compilation would have to start up the environment, and every compiler would have to run as a managed executable.

Additionally, the object creation isn't really required, since we're just going to store the information away.

The compiler therefore validates that it *could* create the object, call the constructor, and set the values for any named parameters. The attribute parameters are then pickled into a chunk of binary information, which is tucked away with the metadata of the object.

A Few More Details

Some attributes can only be used once on a given element. Others, known as multi-use attributes, can be used more than once. This might be used, for example, to apply several different security attributes to a single class. The documentation on the attribute will describe whether an attribute is single-use or multi-use.

In most cases, it's clear that the attribute applies to a specific program element. However, consider the following case:

```
using System.Runtime.InteropServices;
class Test
{
    [return: MarshalAs(UnmanagedType.LPWStr)]
    public static extern string GetMessage();
}
```

In most cases, an attribute in that position would apply to the member function, but this attribute is really related to the return type. How can the compiler tell the difference?

There are several situations in which this can happen:

- Method vs. return value
- Event vs. field or property
- Delegate vs. return value
- Property vs. accessor vs. return value of getter vs. value parameter of setter

For each of these situations, there is a case that is much more common than the other case, and it becomes the default case. To specify an attribute for the non-default case, the element the attribute applies to must be specified:

```
using System.Runtime.InteropServices;
class Test
{
    [return: MarshalAs(UnmanagedType.LPWStr)]
    public static extern string GetMessage();
}
```

The `return:` indicates that this attribute should be applied to the return value.

The element may be specified even if there is no ambiguity. The identifiers are as follows:

SPECIFIER	DESCRIPTION
`assembly`	Attribute is on the assembly
`module`	Attribute is on the module
`type`	Attribute is on a class or struct
`method`	Attribute is on a method
`property`	Attribute is on a property
`event`	Attribute is on an event
`field`	Attribute is on a field
`param`	Attribute is on a parameter
`return`	Attribute is on the return value

Attributes that are applied to assemblies or modules must occur after any `using` clauses and before any code.

```
using System;
[assembly:CLSCompliant(true)]

class Test
{
    Test() {}
}
```

This example applies the `ClsCompliant` attribute to the entire assembly. All assembly-level attributes declared in any file that is in the assembly are grouped together and attached to the assembly.

To use a predefined attribute, start by finding the constructor that best matches the information to be conveyed. Next, write the attribute, passing parameters to the constructor. Finally, use the named parameter syntax to pass additional information that wasn't part of the constructor parameters.

For more examples of attribute use, look at Chapter 31, "Interop."

An Attribute of Your Own

To define attribute classes and reflect on them at runtime, there are a few more issues to consider. This section will discuss some things to consider when designing an attribute.

There are two major things to determine when writing an attribute. The first is the program elements that the attribute may be applied to, and the second is the information that will be stored by the attribute.

Attribute Usage

Placing the `AttributeUsage` attribute on an attribute class controls where the attribute can be used. The possible values for the attribute are listed in the `AttributeTargets` enumerator and are as follows:

RETURNVALUE	MEANING
`Assembly`	The program assembly
`Module`	The current program file
`Class`	A class

(Continued)

RETURNVALUE	MEANING
Struct	A struct
Enum	An enumerator
Constructor	A constructor
Method	A method (member function)
Property	A property
Field	A field
Event	An event
Interface	An interface
Parameter	A method parameter
ReturnValue	The method return value
Delegate	A delegate
All	Anywhere
ClassMembers	Class, Struct, Enum, Constructor, Method, Property, Field, Event, Delegate, Interface

As part of the `AttributeUsage` attribute, one of these can be specified or a list of them can be ORed together.

The `AttributeUsage` attribute is also used to specify whether an attribute is single-use or multi-use. This is done with the named parameter `AllowMultiple`. Such an attribute would look like this:

```
[AttributeUsage(AttributeTargets.Method | AttributeTargets.Event,
               AllowMultiple = true)]
```

Attribute Parameters

The information the attribute will store should be divided into two groups: the information that is required for every use, and the optional items.

The information that is required for every use should be obtained via the constructor for the attribute class. This forces the user to specify all the parameters when they use the attribute.

Optional items should be implemented as named parameters, which allows the user to specify whichever optional items are appropriate.

If an attribute has several different ways in which it can be created, with different required information, separate constructors can be declared for each usage. Don't use separate constructors as an alternative to optional items.

Attribute Parameter Types

The attribute pickling format only supports a subset of all the .NET Runtime types, and therefore, only some types can be used as attribute parameters. The types allowed are the following:

- bool, byte, char, double, float, int, long, short, string
- object
- System.Type
- An enum that has public accessibility (not nested inside something non-public)
- A one-dimensional array of one of the above types

Reflecting on Attributes

Once attributes are defined on some code, it's useful to be able to find the attribute values. This is done through reflection.

The following code shows an attribute class, the application of the attribute to a class, and the reflection on the class to retrieve the attribute.

```
using System;
using System.Reflection;
[AttributeUsage(AttributeTargets.Class, AllowMultiple=true)]
public class CodeReviewAttribute: System.Attribute
{
    public CodeReviewAttribute(string reviewer, string date)
    {
        this.reviewer = reviewer;
        this.date = date;
    }
```

```
    public string Comment
    {
        get
        {
            return(comment);
        }
        set
        {
            comment = value;
        }
    }
    public string Date
    {
        get
        {
            return(date);
        }
    }
    public string Reviewer
    {
        get
        {
            return(reviewer);
        }
    }
    string reviewer;
    string date;
    string comment;
}
[CodeReview("Eric", "01-12-2000", Comment="Bitchin' Code")]
[CodeReview("Gurn", "01-01-2000", Comment="Revisit this section")]
class Complex
{
}
```

```
class Test
{
   public static void Main()
    {
        Type type = typeof(Complex);
        foreach (CodeReviewAttribute att in
                        type.GetCustomAttributes(typeof(CodeReviewAttribute), false))
        {
            CodeReviewAttribute    att = (CodeReviewAttribute) atts[0];
            Console.WriteLine("Reviewer: {0}", att.Reviewer);
            Console.WriteLine("Date: {0}", att.Date);
            Console.WriteLine("Comment: {0}", att.Comment);
        }
    }
}
```

The `Main()` function first gets the type object associated with the type `Complex`. It then iterates over all the `CodeReviewAttribute` attributes attached to the type and writes the values out.

Alternately, the code could get all the attributes by omitting the type in the call to `GetCustomAttributes`:

```
        foreach (object o in type.GetCustomAttributes(false))
        {
            CodeReviewAttribute att = o as CodeReviewAttribute;
            if (att != null)
            {
                // write values here...
            }
        }
```

This example produces the following output:

```
Reviewer: Eric
Date: 01-12-2000
Comment: Bitchin' Code
Reviewer: Gurn
Date: 01-01-2000
Comment: Revisit this section
```

The `false` value in the call to `GetCustomAttributes` tells the runtime to ignore any inherited attributes. In this case, that would ignore any attributes on the base class of `Complex`.

In the example, the type object for the `Complex` type is obtained using `typeof`. It can also be obtained in the following manner:

```
Complex c = new Complex();
Type t = c.GetType();
Type t2 = Type.GetType("Complex");
```

> **NOTE** *The "*`CustomAttributes`*" in the preceding example refers to attributes stored in the section of metadata reserved for attributes. Some .NET Runtime attributes are not stored as custom attributes on the object, but are instead stored as metadata bits on the object. Runtime reflection does not support viewing these attributes through reflection. This restriction may be addressed in future versions of the runtime.*

CHAPTER 22

Delegates

DELEGATES ARE SIMILAR to interfaces, in that they specify a contract between a caller and an implementer. Rather than specifying an entire interface, though, a delegate merely specifies the form of a single function. Also, interfaces are created at compile time, whereas delegates are created at runtime.

Delegates are used as the basis for events in C#, which are the general-purpose notification mechanisms used by the .NET Frameworks.

Using Delegates

The specification of the delegate determines the form of the function, and to create an instance of the delegate, one must use a function that matches that form. Delegates are sometimes referred to as "safe function pointers," which isn't a bad analogy, but they do a lot more than act as function pointers.

Because of their more dynamic nature, delegates are useful when the user may want to change behavior. If, for example, a collection class implements sorting, it might want to support different sort orders. The sorting could be controlled based on a delegate that defines the comparison function:

```
using System;
public class Container
{
    public delegate int CompareItemsCallback(object obj1, object obj2);
    public void Sort(CompareItemsCallback compare)
    {
        // not a real sort, just shows what the
        // inner loop code might do
        int x = 0;
        int y = 1;
        object    item1 = arr[x];
        object item2 = arr[y];
        int order = compare(item1, item2);
    }
    object[]    arr = new object[1];    // items in the collection
}
```

```
public class Employee
{
    Employee(string name, int id)
    {
        this.name = name;
        this.id = id;
    }
    public static int CompareName(object obj1, object obj2)
    {
        Employee emp1 = (Employee) obj1;
        Employee emp2 = (Employee) obj2;
        return(String.Compare(emp1.name, emp2.name));
    }
    public static int CompareId(object obj1, object obj2)
    {
        Employee emp1 = (Employee) obj1;
        Employee emp2 = (Employee) obj2;

        if (emp1.id > emp2.id)
            return(1);
        if (emp1.id < emp2.id)
            return(-1);
        else
            return(0);
    }
    string    name;
    int    id;
}
class Test
{
    public static void Main()
    {
        Container employees = new Container();
        // create and add some employees here

            // create delegate to sort on names, and do the sort
        Container.CompareItemsCallback sortByName =
            new Container.CompareItemsCallback(Employee.CompareName);
        employees.Sort(sortByName);
            // employees is now sorted by name
    }
}
```

The delegate defined in the `Container` class takes the two objects to be compared as parameters and returns an integer that specifies the ordering of the two objects. Two static functions are declared that match this delegate as part of the `Employee` class, with each function describing a different kind of ordering.

When the container needs to be sorted, a delegate can be passed in that describes the ordering that should be used, and the sort function will do the sorting. (Well, it would if it were actually implemented.)

Delegates to Instance Members

Users who are familiar with C++ will find more than a little similarity between delegates and C++ function pointers, but there's more to a delegate than there is to a function pointer.

When dealing with Windows functions, it's fairly common to pass in a function pointer that should be called when a specific event occurs. Since C++ function pointers can only refer to static functions, and not member functions,[1] there needs to be some way to communicate some state information to the function so that it knows what object the event corresponds to. Most functions deal with this by taking an `int` parameter, which is passed through to the callback function. The parameter (in C++ at least) is then cast to a class instance, and then the event is processed.

In C#, delegates can encapsulate both a function to call and an instance to call it on, so there is no need for an extra parameter to carry the instance information. This is also a type-safe mechanism because the instance is specified at the same time the function to call is specified:

```
using System;
public class User
{
    string name;
    public User(string name)
    {
        this.name = name;
    }
    public void Process(string message)
    {
        Console.WriteLine("{0}: {1}", name, message);
    }
}
```

1. Some of you are saying, "What about member function pointers?" Member functions do indeed do something similar, but the syntax is a bit ... opaque. You'll probably find that delegates in C# are both easier to use and more functional.

```
class Test
{
    delegate void ProcessHandler(string message);

    public static void Main()
    {
        User aUser = new User("George");
        ProcessHandler ph = new ProcessHandler(aUser.Process);

        ph("Wake Up!");
    }
}
```

In this example, a delegate is created that points to the `User.Process()` function, with the `aUser` instance, and the call through the delegate is identical to calling `aUser.Process()` directly.

Multicasting

As mentioned earlier, a delegate can refer to more than one function. Basically, a delegate encapsulates a list of functions that should be called in order. The `Delegate` class provides functions to take two delegates and return one that encapsulates both, or to remove a delegate from another.

To combine two delegates, the `Delegate.Combine()` function is used. The last example can be easily modified to call more than one function:

```
using System;
public class User
{
    string name;
    public User(string name)
    {
        this.name = name;
    }
    public void Process(string message)
    {
        Console.WriteLine("{0}: {1}", name, message);
    }
}
```

```
class Test
{
    delegate void ProcessHandler(string message);

    static public void Process(string message)
    {
        Console.WriteLine("Test.Process(\"{0}\")", message);
    }
    public static void Main()
    {
        User user = new User("George");

        ProcessHandler ph = new ProcessHandler(user.Process);
        ph = (ProcessHandler) Delegate.Combine(ph, new ProcessHandler(Process));

        ph("Wake Up!");
    }
}
```

Invoking `ph` now calls both delegates.

There are a couple of problems with this approach, however. The first is that it's ugly. More importantly, however, is that it isn't type-safe at compile time; `Delegate.Combine()` both takes and returns the type `Delegate`, so there's no way at compile time to know whether the delegates are compatible.

To address these issues, C# allows the `+=` and `-=` operators to be used to call `Delegate.Combine()` and `Delegate.Remove()`, and it makes sure the types are compatible. The call in the example is modified to the following:

```
ph += new ProcessHandler(Process);
```

When invoked, the sub-delegates encapsulated in a delegate are called synchronously in the order that they were added to the delegate. If an exception is thrown by one of the sub-delegates, the remaining sub-delegates will not be called. If this behavior is not desirable, the list of sub-delegates (otherwise known as an "invocation list") can be obtained from the delegate, and each sub-delegate can be called directly. Instead of:

```
ph("Wake Up!");
```

the following can be used:

```
foreach (ProcessHandler phDel in ph.GetInvocationList())
{
    try
    {
        phDel("Wake Up!");
    }
    catch (Exception e)
    {
        // log the exception here...
    }
}
```

Code like this could also be used to implement "black-ball" voting, where all delegates could be called once to see if they were able to perform a function and then called a second time if they all voted yes.

Wanting to call more than one function may seem to be a rare situation, but it's common when dealing with events, which will be covered in Chapter 23, "Events."

Delegates as Static Members

One drawback of this approach is that the user who wants to use the sorting has to create an instance of the delegate with the appropriate function. It would be nicer if they didn't have to do that, and that can be done by defining the appropriate delegates as static members of `Employee`:

```
using System;
public class Container
{
    public delegate int CompareItemsCallback(object obj1, object obj2);
    public void Sort(CompareItemsCallback compare)
    {
        // not a real sort, just shows what the
        // inner loop code might do
        int x = 0;
        int y = 1;
        object    item1 = arr[x];
        object item2 = arr[y];
        int order = compare(item1, item2);
    }
```

```
    object[]    arr = new object[1];    // items in the collection
}
class Employee
{
    Employee(string name, int id)
    {
        this.name = name;
        this.id = id;
    }
    public static readonly Container.CompareItemsCallback SortByName =
        new Container.CompareItemsCallback(CompareName);
    public static readonly Container.CompareItemsCallback SortById =
        new Container.CompareItemsCallback(CompareId);

    public static int CompareName(object obj1, object obj2)
    {
        Employee emp1 = (Employee) obj1;
        Employee emp2 = (Employee) obj2;
        return(String.Compare(emp1.name, emp2.name));
    }
    public static int CompareId(object obj1, object obj2)
    {
        Employee emp1 = (Employee) obj1;
        Employee emp2 = (Employee) obj2;

        if (emp1.id > emp2.id)
            return(1);
        if (emp1.id < emp2.id)
            return(-1);
        else
            return(0);
    }
    string    name;
    int    id;
}
class Test
{
    public static void Main()
    {
        Container employees = new Container();
        // create and add some employees here

        employees.Sort(Employee.SortByName);
            // employees is now sorted by name
    }
}
```

This is a lot easier. The users of `Employee` don't have to know how to create the delegate—they can just refer to the static member.

Delegates as Static Properties

One thing that is a bit wasteful, however, is that the delegate is *always* created, even if it is never used. It would be better if the delegate were created on the fly as needed. This can be done by replacing the static members with properties:

```
using System;
class Container
{
    public delegate int CompareItemsCallback(object obj1, object obj2);
    public void SortItems(CompareItemsCallback compare)
    {
        // not a real sort, just shows what the
        // inner loop code might do...
        int x = 0;
        int y = 1;
        object    item1 = arr[x];
        object item2 = arr[y];
        int order = compare(item1, item2);
    }
    object[]    arr;    // items in the collection
}
class Employee
{
    Employee(string name, int id)
    {
        this.name = name;
        this.id = id;
    }
    public static Container.CompareItemsCallback SortByName
    {
        get
        {
            return(new Container.CompareItemsCallback(CompareName));
        }
    }
```

```
    public static Container.CompareItemsCallback SortById
    {
        get
        {
            return(new Container.CompareItemsCallback(CompareId));
        }
    }
    static int CompareName(object obj1, object obj2)
    {
        Employee emp1 = (Employee) obj1;
        Employee emp2 = (Employee) obj2;
        return(String.Compare(emp1.name, emp2.name));
    }
    static int CompareId(object obj1, object obj2)
    {
        Employee emp1 = (Employee) obj1;
        Employee emp2 = (Employee) obj2;

        if (emp1.id > emp2.id)
            return(1);
        if (emp1.id < emp2.id)
            return(-1);
        else
            return(0);
    }
    string    name;
    int    id;
}
class Test
{
    public static void Main()
    {
        Container employees = new Container();
        // create and add some employees here

        employees.SortItems(Employee.SortByName);
            // employees is now sorted by name
    }
}
```

With this version, rather than `Employee.SortByName` being a delegate, it's a function that returns a delegate that can sort by name.

Initially, this example had private static delegate members `SortByName` and `SortById`, and the property created the static member if it hadn't been used before.

This would work well if the creation of the delegate were somewhat costly and the delegate was likely to be used again.

In this case, however, it's much easier to create the delegate on the fly and just return it to the user. As soon as the `Sort` function on `Container` is done with the delegate, it will be available for collection by the garbage collector.

> **NOTE** *This example is only for illustration. To implement a collection class that does sorting, the techniques used by the Frameworks are much easier. See Chapter 27, "Making Friends with the .NET Frameworks," for more information.*

CHAPTER 23

Events

CHAPTER 22 DISCUSSED how delegates could be used to pass a reference to a method so that it could be called in a general way. Being able to call a method in such a way is useful in graphical user interfaces, such as the one provided by the classes in `System.Windows.Forms`. It's fairly easy to build such a framework by using delegates, as shown in this example:

```
using System;

public class Button
{
    public delegate void ClickHandler(object sender, EventArgs e);
    public ClickHandler Click;

    protected void OnClick()
    {
        if (Click != null)
            Click(this, null);

    }

    public void SimulateClick()
    {
        OnClick();
    }
}

class Test
{
    static public void ButtonHandler(object sender, EventArgs e)
    {
        Console.WriteLine("Button clicked");
    }
```

```
    public static void Main()
    {
        Button button = new Button();

        button.Click = new Button.ClickHandler(ButtonHandler);

        button.SimulateClick();
    }
}
```

The `Button` class is supporting a click "event"[1] by having the `ClickHandler` delegate tell what kind of method can be called to hook up, and a delegate instance can then be assigned to the event. The `OnClick()` method then calls this delegate, and everything works fine—at least in this simple case.

The situation gets more complicated in a real-world scenario. In real applications, a button such as this one would live in a form, and a click on the button might be of interest to more than one area of the application. Doing this isn't a problem with delegates because more than one method can be called from a single delegate instance. In the previous example, if another class also wanted to be called when the button was clicked, the += operator could be used, like this:

```
button.Click += new Button.ClickHandler(OtherMethodToCall);
```

Unfortunately, if the other class wasn't careful, it might do the following:

```
button.Click = new Button.ClickHandler(OtherMethodToCall);
```

This would be bad, as it would mean that our `ButtonHandler` would be unhooked and only the new method would be called.

Similarly, to unhook from the click, the right thing to do is use this code:[2]

```
button.Click -= new Button.ClickHandler(OtherMethodToCall);
```

but the following might be used instead:

```
button.Click = null;
```

This is also wrong.

1. This isn't an "event" in the C# sense of the word but just the abstract concept of something happening.
2. This syntax may look weird since a new instance of the delegate is created just so it can be removed from the delegate. When `Delegate.Remove()` is called, it needs to find the delegate in the invocation list, so a delegate instance is required.

What is needed is some way of protecting the delegate field so that it's only accessed using += and -=.

Add and Remove Functions

An easy way to do this is to make the delegate field private and write a couple of methods that can be used to add or remove delegates:

```
using System;

public class Button
{
    public delegate void ClickHandler(object sender, EventArgs e);
    private ClickHandler click;

    public void AddClick(ClickHandler clickHandler)
    {
        click += clickHandler;
    }

    public void RemoveClick(ClickHandler clickHandler)
    {
        click -= clickHandler;
    }

    protected void OnClick()
    {
        if (click != null)
            click(this, null);

    }

    public void SimulateClick()
    {
        OnClick();
    }
}
```

```
class Test
{
    static public void ButtonHandler(object sender, EventArgs e)
    {
        Console.WriteLine("Button clicked");
    }

    public static void Main()
    {
        Button button = new Button();

        button.AddClick(new Button.ClickHandler(ButtonHandler));

        button.SimulateClick();

        button.RemoveClick(new Button.ClickHandler(ButtonHandler));
    }
}
```

In this example, the `AddClick()` and `RemoveClick()` methods have been added, and the delegate field is now private. It's now impossible for users of the class to do the wrong thing when they hook or unhook.

This example is reminiscent of the example in Chapter 18, "Properties." We had two accessor methods, and adding properties made those two methods look like a field. Let's add a feature to our compiler so there's a "virtual" delegate named `Click`. It can write the `AddClick()` and `RemoveClick()` methods for us, and it can also change a use of `+=` or `-=` to the appropriate add or remove call. This gives us the advantage of having the `Add` and `Remove` methods without having to write them.

We need a keyword for this compiler enhancement, and `event` seems like a good choice:

```
using System;

public class Button
{
    public delegate void ClickHandler(object sender, EventArgs e);

    public event ClickHandler Click;

    protected void OnClick()
    {
        if (Click != null)
            Click(this, null);
    }
```

```
    public void SimulateClick()
    {
        OnClick();
    }
}

class Test
{
    static public void ButtonHandler(object sender, EventArgs e)
    {
        Console.WriteLine("Button clicked");
    }

    public static void Main()
    {
        Button button = new Button();

        button.Click += new Button.ClickHandler(ButtonHandler);

        button.SimulateClick();

        button.Click -= new Button.ClickHandler(ButtonHandler);
    }
}
```

When the `event` keyword is added to a delegate, the compiler creates a private field and then writes public `add_Click()` and `remove_Click()` methods. It also emits a bit of metadata that says there is an event named `Click` and that event is associated with add and remove methods with these names so that object browsers and such can tell there's an event on this class.

In `Main()`, the event is accessed as if it were a delegate; but since the add and remove methods are the only ways to access the private delegate, `+=` and `-=` are the only operations that can be performed on the event.

That's the basic story for events. The arguments to the event handler, `object sender` and `EventArgs e`, are by convention and should be followed by other classes that expose events. The `sender` argument allows the user of the code to know which object fired the event, and the `e` argument contains the information associated with the event. In this case, there's no additional information to pass, so `EventArgs` is used. If additional information needed to be passed, a class should be derived from `EventArgs` with the additional information. For example, the `KeyEventArgs` class in the Frameworks looks like this:

```
using System;
using System.Windows.Forms;
class KeyEventArgs: EventArgs
{
    Keys    keyData;

    KeyEventArgs(Keys keyData)
    {
        this.keyData = keyData;
    }

    public Keys KeyData
    {
        get
        {
            return(keyData);
        }
    }

    // other functions here...
}
```

The `OnKey` method will take a parameter of type `Keys`, encapsulate it into a `KeyEventArgs` class, and then call the delegate.

Custom Add and Remove

Because the compiler creates a private delegate field for every event that is declared, a class that declares numerous events will use one field per event. The `Control` class in `System.Windows.Forms` declares 27 events, but there are usually just a couple of these events hooked up for a given control. What's needed is a way to avoid allocating the storage for the delegate unless it is needed.

The C# language supports this by allowing the `add()` and `remove()` methods to be written directly, which lets delegates be stored in a more space-efficient manner. One typical way of doing this is to define a `Hashtable` as part of the object and then to store the delegate in the `Hashtable`, like this:

```
using System;
using System.Collections;
using System.Runtime.CompilerServices;
public class Button
{
    public delegate void ClickHandler(object sender, EventArgs e);

    Hashtable delegateStore = new Hashtable();
    static object clickEventKey = new object();

    public event ClickHandler Click
    {
        [MethodImpl(MethodImplOptions.Synchronized)]
        add
        {
            delegateStore[clickEventKey] =
                Delegate.Combine((Delegate) delegateStore[clickEventKey],
                        value);
        }

        [MethodImpl(MethodImplOptions.Synchronized)]
        remove
        {
            delegateStore[clickEventKey] =
                Delegate.Remove((Delegate) delegateStore[clickEventKey],
                        value);
        }
    }

    protected void OnClick()
    {
        ClickHandler ch = (ClickHandler) delegateStore[clickEventKey];
        if (ch != null)
            ch(this, null);
    }

    public void SimulateClick()
    {
        OnClick();
    }
}
```

```
class Test
{
    static public void ButtonHandler(object sender, EventArgs e)
    {
        Console.WriteLine("Button clicked");
    }

    public static void Main()
    {
        Button button = new Button();

        button.Click += new Button.ClickHandler(ButtonHandler);

        button.SimulateClick();

        button.Click -= new Button.ClickHandler(ButtonHandler);
    }
}
```

The `add()` and `remove()` methods are written using a syntax similar to the one used for properties, and they use the `delegateStore` hash table to store the delegate. One problem with using a hash table is coming up with a key that can be used to store and fetch the delegates. There's nothing associated with an event that can serve as a unique key, so the `clickEventKey` is an object that's included only so that we can use it as a key for the hash table. It's static because the same unique value can be used for all instances of the `Button` class.

The `MethodImpl` attribute is required so two threads won't try to add or remove delegates at the same time (which would be bad). This could also be done with the `lock` statement.

This implementation still results in the use of one field per object for the hash table. To get rid of this, you have a couple of options. The first is to make the hash table static so that it can be shared among all instances of the `Button` class. The second choice would be to make a single global class to be shared among all the controls, which saves the most space.[3]

Both are good choices, but both will require a couple of changes to our approach. First, simply using an object as a key isn't good enough since the hash table is shared among all the instances of the object, so the instance will also have to be used as a key.

A subtle outgrowth of using the instance is that the controls have to call a method to remove their event storage when they are closed. If this didn't happen, the control

3. But perhaps slower access, since this hash table will have more entries than a per-control implementation.

wouldn't be visible anymore, but it would still be referenced through the global event object, and the memory would never be reclaimed by the garbage collector.

Here's the a final version of the example, with a global delegate cache:

```
using System;
using System.Collections;
using System.Runtime.CompilerServices;

    //
    // Global delegate cache. Uses a two-level hashtable. The delegateStore
    //  hashtable stores a hashtable keyed on the object instance, and the
    // instance hashtable is keyed on the unique key. This allows fast tear-down
    // of the object when it's destroyed.
    //
public class DelegateCache
{
    private DelegateCache() {}    // nobody can create one of these

    Hashtable delegateStore = new Hashtable();    // top level hash table

    static DelegateCache dc = new DelegateCache();    // our single instance

    Hashtable GetInstanceHash(object instance)
    {
        Hashtable instanceHash = (Hashtable) delegateStore[instance];

        if (instanceHash == null)
        {
            instanceHash = new Hashtable();
            delegateStore[instance] = instanceHash;

        }
        return(instanceHash);
    }

    public static void Combine(Delegate myDelegate, object instance, object key)
    {
        lock(instance)
        {
            Hashtable instanceHash = dc.GetInstanceHash(instance);

            instanceHash[key] =
                Delegate.Combine((Delegate) instanceHash[key],  myDelegate);
        }
    }
```

```
    public static void Remove(Delegate myDelegate, object instance, object key)
    {
        lock(instance)
        {
            Hashtable instanceHash = dc.GetInstanceHash(instance);

            instanceHash[key] =
                Delegate.Remove((Delegate) instanceHash[key], myDelegate);
        }
    }

    public static Delegate Fetch(object instance, object key)
    {
        Hashtable instanceHash = dc.GetInstanceHash(instance);

        return((Delegate) instanceHash[key]);
    }

    public static void ClearDelegates(object instance)
    {
        dc.delegateStore.Remove(instance);
    }
}

public class Button
{
    public void TearDown()
    {
        DelegateCache.ClearDelegates(this);
    }


    public delegate void ClickHandler(object sender, EventArgs e);

    static object clickEventKey = new object();

    public event ClickHandler Click
    {
        add
        {
            DelegateCache.Combine(value, this, clickEventKey);
        }
```

```
        remove
        {
            DelegateCache.Remove(value, this, clickEventKey);
        }
    }

    protected void OnClick()
    {
        ClickHandler ch = (ClickHandler) DelegateCache.Fetch(this, clickEventKey);

        if (ch != null)
            ch(this, null);
    }

    public void SimulateClick()
    {
        OnClick();
    }
}

class Test
{
    static public void ButtonHandler(object sender, EventArgs e)
    {
        Console.WriteLine("Button clicked");
    }

    public static void Main()
    {
        Button button = new Button();

        button.Click += new Button.ClickHandler(ButtonHandler);

        button.SimulateClick();

        button.Click -= new Button.ClickHandler(ButtonHandler);

        button.TearDown();
    }
}
```

The `DelegateCache` class stores the hash tables for each instance that has stored a delegate in a main hash table. This allows for easier cleanup when a control is finished. The `Combine()`, `Remove()`, and `Fetch()` methods do what is expected. The `ClearDelegates()` method is called by `Button.TearDown()` to remove all delegates stored for a specific control instance.[4]

4. In a real implementation, this could be done through a teardown function, or it could also be done through a finalizer and a `Dispose()` method.

CHAPTER 24

User-Defined Conversions

C# ALLOWS CONVERSIONS to be defined between classes or structs and other objects in the system. User-defined conversions are always static functions, which must either take as a parameter or return as a return value the object in which they are declared. This means that conversions can't be declared between two existing types, which makes the language simpler.

A Simple Example

This example implements a struct that handles roman numerals. It could also be written as a class but since it is a piece of data, a struct makes more sense. .

```
using System;
using System.Text;
struct RomanNumeral
{
    public RomanNumeral(short value)
    {
        if (value > 5000)
            throw(new ArgumentOutOfRangeException());

        this.value = value;
    }
    public static explicit operator RomanNumeral(
        short value)
    {
        RomanNumeral    retval;
        retval = new RomanNumeral(value);
        return(retval);
    }
```

```
    public static implicit operator short(
    RomanNumeral roman)
    {
        return(roman.value);
    }

    static string NumberString(
    ref int value, int magnitude, char letter)
    {
        StringBuilder    numberString = new StringBuilder();

        while (value >= magnitude)
        {
            value -= magnitude;
            numberString.Append(letter);
        }
        return(numberString.ToString());
    }

    public static implicit operator string(
    RomanNumeral roman)
    {
        int        temp = roman.value;

        StringBuilder retval = new StringBuilder();

        retval.Append(RomanNumeral.NumberString(ref temp, 1000, 'M'));
        retval.Append(RomanNumeral.NumberString(ref temp, 500, 'D'));
        retval.Append(RomanNumeral.NumberString(ref temp, 100, 'C'));
        retval.Append(RomanNumeral.NumberString(ref temp, 50, 'L'));
        retval.Append(RomanNumeral.NumberString(ref temp, 10, 'X'));
        retval.Append(RomanNumeral.NumberString(ref temp, 5, 'V'));
        retval.Append(RomanNumeral.NumberString(ref temp, 1, 'I'));

        return(retval.ToString());
    }

    private short value;
}
```

```
class Test
{
    public static void Main()
    {
        short s = 12;
        RomanNumeral numeral = new RomanNumeral(s);

        s = 165;
        numeral = (RomanNumeral) s;

        Console.WriteLine("Roman as int: {0}", (int)numeral);
        Console.WriteLine("Roman as string: {0}", (string)numeral);

        short s2 = numeral;
    }
}
```

This struct declares a constructor that can take a `short` value and it also declares a conversion from an integer to a `RomanNumeral`. The conversion is declared as an `explicit` conversion because it may throw an exception if the number is bigger than the magnitude supported by the struct. There is a conversion to `short` that is declared `implicit`, because the value in a `RomanNumeral` will always fit in a `short`. And finally, there's a conversion to `string` that gives the romanized version of the number.[1]

When an instance of this struct is created, the constructor can be used to set the value. An explicit conversion can be used to convert the integer value to a `RomanNumeral`. To get the romanized version of the `RomanNumeral`, the following would be written:

```
Console.WriteLine(roman);
```

If this is done, the compiler reports that there is an ambiguous conversion present. The class includes `implicit` conversions to both `short` and to `string`, and `Console.WriteLine()` has overloads that take both versions, so the compiler doesn't know which one to call.

In the example, an `explicit` cast is used to disambiguate, but it's a bit ugly. Since this struct would likely be used primarily to print out the romanized notation, it probably makes sense to change the conversion to integer to be an `explicit` one so that the conversion to string is the only `implicit` one.

---

1. No, this struct doesn't handle niceties such as replacing "IIII" with "IV", nor does it handle converting the romanized string to a `short`. The remainder of the implementation is left as an exercise for the reader.

Pre and Post Conversions

In the preceding example, the basic types that were converted to and from the `RomanNumeral` were exact matches to the types that were declared in the struct itself. The user-defined conversions can also be used in situations where the source or destination types are not exact matches to the types in the conversion functions.

If the source or destination types are not exact matches, then the appropriate standard (i.e., built-in) conversion must be present to convert from the source type to the source type of the user-defined conversion and/or from the destination type of the user-defined conversion, and the type of the conversion (`implicit` or `explicit`) must also be compatible.

Perhaps an example will be a bit clearer. In the preceding example, the line

```
short s = numeral;
```

calls the implicit user-defined conversion directly. Since this is an implicit use of the user-defined conversion, there can also be another implicit conversion at the end:

```
int i = numeral;
```

Here, the implicit conversion from `RomanNumeral` to `short` is performed, followed by the implicit conversion from `short` to `long`.

In the explicit case, there was the following conversion in the example:

```
numeral = (RomanNumeral) 165;
```

Since the usage is `explicit`, the explicit conversion from `int` to `RomanNumeral` is used. Also, an additional explicit conversion can occur before the user-defined conversion is called:

```
long bigvalue = 166;
short smallvalue = 12;
numeral = (RomanNumeral) bigvalue;
numeral = (RomanNumeral) smallvalue;
```

In the first conversion, the `long` value is converted by explicit conversion to an integer, and then the user-defined conversion is called. The second conversion is similar, except that an implicit conversion is performed before the explicit user-defined conversion.

Conversions Between Structs

User-defined conversions that deal with classes or structs rather than basic types work in a similar way, except that there are a few more situations to consider. Since the user conversion can be defined in either the source or destination type, there's a bit more design work to do, and the operation is a bit more complex. For details, see the "How It Works" section, later in this chapter.

Adding to the `RomanNumeral` example in the last section, a struct that handles binary numbers can be added:

```
using System;
using System.Text;
struct RomanNumeral
{
    public RomanNumeral(short value)
    {
        if (value > 5000)
            throw(new ArgumentOutOfRangeException());

        this.value = value;
    }
    public static explicit operator RomanNumeral(
    short value)
    {
        RomanNumeral    retval;
        retval = new RomanNumeral(value);
        return(retval);
    }

    public static implicit operator short(
    RomanNumeral roman)
    {
        return(roman.value);
    }

    static string NumberString(
    ref int value, int magnitude, char letter)
    {
        StringBuilder    numberString = new StringBuilder();

        while (value >= magnitude)
        {
            value -= magnitude;
            numberString.Append(letter);
        }
        return(numberString.ToString());
    }
```

```
    public static implicit operator string(
    RomanNumeral roman)
    {
        int          temp = roman.value;

        StringBuilder retval = new StringBuilder();

        retval.Append(RomanNumeral.NumberString(ref temp, 1000, 'M'));
        retval.Append(RomanNumeral.NumberString(ref temp, 500, 'D'));
        retval.Append(RomanNumeral.NumberString(ref temp, 100, 'C'));
        retval.Append(RomanNumeral.NumberString(ref temp, 50, 'L'));
        retval.Append(RomanNumeral.NumberString(ref temp, 10, 'X'));
        retval.Append(RomanNumeral.NumberString(ref temp, 5, 'V'));
        retval.Append(RomanNumeral.NumberString(ref temp, 1, 'I'));

        return(retval.ToString());
    }

    private short value;
}
struct BinaryNumeral
{
    public BinaryNumeral(int value)
    {
        this.value = value;
    }
    public static implicit operator BinaryNumeral(
    int value)
    {
        BinaryNumeral    retval = new BinaryNumeral(value);
        return(retval);
    }

    public static implicit operator int(
    BinaryNumeral binary)
    {
        return(binary.value);
    }

    public static implicit operator string(
    BinaryNumeral binary)
```

```
    {
        StringBuilder    retval = new StringBuilder();

        return(retval.ToString());
    }

    private int value;
}
class Test
{
    public static void Main()
    {
        RomanNumeral    roman = new RomanNumeral(12);
        BinaryNumeral    binary;
        binary = (BinaryNumeral)(int)roman;
    }
}
```

The classes can be used together, but since they don't really know about each other, it takes a bit of extra typing. To convert from a `RomanNumeral` to a `BinaryNumeral` requires first converting to an `int`.

It would be nice to write the `Main()` function as

```
binary = roman;
roman = (RomanNumeral) binary;
```

and make the types look like the built-in types, with the exception that `RomanNumeral` has a smaller range than binary, and therefore will require an explicit conversion in that section.

To get this, a user-defined conversion is required on either the `RomanNumeral` or the `BinaryNumeral` class. In this case, it goes on the `RomanNumeral` class, for reasons that should become clear in the "Design Guidelines" section of this chapter.

The classes are modified as follows, adding two conversions:

```
using System;
using System.Text;
struct RomanNumeral
{
    public RomanNumeral(short value)
    {
        if (value > 5000)
            throw(new ArgumentOutOfRangeException());

        this.value = value;
    }
```

```
public static explicit operator RomanNumeral(
short value)
{
    RomanNumeral    retval;
    retval = new RomanNumeral(value);
    return(retval);
}

public static implicit operator short(
RomanNumeral roman)
{
    return(roman.value);
}

static string NumberString(
ref int value, int magnitude, char letter)
{
    StringBuilder    numberString = new StringBuilder();

    while (value >= magnitude)
    {
        value -= magnitude;
        numberString.Append(letter);
    }
    return(numberString.ToString());
}

public static implicit operator string(
RomanNumeral roman)
{
    int        temp = roman.value;

    StringBuilder retval = new StringBuilder();

    retval.Append(RomanNumeral.NumberString(ref temp, 1000, 'M'));
    retval.Append(RomanNumeral.NumberString(ref temp, 500, 'D'));
    retval.Append(RomanNumeral.NumberString(ref temp, 100, 'C'));
    retval.Append(RomanNumeral.NumberString(ref temp, 50, 'L'));
    retval.Append(RomanNumeral.NumberString(ref temp, 10, 'X'));
    retval.Append(RomanNumeral.NumberString(ref temp, 5, 'V'));
    retval.Append(RomanNumeral.NumberString(ref temp, 1, 'I'));

    return(retval.ToString());
}
```

```
    public static implicit operator BinaryNumeral(RomanNumeral roman)
    {
        return(new BinaryNumeral((short) roman));
    }

    public static explicit operator RomanNumeral(
    BinaryNumeral binary)
    {
        return(new RomanNumeral((short) binary));
    }

    private short value;
}
struct BinaryNumeral
{
    public BinaryNumeral(int value)
    {
        this.value = value;
    }
    public static implicit operator BinaryNumeral(
    int value)
    {
        BinaryNumeral    retval = new BinaryNumeral(value);
        return(retval);
    }

    public static implicit operator int(
    BinaryNumeral binary)
    {
        return(binary.value);
    }

    public static implicit operator string(
    BinaryNumeral binary)
    {
        StringBuilder    retval = new StringBuilder();

        return(retval.ToString());
    }

    private int value;
}
```

```
class Test
{
    public static void Main()
    {
        RomanNumeral    roman = new RomanNumeral(122);
        BinaryNumeral    binary;
        binary = roman;
        roman = (RomanNumeral) binary;
    }
}
```

With these added conversions, conversions between the two types can now take place.

Classes and Pre and Post Conversions

As with basic types, classes can also have standard conversions that occur either before or after the user-defined conversion, or even before *and* after. The only standard conversions that deal with classes, however, are conversions to a base or derived class, so those are the only ones considered.

For implicit conversions, it's pretty simple, and the conversion occurs in three steps:

1. A conversion from a derived class to the source class of the user-defined conversion is optionally performed.

2. The user-defined conversion occurs.

3. A conversion from the destination class of the user-defined conversion to a base class is optionally performed.

To illustrate this, the example will be modified to use classes rather than structs, and a new class that derives from `RomanNumeral` will be added:

```
using System;
using System.Text;
class RomanNumeral
{
    public RomanNumeral(short value)
    {
        if (value > 5000)
            throw(new ArgumentOutOfRangeException());

        this.value = value;
    }
```

```
public static explicit operator RomanNumeral(
short value)
{
    RomanNumeral    retval;
    retval = new RomanNumeral(value);
    return(retval);
}

public static implicit operator short(
RomanNumeral roman)
{
    return(roman.value);
}

static string NumberString(
ref int value, int magnitude, char letter)
{
    StringBuilder    numberString = new StringBuilder();

    while (value >= magnitude)
    {
        value -= magnitude;
        numberString.Append(letter);
    }
    return(numberString.ToString());
}

public static implicit operator string(
RomanNumeral roman)
{
    int        temp = roman.value;

    StringBuilder retval = new StringBuilder();

    retval.Append(RomanNumeral.NumberString(ref temp, 1000, 'M'));
    retval.Append(RomanNumeral.NumberString(ref temp, 500, 'D'));
    retval.Append(RomanNumeral.NumberString(ref temp, 100, 'C'));
    retval.Append(RomanNumeral.NumberString(ref temp, 50, 'L'));
    retval.Append(RomanNumeral.NumberString(ref temp, 10, 'X'));
    retval.Append(RomanNumeral.NumberString(ref temp, 5, 'V'));
    retval.Append(RomanNumeral.NumberString(ref temp, 1, 'I'));

    return(retval.ToString());
}
```

```
    public static implicit operator BinaryNumeral(RomanNumeral roman)
    {
        return(new BinaryNumeral((short) roman));
    }

    public static explicit operator RomanNumeral(
    BinaryNumeral binary)
    {
        return(new RomanNumeral((short)(int) binary));
    }

    private short value;
}
class BinaryNumeral
{
    public BinaryNumeral(int value)
    {
        this.value = value;
    }
    public static implicit operator BinaryNumeral(
    int value)
    {
        BinaryNumeral    retval = new BinaryNumeral(value);
        return(retval);
    }

    public static implicit operator int(
    BinaryNumeral binary)
    {
        return(binary.value);
    }

    public static implicit operator string(
    BinaryNumeral binary)
    {
        StringBuilder    retval = new StringBuilder();

        return(retval.ToString());
    }

    private int value;
}
```

```
class RomanNumeralAlternate : RomanNumeral
{
    public RomanNumeralAlternate(short value): base(value)
    {
    }

    public static implicit operator string(
    RomanNumeralAlternate roman)
    {
        return("NYI");
    }
}
class Test
{
    public static void Main()
    {
            // implicit conversion section
        RomanNumeralAlternate    roman;
        roman = new RomanNumeralAlternate(55);

        BinaryNumeral binary = roman;
            // explicit conversion section
        BinaryNumeral binary2 = new BinaryNumeral(1500);
        RomanNumeralAlternate roman2;

        roman2 = (RomanNumeralAlternate) binary2;
    }
}
```

The operation of the `implicit` conversion to `BinaryNumeral` is as expected; an implicit conversion of `roman` from `RomanNumeralAlternate` to `RomanNumeral` occurs, and then the user-defined conversion from `RomanNumeral` to `BinaryNumeral` is performed.

The `explicit` conversion section may have some people scratching their heads. The user-defined function from `BinaryNumeral` to `RomanNumeral` returns a `RomanNumeral`, and the post-conversion to `RomanNumeralAlternate` can never succeed.

The conversion could be rewritten as follows:

```
using System;
using System.Text;
class RomanNumeral
```

```
{
    public RomanNumeral(short value)
    {
        if (value > 5000)
            throw(new ArgumentOutOfRangeException());

        this.value = value;
    }
    public static implicit operator short(
    RomanNumeral roman)
    {
        return(roman.value);
    }

    static string NumberString(
    ref int value, int magnitude, char letter)
    {
        StringBuilder    numberString = new StringBuilder();

        while (value >= magnitude)
        {
            value -= magnitude;
            numberString.Append(letter);
        }
        return(numberString.ToString());
    }

    public static implicit operator string(
    RomanNumeral roman)
    {
        int        temp = roman.value;

        StringBuilder retval = new StringBuilder();

        retval.Append(RomanNumeral.NumberString(ref temp, 1000, 'M'));
        retval.Append(RomanNumeral.NumberString(ref temp, 500, 'D'));
        retval.Append(RomanNumeral.NumberString(ref temp, 100, 'C'));
        retval.Append(RomanNumeral.NumberString(ref temp, 50, 'L'));
        retval.Append(RomanNumeral.NumberString(ref temp, 10, 'X'));
        retval.Append(RomanNumeral.NumberString(ref temp, 5, 'V'));
        retval.Append(RomanNumeral.NumberString(ref temp, 1, 'I'));

        return(retval.ToString());
    }
```

```
    public static implicit operator BinaryNumeral(RomanNumeral roman)
    {
        return(new BinaryNumeral((short) roman));
    }

    public static explicit operator RomanNumeral(
    BinaryNumeral binary)
    {
        int         val = binary;
        if (val >= 1000)
            return((RomanNumeral)
                    new RomanNumeralAlternate((short) val));
        else
            return(new RomanNumeral((short) val));
    }

    private short value;
}
class BinaryNumeral
{
    public BinaryNumeral(int value)
    {
        this.value = value;
    }
    public static implicit operator BinaryNumeral(
    int value)
    {
        BinaryNumeral    retval = new BinaryNumeral(value);
        return(retval);
    }

    public static implicit operator int(
    BinaryNumeral binary)
    {
        return(binary.value);
    }

    public static implicit operator string(
    BinaryNumeral binary)
    {
        StringBuilder    retval = new StringBuilder();

        return(retval.ToString());
    }
```

```
    private int value;
}
class RomanNumeralAlternate : RomanNumeral
{
    public RomanNumeralAlternate(short value) : base(value)
    {
    }

    public static implicit operator string(
    RomanNumeralAlternate roman)
    {
        return("NYI");
    }
}
class Test
{
    public static void Main()
    {
            // implicit conversion section
        RomanNumeralAlternate    roman;
        roman = new RomanNumeralAlternate(55);
        BinaryNumeral binary = roman;

        // explicit conversion section
        BinaryNumeral binary2 = new BinaryNumeral(1500);
        RomanNumeralAlternate roman2;

        roman2 = (RomanNumeralAlternate) binary2;
    }
}
```

The user-defined conversion operator now doesn't return a `RomanNumeral`, it returns a `RomanNumeral` reference to an object, and it's perfectly legal for that to be a reference to a derived type. Weird, perhaps, but legal. With the revised version of the conversion function, the `explicit` conversion from `BinaryNumeral` to `RomanNumeralAlternate` may succeed, depending on whether the `RomanNumeral` reference is a reference to a `RomanNumeral` object or a `RomanNumeralAlternate` object.

Design Guidelines

When designing user-defined conversions, the following guidelines should be considered.

Implicit Conversions Are Safe Conversions

When defining conversions between types, the only conversions that should be implicit ones are those that don't lose any data and don't throw exceptions.

This is important, because implicit conversions can occur without it being obvious that a conversion has occurred.

Define the Conversion in the More Complex Type

This basically means not cluttering up a simple type with conversions to a more complex one. For conversions to and from one of the predefined types, there is no option but to define the conversion as part of the class, since the source isn't available.

Even if the source *was* available, however, it would be really strange to define the conversions from `int` to `BinaryNumeral` or `RomanNumeral` in the `int` class.

Sometimes, as in the example, the classes are peers to each other, and there is no obvious simpler class. In that case, pick a class, and put both conversions there.

One Conversion to and from a Hierarchy

In my examples, there was only a single conversion from the user-defined type to the numeric types, and one conversion from numeric types to the user-defined type. In general, it is good practice to do this and then to use the built-in conversions to move between the destination types. When choosing the numeric type to convert from or to, choose the one that is the most natural size for the type.

For example, in the `BinaryNumeral` class, there's an implicit conversion to `int`. If the user wants a smaller type, such as `short`, a cast can easily be done.

If there are multiple conversions available, the overloading rules will take effect, and the result may not always be intuitive for the user of the class. This is especially important when dealing with both signed and unsigned types.

Add Conversions Only as Needed

Extraneous conversions only make the user's life harder.

Conversions That Operate in Other Languages

Some of the .NET languages don't support the conversion syntax, and calling conversion functions—which have weird names—may be difficult or impossible.

To make classes easily usable from these languages, alternate versions of the conversions should be supplied. If, for example, an object supports a conversion to `string`, it should also support calling `ToString()` on that function. Here's how it would be done on the `RomanNumeral` class:

```
using System;
using System.Text;

class RomanNumeral
{
    public RomanNumeral(short value)
    {
        if (value > 5000)
            throw(new ArgumentOutOfRangeException());

        this.value = value;
    }
    public static explicit operator RomanNumeral(
    short value)
    {
        RomanNumeral    retval;
        retval = new RomanNumeral(value);
        return(retval);
    }

    public static implicit operator short(
    RomanNumeral roman)
    {
        return(roman.value);
    }

    static string NumberString(
    ref int value, int magnitude, char letter)
    {
        StringBuilder    numberString = new StringBuilder();

        while (value >= magnitude)
        {
            value -= magnitude;
            numberString.Append(letter);
        }
        return(numberString.ToString());
    }
```

```
    public static implicit operator string(
    RomanNumeral roman)
    {
        int       temp = roman.value;

        StringBuilder retval = new StringBuilder();

        retval.Append(RomanNumeral.NumberString(ref temp, 1000, 'M'));
        retval.Append(RomanNumeral.NumberString(ref temp, 500, 'D'));
        retval.Append(RomanNumeral.NumberString(ref temp, 100, 'C'));
        retval.Append(RomanNumeral.NumberString(ref temp, 50, 'L'));
        retval.Append(RomanNumeral.NumberString(ref temp, 10, 'X'));
        retval.Append(RomanNumeral.NumberString(ref temp, 5, 'V'));
        retval.Append(RomanNumeral.NumberString(ref temp, 1, 'I'));

        return(retval.ToString());
    }
    public short ToShort()
    {
        return((short) this);
    }
    public override string ToString()
    {
        return((string) this);
    }

    private short value;
}
```

The `ToString()` function is an override because it overrides the `ToString()` version in `object`.

How It Works

To finish the section on user-defined conversions, there are a few details on how the compiler views conversions that warrant a bit of explanation. Those who are really interested in the gory details can find them in the C# Language Reference.[2]

This section can be safely skipped.

2. The C# Language Reference can be found at `http://msdn.microsoft.com/net/ecma`.

Conversion Lookup

When looking for candidate user-defined conversions, the compiler will search the source class and all of its base classes, and the destination class and all of its base classes.

This leads to an interesting case:

```
public class S
{
    public static implicit operator T(S s)
{
// conversion here
return(new T());
}
}

public class TBase
{
}

public class T: TBase
{

}
public class Test
{
    public static void Main()
    {
        S myS = new S();
        TBase tb = (TBase) myS;
    }
}
```

In this example, the compiler will find the conversion from `S` to `T`, and since the use is explicit, match it for the conversion to `TBase`, which will only succeed if the `T` returned by the conversion is really only a `TBase`.

Revising things a bit, removing the conversion from `S` and adding it to `T`, we get this:

```
// error
class S
{
}
```

```
class TBase
{
}
class T: TBase
{
    public static implicit operator T(S s)
    {
        return(new T());
    }
}
class Test
{
    public static void Main()
    {
        S myS = new S();
        TBase tb = (TBase) myS;
    }
}
```

This code doesn't compile. The conversion is from `S` to `TBase`, and the compiler can't find the definition of the conversion, because class `T` isn't searched.

CHAPTER 25

Operator Overloading

OPERATOR OVERLOADING ALLOWS operators to be defined on a class or struct so that it can be used with operator syntax. This is most useful on data types where there is a good definition for what a specific operator means, thereby allowing an economy of expression for the user.

Overloading the relational operators (==, !=, >, <, >=, <=) is covered in the section that covers overloading the `Equals()` function from the .NET Frameworks, in Chapter 27, "Making Friends with the .NET Frameworks."

Overloading conversion operators is covered in Chapter 24, "User-Defined Conversions."

Unary Operators

All unary operators are defined as static functions that take a single operator of the class or struct type and return an operator of that type. The following operators can be overloaded:

```
+  -  !  ~++  --  true false
```

The first six unary overloaded operators are called when the corresponding operation is invoked on a type. The `true` and `false` operators are available for Boolean types where

```
if (a == true)
```

is not equivalent to

```
if (! (a == false))
```

This happens in the SQL types in the `System.Data.SQL` namespace,, which have a null state that is neither true nor false. In this case, the compiler will use the overloaded `true` and `false` operators to correctly evaluate such statements. These operators must return type `bool`.

There is no way to discriminate between the pre and post increment or decrement operation. Because the operators are static (and therefore have no state), this distinction is not important.

Binary Operators

All binary operators take two parameters, at least one of which must be the class or struct type in which the operator is declared. A binary operator can return any type, but would typically return the type of the class or struct in which it is defined.

The following binary operators can be overloaded:

```
+  -  *  /  %  &  |  ^  <<  >>  ==  !=  >=  <=  >  <
```

An Example

The following class implements some of the overloadable operators:

```
using System;
struct RomanNumeral
{
    public RomanNumeral(int value)
    {
        this.value = value;
    }
    public override string ToString()
    {
        return(value.ToString());
    }
    public static RomanNumeral operator -(RomanNumeral roman)
    {
        return(new RomanNumeral(-roman.value));
    }
    public static RomanNumeral operator +(
    RomanNumeral    roman1,
    RomanNumeral    roman2)
    {
        return(new RomanNumeral(
                    roman1.value + roman2.value));
    }

    public static RomanNumeral operator ++(
    RomanNumeral    roman)
    {
        return(new RomanNumeral(roman.value + 1));
    }
    int value;
}
```

```
class Test
{
    public static void Main()
    {
        RomanNumeral    roman1 = new RomanNumeral(12);
        RomanNumeral    roman2 = new RomanNumeral(125);

        Console.WriteLine("Increment: {0}", roman1++);
        Console.WriteLine("Addition: {0}", roman1 + roman2);
    }
}
```

This example generates the following output:

```
Increment: 12
Addition: 138
```

Restrictions

It is not possible to overload member access, member invocation (function calling), or the `=`, `&&`, `||`, `?:`, or `new` operators. This is for the sake of simplicity; while one can do interesting things with such overloadings, it greatly increases the difficulty in understanding code, since programmers would have to always remember that member invocation (for example) could be doing something special.[1] `New` can't be overloaded because the .NET Runtime is responsible for managing memory, and in the C# idiom, `new` just means "give me a new instance of."

It is also not possible to overload the compound assignment operators `+=`, `*=`, etc., since they are always expanded to the simple operation and an assignment. This avoids cases where one would be defined and the other wouldn't be, or (shudder) they would be defined with different meanings.

Guidelines

Operator overloading is a feature that should be used only when necessary. By "necessary," I mean that it makes things easier and simpler for the user.

Good examples of operator overloading would be defining arithmetic operations on a complex number or matrix class.

1. One could, however, argue that member access can be overloaded through properties.

Bad examples would be defining the increment (++) operator on a `string` class to mean "increment each character in the string." A good guideline is that unless a typical user would understand what the operator does without any documentation, it shouldn't be defined as an operator. Don't make up new meanings for operators.

In practice, the equality (`==`) and inequality (`!=`) operators are the ones that will be defined most often, since if this is not done, there may be unexpected results.[2]

If the type behaves like a built-in data type, such as the `BinaryNumeral` class, it may make sense to overload more operators. At first look, it might seem that since the `BinaryNumeral` class is really just a fancy integer, it could just derive from the `System.Int32` class, and get the operators for free.

This won't work for a couple of reasons. First, value types can't be used as base classes, and `Int32` is a value type. Second, even if it was possible, it wouldn't really work for `BinaryNumeral`, because a `BinaryNumeral` isn't an integer; it only supports a small part of the possible integer range. Because of this, derivation would not be a good design choice. The smaller range means that even if `BinaryNumeral` as derived from `int`, there isn't an implicit conversion from `int` to `BinaryNumeral`, and any expressions would therefore require casts.

Even if these weren't true, however, it still wouldn't make sense, since the whole point of having a data type is to have something that's lightweight, and a struct would be a better choice than a class. Structs, of course, can't derive from other objects.

A Complex Number Class

The following struct implements a complex number, with a few overloaded operators. Note that there are non-overloaded versions for languages that don't support overloaded operators:

```
using System;

struct Complex
{
    float real;
    float imaginary;
```

2. As we saw earlier, if your type is a reference type (class), using == will compare to see if the two things you're comparing reference the same object, rather than seeing if they have the same contents. If your type is a value type, == will compare the contents of the value type, if operator == is defined.

```
public Complex(float real, float imaginary)
{
    this.real = real;
    this.imaginary = imaginary;
}

public float Real
{
    get
    {
        return(real);
    }
    set
    {
        real = value;
    }
}

public float Imaginary
{
    get
    {
        return(imaginary);
    }
    set
    {
        imaginary = value;
    }
}

public override string ToString()
{
    return(String.Format("({0}, {1}i)", real, imaginary));
}

public static bool operator==(Complex c1, Complex c2)
{
    if ((c1.real == c2.real) &&
        (c1.imaginary == c2.imaginary))
        return(true);
    else
        return(false);
}
```

```
public static bool operator!=(Complex c1, Complex c2)
{
    return(!(c1 == c2));
}

public override bool Equals(object o2)
{
    Complex c2 = (Complex) o2;

    return(this == c2);
}

public override int GetHashCode()
{
    return(real.GetHashCode() ^ imaginary.GetHashCode());
}

public static Complex operator+(Complex c1, Complex c2)
{
    return(new Complex(c1.real + c2.real, c1.imaginary + c2.imaginary));
}

public static Complex operator-(Complex c1, Complex c2)
{
    return(new Complex(c1.real - c2.real, c1.imaginary - c2.imaginary));
}

    // product of two complex numbers
public static Complex operator*(Complex c1, Complex c2)
{
    return(new Complex(c1.real * c2.real - c1.imaginary * c2.imaginary,
               c1.real * c2.imaginary + c2.real * c1.imaginary));
}

    // quotient of two complex numbers
public static Complex operator/(Complex c1, Complex c2)
{
    if ((c2.real == 0.0f) &&
        (c2.imaginary == 0.0f))
        throw new DivideByZeroException("Can't divide by zero Complex number");
```

```
        float newReal =
            (c1.real * c2.real + c1.imaginary * c2.imaginary) /
            (c2.real * c2.real + c2.imaginary * c2.imaginary);
        float newImaginary =
            (c2.real * c1.imaginary - c1.real * c2.imaginary) /
            (c2.real * c2.real + c2.imaginary * c2.imaginary);

        return(new Complex(newReal, newImaginary));
    }

        // non-operator versions for other languages...
    public static Complex Add(Complex c1, Complex c2)
    {
        return(c1 + c2);
    }

    public static Complex Subtract(Complex c1, Complex c2)
    {
        return(c1 - c2);
    }

    public static Complex Multiply(Complex c1, Complex c2)
    {
        return(c1 * c2);
    }

    public static Complex Divide(Complex c1, Complex c2)
    {
        return(c1 / c2);
    }
}

class Test
{
    public static void Main()
    {
        Complex c1 = new Complex(3, 1);
        Complex c2 = new Complex(1, 2);
```

```
        Console.WriteLine("c1 == c2: {0}", c1 == c2);
        Console.WriteLine("c1 != c2: {0}", c1 != c2);
        Console.WriteLine("c1 + c2 = {0}", c1 + c2);
        Console.WriteLine("c1 - c2 = {0}", c1 - c2);
        Console.WriteLine("c1 * c2 = {0}", c1 * c2);
        Console.WriteLine("c1 / c2 = {0}", c1 / c2);
    }
}
```

CHAPTER 26

Other Language Details

THIS CHAPTER DEALS WITH some miscellaneous details about the language, including how to use the `Main()` function, how the preprocessor works, and how to write literal values.

The Main Function

The simplest version of the `Main()` function will already be familiar from other examples:

```
using System;
class Test
{
    public static void Main()
    {
        Console.WriteLine("Hello, Universe!");
    }
}
```

Returning an Int Status

It will often be useful to return a status from the `Main()` function. This is done by declaring the return type of `Main()` as an integer:

```
using System;
class Test
{
    public static int Main()
    {
        Console.WriteLine("Hello, Universe!");
        return(0);
    }
}
```

Command-Line Parameters

The command-line parameters to an application can be accessed by declaring the `Main()` function with a `string` array as a parameter. The parameters can then be processed by indexing the array.

```
using System;
class Test
{
    public static void Main(string[] args)
    {
        foreach (string arg in args)
            Console.WriteLine("Arg: {0}", arg);
    }
}
```

Multiple Mains

It is often useful for testing purposes to include a `static` function in a class that tests the class to make sure it does the right thing. In C#, this `static` test function can be written as a `Main()` function, which makes automating such tests easy.

If there is a single `Main()` function encountered during a compilation, the C# compiler will use it. If there is more than one `Main()` function, the class that contains the desired `Main()` can be specified on the command line with the `/main:<classname>` option.

```
// error
using System;
class Complex
{
    static int Main()
    {
        // test code here
        Console.WriteLine("Console: Passed");
        return(0);
    }
}
```

```
class Test
{
    public static void Main(string[] args)
    {
        foreach (string arg in args)
            Console.WriteLine(arg);
    }
}
```

Compiling this file with `/main:Complex` will use the test version of `Main()`, whereas compiling with `/main:Test` will use the real version of `Main()`. Compiling it without either will result in an error.

The `Main()` declared in the `Complex` type isn't declared `public`. In fact, there is no requirement that `Main()` should be public, and keeping it private is very useful in cases such as these where the test function shouldn't be visible to users of the class.

Preprocessing

The most important thing to remember about the C# preprocessor is that it doesn't exist. The features from the C/C++ processor are either totally absent or present in a limited form. In the absent category are `include` files and the ability to do text replacement with `#define`. The `#ifdef` and associated directives are present and are used to control the compilation of code.

Getting rid of the macro version of `#define` allows the programmer to understand more clearly what the program is saying. A name that isn't familiar must come from one of the namespaces, and there's no need to hunt through `include` files to find it.

One reason for this change is that getting rid of preprocessing and `#include` enables a simplified compilation structure, and therefore we get some impressive improvements in compilation speed.[1] Additionally, there is no need to write a separate header file and keep it in sync with the implementation file.

Additionally, getting rid of `#define` ensures that C# code always means what it says and that no time is wasted hunting in include files for macro definitions.

When C# source files are compiled, the order of the compilation of the individual files is unimportant,[2] and it is equivalent to them all being in one big file. There is no need for forward declarations or worrying about the order of `#includes`.

1. When I first installed a copy of the compiler on my system, I typed in a simple example and compiled it, and it came back fast—so fast that I was convinced that something was wrong, and hunted down a developer for assistance. It's *so* much faster than C++ compilers are (or can be).
2. Except for the fact that the output file will automatically use the name of the first compiland.

Preprocessing Directives

The following preprocessing directives are supported:

DIRECTIVE	DESCRIPTION
`#define` identifier	Defines an identifier. Note that a value can't be set for it; it can merely be defined. Identifiers can also be defined via the command line.
`#undef` identifier	Undefines an identifier.
`#if` expression	Code in this section is compiled if the expression is true.
`#elif` expression	Else-if construct. If the previous directive wasn't taken and the expression is true, code in this section is compiled.
`#else`	If the previous directive wasn't taken, code in this section is compiled.
`#endif`	Marks the end of a section.

Here's an example of how they might be used:

```
#define DEBUGLOG
using System;
class Test
{
    public static void Main()
    {
        #if DEBUGLOG
        Console.WriteLine("In Main - Debug Enabled");
        #else
        Console.WriteLine("In Main - No Debug");
        #endif
    }
}
```

`#define` and `#undef` must precede any "real code" in a file, or an error occurs. The previous example can't be written as follows:

```
// error
using System;
class Test
{
    #define DEBUGLOG
    public static void Main()
    {
        #if DEBUGLOG
        Console.WriteLine("In Main - Debug Enabled");
        #else
        Console.WriteLine("In Main - No Debug");
        #endif
    }
}
```

C# also supports the `Conditional` attribute for controlling function calls based upon preprocessor identifiers; see Chapter 37, "Defensive Programming," for more information.

Preprocessor Expressions

The following operators can be used in preprocessor expressions:

OPERATOR	DESCRIPTION
`! ex`	Expression is true if `ex` is false
`ex == value`	Expression is true if `ex` is equal to `value`
`ex != value`	Expression is true if `ex` is not equal to `value`
`ex1 && ex2`	Expression is true if both `ex1` and `ex2` are true
`ex1 || ex2`	Expression is true if either `ex1` or `ex2` are true

Parentheses can be used to group expressions:

```
#if !(DEBUGLOG && (TESTLOG || USERLOG))
```

If `TESTLOG` or `USERLOG` is defined and `DEBUGLOG` is defined, then the expression within the parentheses is true, which is then negated by the "`!`".

Other Preprocessor Functions

In addition to the `#if` and `#define` functions, there are a few other preprocessor functions that can be used.

#warning and #error

`#warning` and `#error` allow warnings or errors to be reported during the compilation process. All text following the `#warning` or `#error` will be output when the compiler reaches that line.

For a section of code, the following could be done:

```
#warning Check algorithm with John
```

This would result in the string "Check algorithm with John" being output when the line was compiled.

#line

With `#line`, the programmer can specify the name of the source file and the line number that are reported when the compiler encounters errors. This would typically be used with machine-generated source code, so the reported lines can be synced with a different naming or numbering system.

Lexical Details

The lexical details of the language deal with things that are important at the single-character level: how to write numerical constants, identifiers, and other low-level entities of the language.

Identifiers

An identifier is a name that is used for some program element, such as a variable or a function.

Identifiers must have a letter or an underscore as the first character, and the remainder of the identifier can also include numeric characters.[3] Unicode characters can be specified using `\udddd`, where `dddd` specifies the hex value of the Unicode character.

When using code that has been written in other languages, some names might be C# keywords. To write such a name, an "at" character (`@`) can be placed before the name, which merely indicates to C# that the name is not a keyword, but an identifier.

3. It's actually a fair bit more complicated than this, since C# has Unicode support. Briefly, letters can be any Unicode letter character, and characters other than the underscore (_) can also be used for combinations. See the C# Language Reference (`http://msdn.microsoft.com/net/ecma`) for a full description.

Similarly, use "@" to use keywords as identifiers:

```
class Test
{
    public void @checked()
    {
    }
}
```

This class declares a member function named `checked`.

Using this feature so that identifiers can be the same as built-in identifiers is not recommended because of the confusion it can create.

Keywords

Keywords are reserved words that cannot be used as identifiers. The keywords in C# are:

abstract	base	bool	break	byte
case	catch	char	checked	class
const	continue	decimal	default	delegate
do	double	else	enum	event
explicit	extern	false	finally	fixed
float	for	foreach	goto	if
implicit	in	int	interface	internal
is	lock	long	namespace	new
null	object	operator	out	override
params	private	protected	public	readonly
ref	return	sbyte	sealed	short
sizeof	static	string	struct	switch
this	throw	true	try	typeof
uint	ulong	unchecked	unsafe	ushort
using	virtual	void	while	

Literals

Literals are the way in which values are written for variables.

Boolean

There are two boolean literals: `true` and `false`.

Integer

Integer literals are written simply by writing the numeric value. Integer literals that are small enough to fit into the `int` data type[4] are treated as `int`s; if they are too big to fit into an `int`, they will be created as the smallest type of `uint`, `long`, or `ulong` in which the literal will fit.

Some integer literal examples:

```
123
-15
```

Integer literals can also be written in hexadecimal format, by placing "0x" in front of the constant:

```
0xFFFF
0x12AB
```

Real

Real literals are used for the types `float`, `double`, and `decimal`. Float literals have "`f`" or "`F`" after them; double literals have "`d`" or "`D`" after them, and `decimal` literals have "`m`" or "`M`" after them. Real literals without a type character are interpreted as `double` literals.

Exponential notation can be used by appending "`e`" followed by the exponent to the real literal.

Examples:

```
1.345                   // double constant
-8.99e12F               // float constant
15.66m                  // decimal constant
```

4. See the "Basic Data Types" section in Chapter 3, "C# Quickstart."

Character

A character literal is a single character enclosed in single quotes, such as 'x'. The following escape sequences are supported:

ESCAPE SEQUENCE	DESCRIPTION
`\'`	Single quote
`\"`	Double quote
`\\`	Backslash
`\0`	Null
`\a`	Alert
`\b`	Backspace
`\f`	Form feed
`\n`	Newline
`\r`	Carriage return
`\t`	Tab
`\v`	Vertical tab
`\xdddd`	Character `dddd`, where `d` is a hexadecimal digit.
`\udddd`	Unicode character dddd, where x is a hexadecimal digit.
`\Udddddddd`	Unicode character dddddddd, where x is a hexadecimal digit.

String

String literals are written as a sequence of characters enclosed in double quotes, such as "`Hello`". All of the character escape sequences are supported within strings.

Strings cannot span multiple lines, but the same effect can be achieved by concatenating them together:

```
string s = "What is your favorite color?" +
           "Blue. No, Red. ";
```

When this code is compiled, a single string constant will be created, consisting of the two strings concatenated together.

Verbatim Strings

Verbatim strings allow some strings to be specified more simply.

If a string contains the backslash character, such as a filename, a verbatim string can be used to turn off the support for escape sequences. Instead of writing something like

```
string s = "c:\\Program Files\\Microsoft Office\\Office";
```

the following can be written:

```
string s = @"c:\Program Files\Microsoft Office\Office";
```

The verbatim string syntax is also useful if the code is generated by a program and there is no way to constrain the contents of the string. All characters can be represented within such a string, though any occurrence of the double-quote character must be doubled:

```
string s = @"She said, ""Hello""";
```

In addition, strings that are written with the verbatim string syntax can span multiple lines, and any whitespace (spaces, tabs, and newlines) is preserved.

```
using System;
class Test
{
    public static void Main()
    {
        string s = @"
        C: Hello, Miss?
        O: What do you mean, 'Miss'?
        C: I'm Sorry, I have a cold. I wish to make a complaint.";
        Console.WriteLine(s);
    }
}
```

Comments

Comments in C# are denoted by a double slash for a single-line comment, and `/*` and `*/` to denote the beginning and ending of a multiline comment.

```
// This is a single-line comment
/*
 * Multiline comment here
 */
```

C# also supports a special type of comment that is used to associate documentation with code; those comments are described in the XML documentation section of Chapter 36, "Deeper into C#."

CHAPTER 27

Making Friends with the .NET Frameworks

THE INFORMATION IN the preceding chapters is sufficient for writing objects that will function in the .NET Runtime, but those objects won't feel like they were written to operate well in the framework. This chapter will detail how to make user-defined objects operate more like the objects in the .NET Runtime and Frameworks.

Things All Objects Will Do

Overriding the `ToString()` function from the `object` class gives a nice representation of the values in an object. If this isn't done, `object.ToString()` will merely return the name of the class.

The `Equals()` function on `object` is called by the .NET Frameworks classes to determine whether two objects are equal.

A class may also override `operator==()` and `operator!=()`, which allows the user to use the built-in operators with instances of the object, rather than calling `Equals()`.

ToString()

Here's an example of what happens by default:

```
using System;
public class Employee
{
    public Employee(int id, string name)
    {
        this.id = id;
        this.name = name;
    }
    int id;
    string name;
}
```

```
class Test
{
    public static void Main()
    {
        Employee herb = new Employee(555, "Herb");
        Console.WriteLine("Employee: {0}", herb);
    }
}
```

The preceding code will result in the following:

```
Employee: Employee
```

By overriding `ToString()`, the representation can be much more useful:

```
using System;
public class Employee
{
    public Employee(int id, string name)
    {
        this.id = id;
        this.name = name;
    }
    public override string ToString()
    {
        return(String.Format("{0}({1})", name, id));
    }
    int id;
    string name;
}
class Test
{
    public static void Main()
    {
        Employee herb = new Employee(555, "Herb");
        Console.WriteLine("Employee: {0}", herb);
    }
}
```

This gives us a far better result:

```
Employee: Herb(555)
```

When `Console.WriteLine()` needs to convert an object to a string representation, it will call the `ToString()` virtual function, which will forward to an object's specific implementation. If more control over formatting is desired, such as implementing a floating point class with different formats, the `IFormattable` interface can be overridden. `IFormattable` is covered in the "Custom Object Formatting" section of Chapter 32, ".NET Frameworks Overview."

Equals()

`Equals()` is used to determine whether two objects have the same contents. This function is called by the collection classes (such as `Array` or `Hashtable`) to determine whether two objects are equal. Extending the employee example:

```
using System;
public class Employee
{
    public Employee(int id, string name)
    {
        this.id = id;
        this.name = name;
    }
    public override string ToString()
    {
        return(name + "(" + id + ")");
    }
    public override bool Equals(object obj)
    {
        return(this == (Employee) obj);
    }
    public override int GetHashCode()
    {
              return(id.GetHashCode() ^ name.GetHashCode());
    }
    public static bool operator==(Employee emp1, Employee emp2)
    {
        if (emp1.id != emp2.id)
            return(false);
        if (emp1.name != emp2.name)
            return(false);
        return(true);
    }
```

```
    public static bool operator!=(Employee emp1, Employee emp2)
    {
        return(!(emp1 == emp2));
    }
    int id;
    string name;
}
class Test
{
    public static void Main()
    {
        Employee herb = new Employee(555, "Herb");
        Employee herbClone = new Employee(555, "Herb");
        Console.WriteLine("Equal: {0}", herb.Equals(herbClone));
        Console.WriteLine("Equal: {0}", herb == herbClone);
    }
}
```

This will produce the following output:

```
Equal: true
Equal: true
```

In this case, `operator==()` and `operator!=()` have also been overloaded, which allows the operator syntax to be used in the last line of `Main()`. These operators must be overloaded in pairs; they cannot be overloaded separately.[1]

Note that in this example, the implementation of `Equals()` forwards to the operator implementation. For this example, it could be done either way, but for structs, there is an extra boxing operation if it's done the other way. Because `Equals()` takes an object parameter, a value type must always be boxed to call `Equals()`, but boxing isn't required to call the strongly typed comparison operators. If the operators forwarded to `Equals()`, they would have to box always.

Hashes and GetHashCode()

The Frameworks include the `Hashtable` class, which is very useful for doing fast lookup of objects by a key. A hash table works by using a hash function, which produces an integer "key" for a specific instance of a class. This key is a condensed version of the contents of the instance. While instances can have the same hash code, it's fairly unlikely to happen.

1. This is required for two reasons. The first is that if a user uses ==, they can expect != to work as well. The other is to support nullable types, for which a == b does *not* imply !(a != b).

A hash table uses this key as a way of drastically limiting the number of objects that must be searched to find a specific object in a collection of objects. It does this by first getting the hash value of the object, which will eliminate all objects with a different hash code, leaving only those with the same hash code to be searched. Since the number of instances with that hash code is small, searches can be much quicker.

That's the basic idea—for a more detailed explanation, please refer to a good data structures and algorithms book.[2] Hashes are a tremendously useful construct. The `Hashtable` class stores objects, so it's easy to use them to store any type.

The `GetHashCode()` function should be overridden in user-written classes because the values returned by `GetHashCode()` are required to be related to the value returned by `Equals()`. Two objects that are the same by `Equals()` must always return the same hash code.

The default implementation of `GetHashCode()` doesn't work this way, and therefore it must be overridden to work correctly. If not overridden, the hash code will only be identical for the same instance of an object, and a search for an object that is equal but not the same instance will fail.

If there is a unique field in an object, it's probably a good choice for the hash code:

```
using System;
using System.Collections;
public class Employee
{
    public Employee(int id, string name)
    {
        this.id = id;
        this.name = name;
    }
    public override string ToString()
    {
        return(String.Format("{0}({1})", name, id));
    }
    public override bool Equals(object obj)
    {
        Employee emp2 = (Employee) obj;
        if (id != emp2.id)
            return(false);
        if (name != emp2.name)
            return(false);
        return(true);
    }
```

2. I've always liked Robert Sedgewick's *Algorithms in C* as a good introduction.

```
    public static bool operator==(Employee emp1, Employee emp2)
    {
        return(emp1.Equals(emp2));
    }
    public static bool operator!=(Employee emp1, Employee emp2)
    {
        return(!emp1.Equals(emp2));
    }
    public override int GetHashCode()
    {
        return(id);
    }
    int id;
    string name;
}
class Test
{
    public static void Main()
    {
        Employee herb = new Employee(555, "Herb");
        Employee george = new Employee(123, "George");
        Employee frank = new Employee(111, "Frank");
        Hashtable    employees = new Hashtable();
        employees.Add(herb, "414 Evergreen Terrace");
        employees.Add(george, "2335 Elm Street");
        employees.Add(frank, "18 Pine Bluff Road");
        Employee herbClone = new Employee(555, "Herb");
        string address = (string) employees[herbClone];
        Console.WriteLine("{0} lives at {1}", herbClone, address);
    }
}
```

In the `Employee` class, the `id` member is unique, so it is used for the hash code. In the `Main()` function, several employees are created, and they are then used as the key values to store the addresses of the employees.

If there isn't a unique value, the hash code should be created out of the values contained in a function. If the employee class didn't have a unique identifier, but did have fields for name and address, the hash function could use those. The following shows a hash function that could be used:[3]

3. This is by no means the only hash function that could be used, or even a particularly good one. See an algorithms book for information on constructing good hash functions.

```
using System;
using System.Collections;
public class Employee
{
    public Employee(string name, string address)
    {
        this.name = name;
        this.address = address;
    }
    public override int GetHashCode()
    {
        return(name.GetHashCode() + address.GetHashCode());
    }
    string name;
    string address;
}
```

This implementation of `GetHashCode()` simply XORs the hash codes of the elements together, and returns them.

Design Guidelines

Any class that overrides `Equals()` should also override `GetHashCode()`. In fact, the C# compiler will issue an error in such a case. The reason for this error is that it prevents strange and difficult-to-debug behavior when the class is used in a `Hashtable`.

The `Hashtable` class depends on the fact that all instances that are equal have the same hash value. The default implementation of `GetHashCode()`, however, returns a value that is unique on a per-instance basis. If this implementation was not overridden, it's very easy to put objects in a hash table, but not be able to retrieve them.

Value Type Guidelines

The `System.ValueType` class contains a version of `Equals()` that works for all value types, but this version of `Equals()` works through reflection and is therefore slow. It's therefore recommended that an implementation of `Equals()` be written for all value types.

Reference Type Guidelines

For most reference types, users will expect that `==` will mean reference comparison and in this case `==` should not be overloaded, even if the object implements `Equals()`. If the type has value semantics (something like a `String` or a `BigNum`), `operator==()` and `Equals()` should be overridden. If a class overloads `+` or `-`, that's a pretty good indication that it should also override `==` and `Equals()`.

A subtler area of concern is how `Equals()` operates when inheritance hierarchies come into play. Consider the following example:

```
using System;
class Base
{
    int val;

    public Base(int val)
    {
        this.val = val;
    }

    public override bool Equals(object o2)
    {
        Base b2 = (Base) o2;

        return(val == b2.val);
    }

    public override int GetHashCode()
    {
        return(val.GetHashCode());
    }
}
class Derived: Base
{
    int val2;

    public Derived(int val, int val2) : base(val)
    {
        this.val2 = val2;
    }
}
```

```
class Test
{
    public static void Main()
    {
        Base b1 = new Base(12);
        Base b2 = new Base(12);
        Derived d1 = new Derived(12, 15);
        Derived d2 = new Derived(12, 25);

        Console.WriteLine("b1 equals b2: {0}", b1.Equals(b2));
        Console.WriteLine("d1 equals d2: {0}", d1.Equals(d2));
        Console.WriteLine("d1 equals b1: {0}", b1.Equals(d1));
    }
}
```

This code generates the following results:

```
b1 equals b2: True
d1 equals d2: True
b1 equals d1: True
```

The `Base` class implements `Equals()`, and it works as expected for objects of type `Base`. Classes derived directly from `object` (or from classes that don't override `Equals()`) will work fine since they will use `object.Equals()`, which compares references.

But any class derived from `Base` will inherit the implementation of `Equals()` from `Base` and will therefore generate the wrong results. Because of this, any class that derives from a class that overrides `Equals()` should also override `Equals()`.[4] This situation can be guarded against by adding a check to make sure the object is the expected type:

```
    public override bool Equals(object o2)
    {
        if (o2.GetType() != typeof(Base) || GetType() != typeof(Base))
            return(false);

        Base b2 = (Base) o2;

        return(val == b2.val);
    }
```

4. There is the rare case where the derived class has exactly the same concept of equality as the base class.

This gives the following output:

```
b1 equals b2: True
d1 equals d2: False
b1 equals d1: False
```

which is correct, and prevents a derived class from accidentally using the base class `Equals()` accidentally. It's now obvious that `Derived` needs its own version of `Equals()`. The code for `Derived.Equals()` will use `Base.Equals()` to check whether the base objects are equal and then compare the derived fields. The code for `Derived.Equals()` looks like this:

```
public override bool Equals(object o2)
{
    if (o2.GetType() != typeof(Derived) || GetType() != typeof(Derived))
        return(false);

    Derived d2 = (Derived) o2;
    return(base.Equals(o2) && val2 == d2.val2);
}
```

Adding this code generates the following output:

```
b1 equals b2: True
d1 equals d2: False
b1 equals d1: False
```

That's clearly wrong. What's causing the problem is the type check in the base class will always return false when called from `Derived.Equals()`.

Since it doesn't work to check for an exact type, the next best thing is to check that the types are the same. The code for `Base.Equals()` becomes:

```
public override bool Equals(object o2)
{
    if (o2 == null || GetType() != o2.GetType())
        return false;

    Base b2 = (Base) o2;

    return(val == b2.val);
}
```

And the code for `Derived.Equals()` uses the same check and also calls `base.Equals()`. This code also checks for `null` to prevent an exception when comparing to a null reference.
To summarize:

- Reference types should make sure that both types are the same in `Equals()`.
- If the type is derived from a type that overrides `Equals()`, `Base.Equals()` should be called to check whether the base portion of the type is equal.
- If the type is derived from a type that doesn't override `Equals()`, `Base.Equals()` should not called since it would be `object.Equals()`, which implements reference comparison.

CHAPTER 28

System.Array and the Collection Classes

CONCEPTUALLY, THIS CHAPTER will give an overview of what classes are available. It will then cover them by class and give examples of what interfaces and functions are required to enable specific functionality.

Sorting and Searching

The Frameworks collection classes provide some useful support for sorting and searching, with built-in functions to do sorting and binary searching. The `Array` class provides the same functionality but as static functions rather than member functions.

Sorting an array of integers is as easy as this:

```
using System;
class Test
{
    public static void Main()
    {
        int[]    arr = {5, 1, 10, 33, 100, 4};
        Array.Sort(arr);
        foreach (int v in arr)
            Console.WriteLine("Element: {0}", v);
    }
}
```

The preceding code gives the following output:

```
4
5
10
33
100
```

This is very convenient for the built-in types, but it doesn't work for classes or structs because the sort routine doesn't know how to order them.

Implementing IComparable

The Frameworks have some very nice ways for a class or struct to specify how to order instances of the class or struct. In the simplest one, the object implements the `IComparable` interface:

```
using System;
public class Employee: IComparable
{
    public Employee(string name, int id)
    {
        this.name = name;
        this.id = id;
    }

    int IComparable.CompareTo(object obj)
    {
        Employee emp2 = (Employee) obj;
        if (this.id > emp2.id)
            return(1);
        if (this.id < emp2.id)
            return(-1);
        else
            return(0);
    }

    public override string ToString()
    {
        return(String.Format("{0}:{1}", name, id));
    }

    string    name;
    int    id;
}
```

```
class Test
{
    public static void Main()
    {
        Employee[] arr = new Employee[4];
        arr[0] = new Employee("George", 1);
        arr[1] = new Employee("Fred", 2);
        arr[2] = new Employee("Tom", 4);
        arr[3] = new Employee("Bob", 3);

        Array.Sort(arr);
        foreach (Employee emp in arr)
            Console.WriteLine("Employee: {0}", emp);
            // Find employee id 2 in the list;
        Employee employeeToFind = new Employee(null, 2);
        int index = Array.BinarySearch(arr, employeeToFind);
        if (index != -1)
            Console.WriteLine("Found: {0}", arr[index]);
    }
}
```

This program gives us the following output:

```
Employee: George:1
Employee: Fred:2
Employee: Bob:3
Employee: Tom:4
Found: Fred:2
```

This sort implementation only allows one sort ordering; the class could be defined to sort based on employee ID or based on name, but there's no way to allow the user to choose which sort order they prefer.

This example also uses the `BinarySearch()` method to find an employee in the list. For this to work, the array (or `ArrayList`) must be sorted, or the results will not be correct.

Using IComparer

The designers of the Frameworks have provided the capability to define multiple sort orders. Each sort order is expressed through the `IComparer` interface, and the appropriate interface is passed to the sort or search function.

The IComparer interface can't be implemented on Employee, however, because each class can only implement an interface once, which would allow only a single sort order.[1] A separate class is needed for each sort order, with the class implementing IComparer. The class will be very simple, since all it will do is implement the Compare() function:

```
using System;
using System.Collections;
class Employee
{
    public string name;
}
class SortByNameClass: IComparer
{
    public int Compare(object obj1, object obj2)
    {
        Employee emp1 = (Employee) obj1;
        Employee emp2 = (Employee) obj2;
        return(String.Compare(emp1.name, emp2.name));
    }
}
```

The Compare() member takes two objects as parameters. Since the class should only be used for sorting employees, the object parameters are cast to Employee. The Compare() function built into string is then used for the comparison.

The Employee class is then revised as follows. The sort-ordering classes are placed inside the Employee class as nested classes:

```
using System;
using System.Collections;

public class Employee: IComparable
{
    public Employee(string name, int id)
    {
        this.name = name;
        this.id = id;
    }
```

1. IComparable *could* implement one sort order and IComparer another, but that would be very confusing to the user.

```
    int IComparable.CompareTo(object obj)
    {
        Employee emp2 = (Employee) obj;
        if (this.id > emp2.id)
            return(1);
        if (this.id < emp2.id)
            return(-1);
        else
            return(0);
    }

    public override string ToString()
    {
        return(name + ":" + id);
    }

    public class SortByNameClass: IComparer
    {
        public int Compare(object obj1, object obj2)
        {
            Employee emp1 = (Employee) obj1;
            Employee emp2 = (Employee) obj2;

            return(String.Compare(emp1.name, emp2.name));
        }
    }

    public class SortByIdClass: IComparer
    {
        public int Compare(object obj1, object obj2)
        {
            Employee emp1 = (Employee) obj1;
            Employee emp2 = (Employee) obj2;

            return(((IComparable) emp1).CompareTo(obj2));
        }
    }

    string    name;
    int    id;
}
```

```
class Test
{
    public static void Main()
    {
        Employee[] arr = new Employee[4];
        arr[0] = new Employee("George", 1);
        arr[1] = new Employee("Fred", 2);
        arr[2] = new Employee("Tom", 4);
        arr[3] = new Employee("Bob", 3);

        Array.Sort(arr, (IComparer) new Employee.SortByNameClass());
            // employees is now sorted by name

        foreach (Employee emp in arr)
            Console.WriteLine("Employee: {0}", emp);

        Array.Sort(arr, (IComparer) new Employee.SortByIdClass());
            // employees is now sorted by id

        foreach (Employee emp in arr)
            Console.WriteLine("Employee: {0}", emp);

        ArrayList arrList = new ArrayList();
        arrList.Add(arr[0]);
        arrList.Add(arr[1]);
        arrList.Add(arr[2]);
        arrList.Add(arr[3]);
        arrList.Sort((IComparer) new Employee.SortByNameClass());

        foreach (Employee emp in arrList)
            Console.WriteLine("Employee: {0}", emp);

        arrList.Sort();    // default is by id

        foreach (Employee emp in arrList)
            Console.WriteLine("Employee: {0}", emp);
    }
}
```

The user can now specify the sort order and switch between the different sort orders as desired. This example shows how the same functions work using the `ArrayList` class, though `Sort()` is a member function rather than a static function.

`IComparer` *as a Property*

Sorting with the `Employee` class is still a bit cumbersome, since the user has to create an instance of the appropriate ordering class and then cast it to `IComparer`. This can be simplified a bit further by using static properties to do this for the user:

```
using System;
using System.Collections;

public class Employee: IComparable
{
    public Employee(string name, int id)
    {
        this.name = name;
        this.id = id;
    }

    int IComparable.CompareTo(object obj)
    {
        Employee emp2 = (Employee) obj;
        if (this.id > emp2.id)
            return(1);
        if (this.id < emp2.id)
            return(-1);
        else
            return(0);
    }

    public static IComparer SortByName
    {
        get
        {
            return((IComparer) new SortByNameClass());
        }
    }

    public static IComparer SortById
    {
        get
        {
            return((IComparer) new SortByIdClass());
        }
    }
```

```
    public override string ToString()
    {
        return(name + ":" + id);
    }

    class SortByNameClass: IComparer
    {
        public int Compare(object obj1, object obj2)
        {
            Employee emp1 = (Employee) obj1;
            Employee emp2 = (Employee) obj2;

            return(String.Compare(emp1.name, emp2.name));
        }
    }

    class SortByIdClass: IComparer
    {
        public int Compare(object obj1, object obj2)
        {
            Employee emp1 = (Employee) obj1;
            Employee emp2 = (Employee) obj2;

            return(((IComparable) emp1).CompareTo(obj2));
        }
    }

    string    name;
    int    id;
}
class Test
{
    public static void Main()
    {
        Employee[] arr = new Employee[4];
        arr[0] = new Employee("George", 1);
        arr[1] = new Employee("Fred", 2);
        arr[2] = new Employee("Tom", 4);
        arr[3] = new Employee("Bob", 3);

        Array.Sort(arr, Employee.SortByName);
            // employees is now sorted by name
```

```
        foreach (Employee emp in arr)
            Console.WriteLine("Employee: {0}", emp);

        Array.Sort(arr, Employee.SortById);
            // employees is now sorted by id

        foreach (Employee emp in arr)
            Console.WriteLine("Fmployee: {0}", emp);

        ArrayList arrList = new ArrayList();
        arrList.Add(arr[0]);
        arrList.Add(arr[1]);
        arrList.Add(arr[2]);
        arrList.Add(arr[3]);
        arrList.Sort(Employee.SortByName);

        foreach (Employee emp in arrList)
            Console.WriteLine("Employee: {0}", emp);

        arrList.Sort();     // default is by id

        foreach (Employee emp in arrList)
            Console.WriteLine("Employee: {0}", emp);
    }
}
```

The static properties `SortByName` and `SortById` create an instance of the appropriate sorting class, cast it to `IComparer`, and return it to the user. This simplifies the user model quite a bit; the `SortByName` and `SortById` properties return an `IComparer`, so it's obvious that they can be used for sorting, and all the user has to do is specify the appropriate ordering property for the `IComparer` parameter.

Overloading Relational Operators

If a class has an ordering that is expressed in `IComparable`, it may also make sense to overload the other relational operators. As with `=` and `!=`, other operators must be declared as pairs, with `<` and `>` being one pair, and `>=` and `<=` being the other pair:

```
using System;
public class Employee: IComparable
{
    public Employee(string name, int id)
    {
        this.name = name;
        this.id = id;
    }

    int IComparable.CompareTo(object obj)
    {
        Employee emp2 = (Employee) obj;
        if (this.id > emp2.id)
            return(1);
        if (this.id < emp2.id)
            return(-1);
        else
            return(0);
    }
    public static bool operator <(
    Employee emp1,
    Employee emp2)
    {
        IComparable    icomp = (IComparable) emp1;
        return(icomp.CompareTo (emp2) < 0);
    }
    public static bool operator >(
    Employee emp1,
    Employee emp2)
    {
        IComparable    icomp = (IComparable) emp1;
        return(icomp.CompareTo (emp2) > 0);
    }
    public static bool operator <=(
    Employee emp1,
    Employee emp2)
    {
        IComparable    icomp = (IComparable) emp1;
        return(icomp.CompareTo (emp2) <= 0);
    }
```

```
    public static bool operator >=(
    Employee emp1,
    Employee emp2)
    {
        IComparable    icomp = (IComparable) emp1;
        return(icomp.CompareTo (emp2) >= 0);
    }

    public override string ToString()
    {
        return(name + ":" + id);
    }

    string    name;
    int    id;
}
class Test
{
    public static void Main()
    {
        Employee george = new Employee("George", 1);
        Employee fred = new Employee("Fred", 2);
        Employee tom = new Employee("Tom", 4);
        Employee bob = new Employee("Bob", 3);

        Console.WriteLine("George < Fred: {0}", george < fred);
        Console.WriteLine("Tom >= Bob: {0}", tom >= bob);
    // Find employee id 2 in the list;
        Employee employeeToFind = new Employee(null, 2);
        int index = Array.BinarySearch(arr, employeeToFind);
        if (index != -1)
            Console.WriteLine("Found: {0}", arr[index]);
    }
}
```

This example produces the following output:

```
George < Fred: true
Tom >= Bob: true
```

Advanced Use of Hashes

In some situations, it may be desirable to define more than one hash code for a specific object. This could be used, for example, to allow an Employee to be searched for based on the employee ID or on the employee name. This is done by implementing the `IHashCodeProvider` interface to provide an alternate hash function, and it also requires a matching implementation of `IComparer`. These new implementations are passed to the constructor of the `Hashtable`:

```
using System;
using System.Collections;

public class Employee: IComparable
{
    public Employee(string name, int id)
    {
        this.name = name;
        this.id = id;
    }

    int IComparable.CompareTo(object obj)
    {
        Employee emp2 = (Employee) obj;
        if (this.id > emp2.id)
            return(1);
        if (this.id < emp2.id)
            return(-1);
        else
            return(0);
    }
    public override int GetHashCode()
    {
        return(id);
    }
    public static IComparer SortByName
    {
        get
        {
            return((IComparer) new SortByNameClass());
        }
    }

    public static IComparer SortById
    {
        get
        {
            return((IComparer) new SortByIdClass());
        }
    }
```

```
public static IHashCodeProvider HashByName
{
    get
    {
        return((IHashCodeProvider) new HashByNameClass());
    }
}
public override string ToString()
{
    return(name + ":" + id);
}

class SortByNameClass: IComparer
{
    public int Compare(object obj1, object obj2)
    {
        Employee emp1 = (Employee) obj1;
        Employee emp2 = (Employee) obj2;

        return(String.Compare(emp1.name, emp2.name));
    }
}

class SortByIdClass: IComparer
{
    public int Compare(object obj1, object obj2)
    {
        Employee emp1 = (Employee) obj1;
        Employee emp2 = (Employee) obj2;

        return(((IComparable) emp1).CompareTo(obj2));
    }
}
class HashByNameClass: IHashCodeProvider
{
    public int GetHashCode(object obj)
    {
        Employee emp = (Employee) obj;
        return(emp.name.GetHashCode());
    }
}
```

```
    string    name;
    int    id;
}
class Test
{
    public static void Main()
    {
        Employee herb = new Employee("Herb", 555);
        Employee george = new Employee("George", 123);
        Employee frank = new Employee("Frank", 111);
        Hashtable employees =
            new Hashtable(Employee.HashByName, Employee.SortByName);
        employees.Add(herb, "414 Evergreen Terrace");
        employees.Add(george, "2335 Elm Street");
        employees.Add(frank, "18 Pine Bluff Road");
        Employee herbClone = new Employee("Herb", 000);
        string address = (string) employees[herbClone];
        Console.WriteLine("{0} lives at {1}", herbClone, address);
    }
}
```

This technique should be used sparingly. It's often simpler to expose a value, such as the employee name as a property, and allow that to be used as a hash key instead.

Synchronized Collections

When a collection class—such as `ArrayList`–is created, it is not thread-safe, because adding synchronization to such a class imposes some overhead. If a thread-safe version is needed, simply call the `Synchronized()` method to get a thread-safe wrapper to the list.
In other words, the following can be used to create a thread-safe `ArrayList`:

```
ArrayList arr = ArrayList.Synchronized(new ArrayList());
```

For more information on threading and synchronization, see Chapter 29, "Threading and Asynchronous Operations."

Case-Insensitive Collections

To deal with strings in a case-insensitive manner, the Frameworks provide a way to create case-insensitive versions of the `SortedList` and `Hashtable` collection classes. This support is supplied through the `CollectionsUtil` class in the

`System.Collections.Specialized` namespace by calling the `CreateCaseInsensitiveSortedList()` or `CreateCaseInsensitiveHashtable()` functions.

ICloneable

The `object.MemberWiseClone()` function can be used to create a clone of an object. The default implementation of this function produces a shallow copy of an object; the fields of an object are copied exactly rather than duplicated. Consider the following:

```
using System;
class ContainedValue
{
    public ContainedValue(int count)
    {
        this.count = count;
    }
    public int count;
}
class MyObject
{
    public MyObject(int count)
    {
        this.contained = new ContainedValue(count);
    }
    public MyObject Clone()
    {
        return((MyObject) MemberwiseClone());
    }
    public ContainedValue contained;
}
class Test
{
    public static void Main()
    {
        MyObject    my = new MyObject(33);
        MyObject    myClone = my.Clone();
        Console.WriteLine(    "Values: {0} {1}",
                    my.contained.count,
                    myClone.contained.count);
        myClone.contained.count = 15;
        Console.WriteLine(    "Values: {0} {1}",
                    my.contained.count,
                    myClone.contained.count);
    }
}
```

This example produces the following output:

```
Values: 33 33
Values: 15 15
```

Because the copy made by `MemberWiseClone()` is a shallow copy, the value of `contained` is the same in both objects, and changing a value inside the `ContainedValue` object affects both instances of `MyObject`.

What is needed is a deep copy, where a new instance of `ContainedValue` is created for the new instance of `MyObject`. This is done by implementing the `ICloneable` interface:

```
using System;
class ContainedValue
{
    public ContainedValue(int count)
    {
        this.count = count;
    }
    public int count;
}
class MyObject: ICloneable
{
    public MyObject(int count)
    {
        this.contained = new ContainedValue(count);
    }
    public object Clone()
    {
        Console.WriteLine("Clone");
        return(new MyObject(this.contained.count));
    }
    public ContainedValue contained;
}
```

```
class Test
{
    public static void Main()
    {
        MyObject    my = new MyObject(33);
        MyObject    myClone = (MyObject) my.Clone();
        Console.WriteLine(    "Values: {0} {1}",
                    my.contained.count,
                    myClone.contained.count);
        myClone.contained.count = 15;
        Console.WriteLine(    "Values: {0} {1}",
                    my.contained.count,
                    myClone.contained.count);
    }
}
```

This example produces the following output:

```
Values: 33 33
Values: 33 15
```

The call to `MemberWiseClone()` will now result in a new instance of `ContainedValue`, and the contents of this instance can be modified without affecting the contents of `my`.

Unlike some of the other interfaces that might be defined on an object, `ICloneable` is not called by the runtime; it is provided merely to ensure that the `Clone()` function has the proper signature. Some objects may choose to implement a constructor that takes an instance as a parameter instead.

Other Collections

In addition to the collection classes that have already been discussed, the Frameworks provides a number of others:

`BitArray`	A compact array of bit values
`Queue`	A first-in, first-out collection
`Stack`	A last-in, first-out collection
`ListDictionary`	A lightweight implementation of `IDictionary` that's faster than `Hashtable` for small lists
`StringCollection`	A collection of strings
`StringDictionary`	A hash table, but with a `string` as a key instead of an `object`
`BitVector32`	A lightweight value type to allow integer or boolean access to a 32-bit `int`

Design Guidelines

The intended use of an object should be considered when deciding which virtual functions and interfaces to implement. The following table provides guidelines for this:

OBJECT USE	FUNCTION OR INTERFACE
General	ToString()
Arrays or collections	Equals(), operator==(), operator!=(), GetHashCode()
Sorting or binary search	IComparable
Multiple sort orders	IComparer
Multiple has lookups	IHashCodeProvider

Functions and Interfaces by Framework Class

The following tables summarize which functions or interfaces on an object are used by each collection class.

Array

FUNCTION	USES
IndexOf()	Equals()
LastIndexOf()	Equals()
Contains()	Equals()
Sort()	Equals(), IComparable
BinarySearch()	Equals(), IComparable

ArrayList

FUNCTION	USES
IndexOf()	Equals()
LastIndexOf()	Equals()
Contains()	Equals()
Sort()	Equals(), IComparable
BinarySearch()	Equals(), IComparable

Hashtable

FUNCTION	USES
HashTable()	IHashCodeProvider, IComparable (optional)
Contains()	GetHashCode(), Equals()
Item	GetHashCode(), Equals()

SortedList

FUNCTION	USES
SortedList()	IComparable
Contains()	IComparable
ContainsKey()	IComparable
ContainsValue()	Equals()
IndexOfKey()	IComparable
IndexOfValue()	Equals()
Item	IComparable

CHAPTER 29

Threading and Asynchronous Operations

MODERN COMPUTER OPERATING SYSTEMS allow a program to have multiple threads of execution at one time. At least, they allow the appearance of having multiple things going on at the same time.

It's often useful to take advantage of this feature with a programming language, allowing several operations to take place in parallel. This can be used to prevent a program's user interface from becoming unresponsive while a time-consuming task is being performed, or it can be used to execute some other task while waiting for a blocking operation (an I/O, for example) to complete.

The Common Language Runtime provides two different ways to perform such operations: through the threading and asynchronous call mechanisms.

Note that this is a big topic, and the material in this chapter may not be sufficient for your own application.

Data Protection and Synchronization

Performing more than one operation at once provides a valuable facility to a program, but it also increases the complexity of the programming task.

A Slightly Broken Example

Consider the following code:

```
using System;
class Val
{
    int number = 1;
```

```
    public void Bump()
    {
        int temp = number;
        number = temp + 2;
    }

    public override string ToString()
    {
        return(number.ToString());
    }

    public void DoBump()
    {
        for (int i = 0; i < 5; i++)
        {
            Bump();
            Console.WriteLine("number = {0}", number);
        }
    }
}

class Test
{
    public static void Main()
    {
        Val v = new Val();

        v.DoBump();
    }
}
```

In this example, the `Val` class holds a number and has a way to add 2 to it. When this program is run, it generates the following output:

```
number = 3
number = 5
number = 7
number = 9
number = 11
```

While that program is being executed, the operating system may be performing other tasks simultaneously. Our code can be interrupted at any spot in the code,[1] but after the interruption, everything will be in the same state as before, and there's no way to know that the interruption took place.

Let's modify the program to use some threads:

```
using System;
using System.Threading;
class Val
{
    int number = 1;

    public void Bump()
    {
        int temp = number;
        number = temp + 2;
    }

    public override string ToString()
    {
        return(number.ToString());
    }

    public void DoBump()
    {
        for (int i = 0; i < 5; i++)
        {
            Bump();
            Console.WriteLine("number = {0}", number);
        }
    }
}
```

1. Not quite *any* spot; the situations where it won't be interrupted are covered later.

```
class Test
{
    public static void Main()
    {
        Val v = new Val();

        for (int threadNum = 0; threadNum < 5; threadNum++)
        {
            Thread thread = new Thread(new ThreadStart(v.DoBump));
            thread.Start();
        }
    }
}
```

In this code, a `ThreadStart` delegate is created that refers to the function the thread should execute. When this program is run, it generates the following output:

```
number = 3
number = 5
number = 7
number = 9
number = 11
number = 13
number = 15
number = 17
number = 19
number = 21
number = 23
number = 25
number = 27
number = 29
number = 31
number = 33
number = 35
number = 37
number = 39
number = 41
number = 43
number = 45
number = 47
number = 49
number = 51
```

Can you find the error in the output? No?

This example illustrates one of the common problems with writing multi-threaded programs. The example has a latent error that might show up in some situations, but it doesn't show up when the example is run under normal conditions. Bugs like this are some of the worst to find, and they usually show up only under stressful conditions.[2]

Let's change the code a bit to simulate an interruption by the operating system:

```
public void Bump()
{
    int temp = number;
    Thread.Sleep(1);
    number = temp + 2;
}
```

This small change leads to the following output:

```
number = 3
number = 3
number = 3
number = 3
number = 3
number = 5
number = 5
number = 5
number = 5
number = 5
number = 7
number = 7
number = 7
number = 7
number = 7
number = 9
number = 9
number = 9
number = 9
number = 9
number = 11
number = 11
number = 11
number = 11
number = 11
```

2. Such as at a customer's site.

Not exactly the desired result.

The call to `Thread.Sleep()` will cause the current thread to sleep for one millisecond, before it has saved away the bumped value. When this happens, another thread will come in and also fetch the current value.

The underlying bug in the code is that there's no protection against this situation happening. Unfortunately, it's rare enough that it's hard to find. Creating multi-threaded applications is one area where good design techniques are very important.

Protection Techniques

You can use several different techniques prevent problems. Code that is written to keep this in mind is known as "thread-safe."

In general, most code isn't thread-safe because there is usually a performance penalty in writing thread-safe code.

Don't Share Data

One of the best techniques to prevent such problems is to not share data in the first place. It is often possible to architect an application so that each thread has its own data to deal with. An application that fetches data from several web sites simultaneously can create a separate object for each thread.

This is obviously the best option, as it imposes no performance penalty and doesn't clutter the code. It requires some care, however, since a modification to the code may introduce the errors that were so carefully avoided. For example, a programmer who doesn't know that a class uses threading might add shared data.

Exclusion Primitives

The `System.Threading` namespace contains a number of useful classes for preventing the problems in the earlier example. The most commonly used one is the `Monitor` class. Our slightly broken example can be modified by surrounding the problem region of code with exclusion primitives:

```
public void Bump()
{
    Monitor.Enter(this);
    int temp = number;
    Thread.Sleep(1);
    number = temp + 2;
    Monitor.Exit(this);
}
```

The call to `Monitor.Enter()` passes in the `this` reference for this object. The monitor's job is to make sure that if a thread has called `Monitor.Enter()` with a specific value, any other call to `Monitor.Enter()` with the same value will block until the first thread has called `Monitor.Exit()`. When the first thread calls `Thread.Sleep()`, the second thread will call `Monitor.Enter()` and pass the same object as the first thread did, and therefore the second thread will block.

> **NOTE** *Note: Those of you who've done Win32 programming may be familiar with using* `EnterCriticalSection()` *and* `LeaveCriticalSection()` *to block access. Unlike the Win32 functions, the* `Monitor` *functions lock on a specific object.*

There's a slight problem with the implementation of `Bump()`. If an exception was thrown in the block that is protected, `Monitor.Exit()` will never be called, which is bad. To make sure `Monitor.Exit()` is always called, the calls need to be wrapped in a `try-finally`. This is important enough that C# provides a special statement to do just that.

The `lock` *Statement*

The `lock` statement is simply a thin wrapper around calls to `Monitor.Enter()` and `Monitor.Exit()`. This code:

```
lock(this)
{
    // statements
}
```

is translated to:

```
try
{
    System.Threading.Monitor.Enter(this);
    // statements
}
finally
{
    System.Threading.Monitor.Exit(this);
}
```

The object that is used in the `lock` statement reflects the granularity at which the lock should be obtained. If the data to be protected is instance data, it's typical to lock on `this`, though if the data is a reference type, the reference instance could be used instead.

If the data to be protected is a static data item, it will need to be locked using a unique static reference object. This is done simply by adding a static field of type `object` to the class:

```
static object staticLock = new object();
```

This object is then used in the `lock` statement.

Synchronized Methods

An alternate to using the `lock` statement is to mark the entire method as synchronized, which has the same effect as enclosing the entire method in `lock(this)`. To do this, mark the method with the following attribute:

```
[MethodImpl(MethodImplOptions.Synchronized)]
```

This attribute is found in the `System.Runtime.CompilerServices` namespace.

In general, the use of `lock` is preferred over the use of the attribute for two reasons. First, the performance is better because the region in which there is a lock is often a subset of the whole method.[3] Second, it's easy to miss the attribute (or forget what it does) when reading code, while the use of `lock is more explicit.`

Interlocked Operations

Many processors support some instructions that cannot be interrupted. These are useful when dealing with threads, as no locking is required to use them. In the Common Language Runtime, these operations are encapsulated in the `Interlocked` class in the `System.Threading` namespace. This class exposes the `Increment()`, `Decrement()`, `Exchange()`, and `CompareExchange()` methods, which can be used on `int` or `long` data types.

The problem example could be rewritten using these instructions:

```
public void Bump()
{
    Interlocked.Increment(ref number);
    Interlocked.Increment(ref number);
}
```

3. In the Beta 1 release, the attribute performed better than the use of `lock`. This has been addressed in Beta 2.

It is guaranteed by the runtime that the increment operations will not be interrupted. If interlocked works for an application, it can provide a nice performance boost as it avoids the overhead of locking.

Access Reordering and Volatile

To avoid the overhead of synchronization, some programmers will build their own optimization primitives. In C#, however, there are some surprising subtleties in what the language and runtime guarantee with respect to instruction ordering, especially to those who are familiar with the x86 architecture, which doesn't typically perform these operations.

This topic is complex, but it isn't necessary to fully understand it if you stick to the synchronization methods discussed earlier in this chapter.

To illustrate this, consider the following example:

```
using System;
using System.Threading;

class Problem
{
    int x;
    int y;
    int curx;
    int cury;

    public Problem()
    {
        x = 0;
        y = 0;
    }

    public void Process1()
    {
        x = 1;
        cury = y;
    }

    public void Process2()
    {
        y = 1;
        curx = x;
    }
```

```
    public void TestCurrent()
    {
        Console.WriteLine("curx, cury: {0} {1}", curx, cury);
    }
}

class Test
{
    public static void Main()
    {
        Problem p = new Problem();

        Thread t1 = new Thread(new ThreadStart(p.Process1));
        Thread t2 = new Thread(new ThreadStart(p.Process2));
        t1.Start();
        t2.Start();

        t1.Join();
        t2.Join();

        p.TestCurrent();
    }
}
```

In this example, two threads are started: one that calls `p.Process1()` and another that calls `p.Process2()`. This process is shown in Figure 29-1.

What possible values can be printed for `curx` and `cury`? It's not surprising that two possible values are:

```
curx, cury: 1 0
curx, cury: 0 1
```

This makes sense from the serial nature of the code in `Process1()` and `Process2()`; either function can complete before the other one starts.

A bit less obvious[4] is the following output:

```
curx, cury: 1 1
```

This is a possibility because one of threads could be interrupted after the first instruction and the other thread could run.

4. Though I hope it's still somewhat obvious, given the earlier content of the chapter.

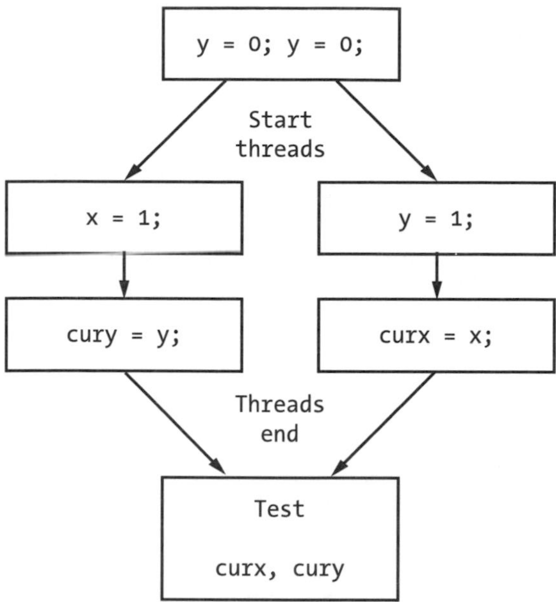

Figure 29-1. Reordering example

The point of the example, however, is that there's a fourth possible output:

```
curx, cury: 0 0
```

This happens because of one of those things that's assumed to be true but isn't really always true. The common assumption when looking at the code in `Process1()` is that the lines always execute in the order in which they are written. Surprisingly, that isn't true; there are a few cases where the instructions might execute out of order:

- First, the compiler could choose to reorder the statements, as there's no way for the compiler to know this isn't safe.
- Second, the JIT could decide to load the values for both `x` and `y` into registers before executing either line of code.
- Third, the processor could reorder the execution of the instructions to be faster.[5]
- Fourth, on a multi-processor system, the values might not be synchronized in global memory.

5. x86 processors don't do this, but there are other processors—including Intel's IA64 architecture—where reordering is common.

What is needed to address this is a way to annotate a field so that such optimizations are inhibited. C# does this with the `volatile` keyword.

When a field is marked as `volatile`, reordering of instructions is inhibited, so that:

- A write cannot be moved forward across a volatile write.
- A read cannot be move backward across a volatile read.

In the example, if `curx` and `cury` are marked volatile, the code in `Process1()` and `Process2()` cannot be reordered:

```
public void Process1()
{
    x = 1;
    cury = y;
}
```

Since `cury` is now volatile, the write to `x` cannot be moved after the write to `cury`.

In addition to precluding such reordering, `volatile` also means that the JIT can't keep the variable in the register and that the variable must be stored in global memory on a multi-processor system.

So what is `volatile` good for, when we already have ways of doing synchronization?

Use of Volatile

Volatile can be used to implement a thread-safe version of a singleton class. The traditional implementation would use `lock`:

```
using System;
class Singleton
{
    static object sync = new object();
    static Singleton singleton = null;

    private Singleton()
    {
    }
```

```
    public static Singleton GetSingleton()
    {
        lock(sync)
        {
            if (singleton == null)
                singleton = new Singleton();

            return(singleton);
        }
    }
}
```

This works fine, but it's pretty wasteful; the synchronization is really only needed the first time the function is called. In this case, the lock needs to be on a static variable, because the function is a static function.

With `volatile`, a nicer version can be written:

```
using System;

class Singleton
{
    static object sync = new object();

    static volatile Singleton singleton = null;

    private Singleton()
    {
    }

    public static Singleton GetSingleton()
    {
        if (singleton == null)
        {
            lock(sync)
            {
                if (singleton == null)
                    singleton = new Singleton();
            }
        }

        return(singleton);
    }
}
```

This version has much better performance since the synchronization is only required if the object hasn't been created.

Threads

The previous example has shown a bit about threads, but there are a few more details to cover. When a `Thread` instance is created, a delegate to the function the thread should run is created and passed to the constructor. Since a delegate can refer to a member function and a specific instance, there's no need to pass anything else to the thread.

The thread instance can be used to control the priority of the thread, set the name of the thread, or perform other thread operations, so it's necessary to save that thread instance if such operations will be performed later. A thread can get its own thread instance through the `Thread.CurrentThread` property.

Joining

After a thread has been created to perform a task, such as doing a computation-intensive calculation, it's sometimes necessary to wait for that thread to complete. The following example illustrates this:

```
using System;
using System.Threading;

class ThreadSleeper
{
    int seconds;

    private ThreadSleeper(int seconds)
    {
        this.seconds = seconds;
    }

    public void Nap()
    {
        Console.WriteLine("Napping {0} seconds", seconds);
        Thread.Sleep(seconds * 1000);
    }
```

```
    public static Thread DoSleep(int seconds)
    {
        ThreadSleeper ts = new ThreadSleeper(seconds);
        Thread thread = new Thread(new ThreadStart(ts.Nap));
        thread.Start();
        return(thread);
    }
}

class Test
{
    public static void Main()
    {
        Thread thread = ThreadSleeper.DoSleep(5);

        Console.WriteLine("Waiting for thread to join");
        thread.Join();
        Console.WriteLine("Thread Joined");
    }
}
```

The `ThreadSleeper.Nap()` function simulates an operation that takes a while to perform. `ThreadSleeper.DoSleep()` creates an instance of a `ThreadSleeper`, executes the `Nap()` function, and then returns the thread instance to the main program. The main program then calls `Join()` on that thread to wait for it to complete.

Using `Join()` works well when waiting for a single thread, but if there is more than one active thread, a call to `Join()` must be made for each, which is a bit unwieldy.

A nicer solution is to use one of the utility classes.

Waiting with WaitHandle

The `WaitHandle` abstract class provides a simple way to wait for an event to occur.[6] In addition to waiting for a single event to occur, it can be used to wait for more than one event and return when one or all of them occur. The `AutoResetEvent` and `ManualResetEvent` classes derive from `WaitHandle`. The `AutoResetEvent` will only release a single thread when the `Set()` function is called and will then reset. The `ManualResetEvent` may release many threads from a single call to `Set() and must be cleared by calling Reset()`.

The previous example can be modified to use an `AutoResetEvent` to signal when an event is complete and to wait for more than one thread to complete:

6. Note that this is an event in the general sense, not in the "C# event" sense.

```
using System;
using System.Threading;

class ThreadSleeper
{
    int seconds;
    AutoResetEvent napDone = new AutoResetEvent(false);

    private ThreadSleeper(int seconds)
    {
        this.seconds = seconds;
    }

    public void Nap()
    {
        Console.WriteLine("Napping {0} seconds", seconds);
        Thread.Sleep(seconds * 1000);
        Console.WriteLine("{0} second nap finished", seconds);
        napDone.Set();
    }

    public static WaitHandle DoSleep(int seconds)
    {
        ThreadSleeper ts = new ThreadSleeper(seconds);
        Thread thread = new Thread(new ThreadStart(ts.Nap));
        thread.Start();
        return(ts.napDone);
    }
}

class Test
{
    public static void Main()
    {
        WaitHandle[] waits = new WaitHandle[2];
        waits[0] = ThreadSleeper.DoSleep(8);
        waits[1] = ThreadSleeper.DoSleep(4);

        Console.WriteLine("Waiting for threads to finish");
        WaitHandle.WaitAll(waits);
        Console.WriteLine("Threads finished");
    }
}
```

The output is:

```
Waiting for threads to finish
Napping 8 seconds
Napping 4 seconds
4 second nap finished
8 second nap finished
Threads finished
```

Instead of returning a `Thread`, the `DoSleep()` function now returns a `WaitHandle` that will be set when the thread has completed. An array of `WaitHandle` is created and then is passed to `WaitHandle.WaitAll()` to wait for all the events to be set.

Thread-Local Storage

It is sometimes useful to store information on a per-thread basis rather than as part of an instance, using what is often known as "thread-local storage." This storage can be accessed through the data slot methods of `Thread` class.

Asynchronous Calls

When using threads, the programmer is responsible for taking care of all the details of execution and determining how to transfer data from the caller to the thread and then back from the thread. This normally involves creating a class to encapsulate the data to be exchanged, which is a fair bit of extra work.

Writing this class isn't difficult, but it's a bit of pain to do if all that is needed is a single asynchronous call. Luckily, the runtime and compiler provide a way to get asynchronous execution without a separate class.

The runtime will handle the details of managing the thread on which the function will be called[7] and provide an easy mechanism for exchanging data. Nicer still, the runtime will allow *any* function to be called with this mechanism; it doesn't have to be designed to be asynchronous to call it asynchronously. This can be a nice way to start an operation and then continue with the main code.

It all happens through a little magic in delegates.

To set up an asynchronous call, the first step is to define a delegate that matches the function to be called. For example, if the function is:

```
Console.WriteLine(string s);
```

7. Using a thread pool.

The delegate would be:

```
delegate void FuncToCall(string s);
```

If this delegate is placed in a class and compiled, it can be viewed using the ILDASM utility. There's an `Invoke()` member that takes a string, which is used to invoke a delegate, and then there are two strange-looking functions:

```
public IAsyncResult BeginInvoke(string s, System.AsyncCallback callback, object o);
public void EndInvoke(IAsyncResult);
```

These functions are generated by the compiler to make doing asynchronous calls easier and are defined based upon the parameters and return type of the delegate, as detailed in the following table:

DATA	MECHANISM
Value parameters	Passed to `BeginInvoke()`
Ref parameters	Passed as `ref` to `BeginInvoke()` and `EndInvoke()`
Out parameters	Passed as `out` to `EndInvoke()`
Return value	Returned from `EndInvoke()`

In addition to the parameters defined for the delegate, `BeginInvoke()` also takes an optional callback to call when the function call has completed and an object that can be used by the caller to pass some state information. `BeginInvoke()` returns an `IAsyncResult` that is passed to `EndInvoke()`.

A Simple Example

The following example shows a simple async call:

```
using System;
public class AsyncCaller
{
    // Declare a delegate that will match Console.WriteLine("string");
    delegate void FuncToCall(string s);
```

```
    public void CallWriteLine(string s)
    {
            // delegate points to function to call
            // start the async call
            // wait for completion
        FuncToCall func = new FuncToCall(Console.WriteLine);
        IAsyncResult iar = func.BeginInvoke(s, null, null);
        func.EndInvoke(iar);
    }
}

class Test
{
    public static void Main()
    {
        AsyncCaller ac = new AsyncCaller();
        ac.CallWriteLine("Hello");
    }
}
```

The `CallWriteLine()` function takes a `string` parameter, creates a delegate to `Console.WriteLine()`, and then calls `BeginInvoke()` and `EndInvoke()` to call the function asynchronously and wait for it to complete.

That's not terribly exciting. Let's modify the example to use a callback function:

```
using System;

public class AsyncCaller
{
    // Declare a delegate that will match Console.WriteLine("string");
    delegate void FuncToCall(string s);

    public void WriteLineCallback(IAsyncResult iar)
    {
        Console.WriteLine("In WriteLineCallback");
        FuncToCall func = (FuncToCall) iar.AsyncState;
        func.EndInvoke(iar);
    }
```

```
    public void CallWriteLineWithCallback(string s)
    {
        FuncToCall func = new FuncToCall(Console.WriteLine);
        func.BeginInvoke(s,
                                        new AsyncCallback(WriteLineCallback),
                                        func); // iar.AsyncState in callback
    }
}
class Test
{
    public static void Main()
    {
        AsyncCaller ac = new AsyncCaller();

        ac.CallWriteLineWithCallback("Hello There");

        System.Threading.Thread.Sleep(1000);
    }
}
```

The `CallWriteLineWithCallback()` function calls `BeginInvoke()`, passing a callback function and the delegate. The callback routine takes the callback function passed in the state object and calls `EndInvoke()`.

Because the call to `CallWriteLineWithCallback()` returns immediately, the `Main()` function sleeps for a second so that the asynchronous call can complete before the program exits.

Return Values

This example calls `Math.Sin()` asynchronously:

```
using System;
using System.Threading;

public class AsyncCaller
{
    public delegate double MathFunctionToCall(double arg);
```

```
    public void MathCallback(IAsyncResult iar)
    {
        MathFunctionToCall mc = (MathFunctionToCall) iar.AsyncState;
        double result = mc.EndInvoke(iar);
        Console.WriteLine("Function value = {0}", result);
    }
    public void CallMathCallback(MathFunctionToCall mathFunc,
                                              double start,
                                              double end,
                                              double increment)
    {
        AsyncCallback cb = new AsyncCallback(MathCallback);

        while (start < end)
        {
            Console.WriteLine("BeginInvoke: {0}", start);
            mathFunc.BeginInvoke(start, cb, mathFunc);
            start += increment;
        }
    }
}

class Test
{
    public static void Main()
    {
        AsyncCaller ac = new AsyncCaller();

        ac.CallMathCallback(
             new AsyncCaller.MathFunctionToCall(Math.Sin), 0.0, 1.0, 0.2);
        Thread.Sleep(2000);
    }
}
```

The following output is generated:

```
BeginInvoke: 0
BeginInvoke: 0.2
BeginInvoke: 0.4
BeginInvoke: 0.6
BeginInvoke: 0.8
Function value = 0
Function value = 0.198669330795061
Function value = 0.389418342308651
Function value = 0.564642473395035
Function value = 0.717356090899523
```

This time, the call to `EndInvoke()` in the callback returns the result of the function, which is then written out. Note that `BeginInvoke()` gets called before any of the calls to `Math.Sin()` occur.

Because there's no synchronization in the example, the call to `Thread.Sleep` is required to make sure the callbacks execute before main finishes.

Waiting for Completion

It's possible to wait for several asynchronous calls to finish, using `WaitHandle` as in the threads section. The `IAsyncResult` returned from `BeginInvoke()` has an `AsyncWaitHandle` member that can be used to know when the asynchronous call completes. Here's a modification to our previous example:

```
using System;
using System.Threading;

public class AsyncCaller
{
    public delegate double MathFunctionToCall(double arg);

    public void MathCallback(IAsyncResult iar)
    {
        MathFunctionToCall mc = (MathFunctionToCall) iar.AsyncState;
        double result = mc.EndInvoke(iar);
        Console.WriteLine("Function value = {0}", result);
    }
```

```
    WaitHandle DoInvoke(MathFunctionToCall mathFunc, double value)
    {
        AsyncCallback cb = new AsyncCallback(MathCallback);

        IAsyncResult asyncResult =
            mathFunc.BeginInvoke(value, cb, mathFunc);
        return(asyncResult.AsyncWaitHandle);
    }

    public void CallMathCallback(MathFunctionToCall mathFunc)
    {
        WaitHandle[] waitArray = new WaitHandle[4];

        Console.WriteLine("Begin Invoke");
        waitArray[0] = DoInvoke(mathFunc, 0.1);
        waitArray[1] = DoInvoke(mathFunc, 0.5);
        waitArray[2] = DoInvoke(mathFunc, 1.0);
        waitArray[3] = DoInvoke(mathFunc, 3.14159);
        Console.WriteLine("Begin Invoke Done");

        Console.WriteLine("Waiting for completion");
        WaitHandle.WaitAll(waitArray, 10000, false);
        Console.WriteLine("Completion achieved");
    }
}

public class Test
{
    public static double DoCalculation(double value)
    {
        Console.WriteLine("DoCalculation: {0}", value);
        Thread.Sleep(250);
        return(Math.Cos(value));
    }

    public static void Main()
    {
        AsyncCaller ac = new AsyncCaller();

        ac.CallMathCallback(new AsyncCaller.MathFunctionToCall(DoCalculation));
        //Thread.Sleep(500);        // no longer needed
    }
}
```

The `DoInvoke()` function returns the `WaitHandle` for a specific call, and `CallMathCallback()` waits for all the calls to complete and then returns. Because of the wait, the sleep call in `main` is no longer needed.

The following output is generated by this example:

```
Begin Invoke
Begin Invoke Done
Waiting for completion
DoCalculation: 0.1
Function value = 0.995004165278026
DoCalculation: 0.5
Function value = 0.877582561890373
DoCalculation: 1
Function value = 0.54030230586814
DoCalculation: 3.14159
Completion achieved
```

The return value for the last calculation is missing.

This illustrates a problem with using the `WaitHandle` that's provided in the `IAsyncResult`. The `WaitHandle` is set when `EndInvoke()` is called, but before the callback routine completes. In this example, it's obvious that something's wrong, but in a real program, this could result in a really nasty race condition, where some results are dropped. This means that using the provided `WaitHandle` is only safe if there isn't any processing done after `EndInvoke()`.

The way to deal with this problem is to ignore the provided `WaitHandle` and add a `WaitHandle` that's called at the end of the callback function:

```
using System;
using System.Threading;

public class AsyncCallTracker
{
    Delegate function;
    AutoResetEvent doneEvent;

    public AutoResetEvent DoneEvent
    {
        get
        {
            return(doneEvent);
        }
    }
```

```
    public Delegate Function
    {
        get
        {
            return(function);
        }
    }

    public AsyncCallTracker(Delegate function)
    {
        this.function = function;
        doneEvent = new AutoResetEvent(false);
    }
}

public class AsyncCaller
{
    public delegate double MathFunctionToCall(double arg);

    public void MathCallback(IAsyncResult iar)
    {
        AsyncCallTracker callTracker = (AsyncCallTracker) iar.AsyncState;
        MathFunctionToCall func = (MathFunctionToCall) callTracker.Function;
        double result = func.EndInvoke(iar);
        Console.WriteLine("Function value = {0}", result);
        callTracker.DoneEvent.Set();
    }

    WaitHandle DoInvoke(MathFunctionToCall mathFunc, double value)
    {
        AsyncCallTracker callTracker = new AsyncCallTracker(mathFunc);

        AsyncCallback cb = new AsyncCallback(MathCallback);
        IAsyncResult asyncResult = mathFunc.BeginInvoke(value, cb, callTracker);
        return(callTracker.DoneEvent);
    }

    public void CallMathCallback(MathFunctionToCall mathFunc)
    {
        WaitHandle[] waitArray = new WaitHandle[4];
```

```
            Console.WriteLine("Begin Invoke");
            waitArray[0] = DoInvoke(mathFunc, 0.1);
            waitArray[1] = DoInvoke(mathFunc, 0.5);
            waitArray[2] = DoInvoke(mathFunc, 1.0);
            waitArray[3] = DoInvoke(mathFunc, 3.14159);
            Console.WriteLine("Begin Invoke Done");

            Console.WriteLine("Waiting for completion");
            WaitHandle.WaitAll(waitArray, 10000, false);
            Console.WriteLine("Completion achieved");
        }
    }

    public class Test
    {
        public static double DoCalculation(double value)
        {
            Console.WriteLine("DoCalculation: {0}", value);
            Thread.Sleep(250);
            return(Math.Cos(value));
        }

        public static void Main()
        {
            AsyncCaller ac = new AsyncCaller();

            ac.CallMathCallback(new AsyncCaller.MathFunctionToCall(DoCalculation));
        }
    }
```

It's now necessary to pass both the delegate and an associated `AutoResetEvent` to the callback function, so these are encapsulated in the `AsyncCallTracker` class. The `AutoResetEvent` is returned from `DoInvoke()`, and this event isn't set until the last line of the callback, so there are no longer any race conditions.

Classes That Support Asynchronous Calls Directly

Some framework classes provide explicit support for asynchronous calls, which allows them to have full control over how asynchronous calls are processed. The `HttpWebRequest` class, for example, provides `BeginGetResponse()` and `EndGetResponse()` functions, so creating a delegate isn't required.

All the framework classes that provide such support adhere to the same pattern as the do-it-yourself approach and are used in the same manner.

Design Guidelines

Both threading and asynchronous calls provide a way to have more than one process happen at once. In most situations, either method can be used.

Asynchronous calls are best-suited to situations where you're doing one or two asynchronous calls, and you don't want the hassle of setting up a separate thread or dealing with data transfer. The system uses a thread pool to implement asynchronous calls (see the "Thread Pools" sidebar), and there's no way to control how many threads it assigns to processing asynchronous calls or anything else about the thread pool. Because of this, asynchronous calls aren't suited for more than a few active calls at once.

Threads allow more flexibility than asynchronous calls but often require more design and implementation work, especially if a thread pool needs to be implemented. It's also more work to transfer data around, and synchronization details may require more thought.

There's also a readability issue. Thread-based code is often easier to understand (though it's probably more likely to harbor hard-to-find problems), and it's a more familiar idiom.

Thread Pools

A program with simple threading will often create a separate thread for every operation. Not only is this wasteful, as threads are being created and destroyed continuously, but it scales very poorly, as having 1,000 threads isn't good design (if it works at all).

A way to get around this is to use a thread pool. Rather than having a thread dedicated to a specific operation, a small number of worker threads are created. Incoming operations are assigned to a specific worker thread (or queued if all threads are busy), so when a thread is done with an operation, it waits for another one to perform.

Advanced thread pools manage the number of worker threads on the fly based on the queue length and other factors.

CHAPTER 30

Execution-Time Code Generation

IF YOU COME FROM A C++ background, it's likely you have a very "compile-time" view of the world. Because a C++ compiler does all code generation when the code is compiled, C++ programs are static systems that are fully known at compile time.

The Common Language Runtime provides a new way of doing things. The compile-time world still exists, but it's also possible to build dynamic systems where new code is added by loading assemblies or even by writing custom code on the fly.

Loading Assemblies

In the .NET Common Language Runtime, it's possible to load an assembly from disk and to create instances of classes from that assembly. To demonstrate this, we're going to build a simple logging facility that can be extended by the customer at runtime to send informational messages elsewhere.

The first step is to define the standard part of the facility:

```
// file=LogDriver.cs
// compile with: csc /target:library LogDriver.cs
using System;
using System.Collections;

public interface ILogger
{
    void Log(string message);
}

public class LogDriver
{
    ArrayList loggers = new ArrayList();
```

```
    public LogDriver()
    {
    }

    public void AddLogger(ILogger logger)
    {
        loggers.Add(logger);
    }

    public void Log(string message)
    {
        foreach (ILogger logger in loggers)
        {
            logger.Log(message);
        }
    }
}

public class LogConsole: ILogger
{
    public void Log(string message)
    {
        Console.WriteLine(message);
    }
}
```

First, we define the `ILogger` interface that our loggers will implement and the `LogDriver` class that calls all the registered loggers whenever the `Log()` function is called. There's also a `LogConsole` implementation that logs messages to the console. This file is compiled to an assembly named `LogDriver.dll`.

In addition to this file, there's a small class to exercise the loggers:

```
using System;

class Test
{
    public static void Main()
    {
        LogDriver logDriver = new LogDriver();

        logDriver.AddLogger(new LogConsole());

        logDriver.Log("Log start: " + DateTime.Now.ToString());
```

```
        for (int i = 0; i < 5; i++)
        {
            logDriver.Log("Operation: " + i.ToString());
        }

        logDriver.Log("Log end: " + DateTime.Now.ToString());
    }
}
```

This code merely creates a `LogDriver`, adds a `LogConsole` to the list of loggers, and does some logging.

Making It Dynamic

It's now time to add some dynamic ability to our system. A mechanism is needed so the `LogDriver` class discovers there is a new assembly that contains an additional logger. To keep the sample simple, the code will look for assemblies named `LogAddIn*.dll`.

The first step is to come up with another implementation of `ILogger`. The `LogAddInToFile` class logs messages to `logger.log`:

```
// file=LogAddInToFile.cs
// compile with: csc /r:..\logdriver.dll /target:library logaddintofile.cs
using System;
using System.Collections;
using System.IO;

public class LogAddInToFile: ILogger
{
    StreamWriter streamWriter;

    public LogAddInToFile()
    {
        streamWriter = File.CreateText(@"logger.log");
        streamWriter.AutoFlush = true;
    }

    public void Log(string message)
    {
        streamWriter.WriteLine(message);
    }
}
```

This class doesn't require much explanation. Next, the code to load the assembly needs to be added to the `LogDriver` class:

```
    void ScanDirectoryForLoggers()
    {
        DirectoryInfo dir = new DirectoryInfo(@".");
        foreach (FileInfo f in dir.GetFiles(@"LogAddIn*.dll"))
        {
            ScanAssemblyForLoggers(f.FullName);
        }
    }
    void ScanAssemblyForLoggers(string filename)
    {
        Assembly a = Assembly.LoadFrom(filename);

        foreach (Type t in a.GetTypes())
        {
            if (t.GetInterface("ILogger") != null)
            {
                ILogger iLogger = (ILogger) Activator.CreateInstance(t);
                loggers.Add(iLogger);
            }
        }
    }
}
```

The `ScanDirectoryForLoggers()` function looks in the current directory for any files that match our specification. When one of the files is found, `ScanAssemblyForLoggers()` is called. This function loads the assembly and then iterates through each of the types contained in the assembly. If the type implements the `ILogger` interface, then an instance of the type is created using `Activator.CreateInstance()`, the instance is cast to the interface, and the interface is added to the list of loggers.

If an even more dynamic implementation is desirable, a `FileChangeWatcher` object could be used to watch a specific directory, and any assemblies copied to that directory could be then be loaded.

There are a few caveats in loading assemblies from a disk. First, the runtime locks assemblies when they are loaded. Second, it's not possible to unload a single assembly, so if unloading an assembly is required (to update a class, for example), it will need to be loaded in a separate application domain since application domains can be unloaded. For more information on application domains, consult the .NET Common Language Runtime documentation.

Custom Code Generation

It's sometimes necessary to have the utmost in performance for a class. For some algorithms, it's easy to write a general solution to a problem, but the overhead of the general solution may be undesirable. A custom solution to the problem may be possible but cannot be generated ahead of time because the particulars of the problem aren't known until the runtime.

In such situations, it may be useful to generate the custom solution at execution time. This technique is often known as "self-modifying code."

Polynomial Evaluation

This section will implement a polynomial evaluator, for polynomials in the form:

$$Y = a_n x^n + \ldots + a_2 x^2 + a_1 x + a_0$$

To get rid of the exponentiation operation, which is slow, the equation can be nicely rearranged into:

$$Y = a_0 + x\ (a_1 + x\ (a_2 + \ldots x\ (a_n)\ )\ )$$

The first step in this exercise is to write the simple general solution to the problem. Since there are going to be several different solutions, it will take a few files to build up a framework. The first is a utility class to do timing:

```
using System;
namespace Polynomial
{
    class Counter
    {
        public static long Frequency
        {
            get
            {
                long freq = 0;
                QueryPerformanceFrequency(ref freq);
                return freq;
            }
        }
```

```
            public static long Value
            {
                get
                {
                    long count = 0;
                    QueryPerformanceCounter(ref count);
                    return count;
                }
            }

            [System.Runtime.InteropServices.DllImport("KERNEL32")]
            private static extern bool
                QueryPerformanceCounter(  ref long lpPerformanceCount);

            [System.Runtime.InteropServices.DllImport("KERNEL32")]
            private static extern bool
                QueryPerformanceFrequency( ref long lpFrequency);
        }
    }
```

The `Counter` class encapsulates the Win32 performance counter functions and can be used to get accurate timings.

Next, a helper class to hold the information about a `Polynomial`:

```
namespace Polynomial
{
    using System;
    using PolyInterface;

        /// <summary>
        /// The abstract class all implementations inherit from
        /// </summary>
    public abstract class Polynomial
    {
        public Polynomial(params double[] coefficients)
        {
            this.coefficients = new double[coefficients.Length];

            for (int i = 0; i < coefficients.Length; i++)
                this.coefficients[i] = coefficients[i];
        }
```

```
        public abstract double Evaluate(double value);
        public abstract IPolynomial GetEvaluate();

        protected double[] coefficients = null;
    }
}
```

The Polynomial class is an abstract class that holds the polynomial coefficients.

There's a small interface that defines the evaluation function:

```
namespace PolyInterface
{
        /// <summary>
        /// The interface that implementations will implement
        /// </summary>
    public interface IPolynomial
    {
        double Evaluate(double value);
    }
}
```

There's a class to implement the general method of evaluation:

```
namespace Polynomial
{
    using System;
    /// <summary>
    /// The simplest polynomial implementation
    /// </summary>
    /// <description>
    /// This implementation loops through the coefficients and evaluates each
    /// term of the polynomial.
    /// </description>
    class PolySimple: Polynomial
    {
        public PolySimple(params double[] coefficients): base(coefficients)
        {
        }

        public override IPolynomial GetEvaluate()
        {
            return((IPolynomial) this);
        }
```

```
        public override double Evaluate(double value)
        {
            double retval = coefficients[0];

            double f = value;

            for (int i = 1; i < coefficients.Length; i++)
            {
                retval += coefficients[i] * f;
                f *= value;
            }
            return(retval);
        }
    }
}
```

This is a very simple evaluator that merely walks through the polynomial term by term, accumulates the values, and returns the result.

Finally, there's the driver that ties it all together:

```
namespace Polynomial
{
    using System;
    using System.Diagnostics;

    /// <summary>
    /// Driver class for the project
    /// </summary>
    public class Driver
    {
        /// <summary>
        /// Times the evaluation of a polynomial
        /// </summary>
        /// <param name="p">The polynomial to evaluate</param>
        public static double TimeEvaluate(Polynomial p)
        {
            double value = 2.0;

            Console.WriteLine("{0}", p.GetType().Name);

                // Time the first iteration. This one is done
                // separately so that we can figure out the startup
                // overhead separately...
            long start = Counter.Value;
```

```
    IPolynomial iPoly = p.GetEvaluate();
    long delta = Counter.Value - start;
    Console.WriteLine("Overhead = {0:f2} seconds",
          (double) delta/Counter.Frequency);
    Console.WriteLine("Eval({0}) = {1}", value, iPoly.Evaluate(value));

    int limit = 100000;
    start = Counter.Value;

        // Evaluate the polynomial the required number of
        // times.
    double result = 0;
    for (int i = 0; i < limit; i++)
    {
        result += iPoly.Evaluate(value);
    }
    delta = Counter.Value - start;

    double ips = (double) limit * ((double)Counter.Frequency /
                    (double) delta);
    Console.WriteLine("Evalutions/Second = {0:f0}", ips);
    Console.WriteLine();

    return(ips);
}
/// <summary>
/// Run all implementations for a given set of coefficients
/// </summary>
/// <param name="coeff"> </param>
public static void Eval(double[] coeff)
{
    Polynomial[] imps = new Polynomial []
    {
            new PolySimple(coeff),
    };

    double[] results = new double[imps.Length];
    for (int index = 0; index < imps.Length; index++)
    {
        results[index] = TimeEvaluate(imps[index]);
    }
```

```
            Console.WriteLine("Results for length = {0}", coeff.Length);
            for (int index = 0; index < imps.Length; index++)
            {
                Console.WriteLine("{0} = {1:f0}", imps[index], results[index]);
            }
            Console.WriteLine();
        }

        /// <summary>
        /// Maim function.
        /// </summary>
        public static void Main()
        {
            Eval(new Double[] {5.5});

                // Evaluate the first polynomial, with 7 elements
            double[] coeff = new double[] {5.5, 7.0, 15, 30, 500, 100, 1};

            Eval(coeff);

                // Evaluate the second polynomial, with 50 elements
            coeff = new double[50];
            for (int index = 0; index < 50; index++)
            {
                coeff[index] = index;
            }
            Eval(coeff);
        }
    }
}
```

The `TimeEvaluate()` function takes a class that derives from `Polynomial` and calls `GetEvaluate()` to obtain the `IPolynomial` interface to do the evaluation. It times the `GetEvaluate()` function to determine the initialization overhead and then calls the evaluation function 100,000 times.

The driver evaluates polynomials with 1, 7, and 50 coefficients and writes out timing information.

For the initial run, the following results (which are counts in evaluations/second) are generated:

METHOD	C=1	C=7	C=50
Simple	18,000,000	6,400,000	1,600,000

Those results are really quite good, but it will be interesting to see if a custom solution can do better.

A Custom C# Class

The general solution has some loop overhead, and it would be nice to get rid of this. To do this, there would need to be a version of `eval` that evaluates an expression directly.

This example will generate a class that evaluates the polynomial in a single expression. It will generate a class like this:

```
// Polynomial evaluator
// Evaluating Y = 5.5 + 7 X^1 + 15 X^2 + 30 X^3 + 500 X^4 + 100 X^5 + 1 X^6
public class Poly_1001 : PolyInterface.IPolynomial {

    public double Eval(double x) {
        return (5.5
                    + (x * (7
                    + (x * (15
                    + (x * (30
                    + (x * (500
                    + (x * (100
                    + (x * (1 + 0))))))))))))));
    }
}
```

The class to generate this file, compile it, and load it is as follows:

```
using System;
using System.IO;
using System.Diagnostics;
using System.Reflection;

class PolyCodeSlow: Polynomial
{
    public PolyCodeSlow(params double[] coefficients): base(coefficients)
    {
    }

    void WriteCode()
    {
        string timeString = polyNumber.ToString();
        polyNumber++;
```

```
string filename = "PS_" + timeString;
Stream s = File.Open(filename + ".cs", FileMode.Create);
StreamWriter t = new StreamWriter(s);

t.WriteLine("// polynomial evaluator");
t.Write("// Evaluating y = ");

string[] terms = new string[coefficients.Length];
terms[0] = coefficients[0].ToString();

for (int i = 1; i < coefficients.Length; i++)
    terms[i] = String.Format("{0} X^{1}", coefficients[1], i);

t.Write("{0}", String.Join(" + ", terms));
t.WriteLine();

t.WriteLine("");

string className = "Poly_" + timeString;
t.WriteLine("class {0}", className);
t.WriteLine("{");
t.WriteLine("public double Eval(double value)");
t.WriteLine("{");
t.WriteLine("    return(");
t.WriteLine("        {0}", coefficients[0]);

string closing = "";
for (int i = 1; i < coefficients.Length; i++)
{
    t.WriteLine("        + value * ({0} ", coefficients[i]);
    closing += ")";
}
t.Write("\t{0}", closing);
t.WriteLine(");");

t.WriteLine("}");
t.WriteLine("}");
t.Close();
s.Close();
```

```
            // Build the file
        ProcessStartInfo psi = new ProcessStartInfo();
        psi.FileName = "cmd.exe";
        psi.Arguments = String.Format(
            "/c csc /o+ /r:polynomial.exe /target:library {0}.cs > compile.out",
            filename);
        psi.WindowStyle = ProcessWindowStyle.Minimized;

        Process proc = Process.Start(psi);
        proc.WaitForExit();

            // Open the file, and get a pointer to the method info
        Assembly a = Assembly.LoadFrom(filename + ".dll");

        func = a.CreateInstance(className);

        invokeType = a.GetType(className);

        File.Delete(filename + ".cs");
    }
    public override IPolynomial GetEvaluate()
    {
        return((IPolynomial) this);
    }

    public override double Evaluate(double value)
    {
        object[] args = new Object[] {value};
        object retValue =
            invokeType.InvokeMember("Eval",
                    BindingFlags.Default | BindingFlags.InvokeMethod,
                    null,
                    func,
                    args);
        return((double) retValue);
    }

    object func = null;
    Type invokeType = null;

    static int polyNumber = 0;     // which number we're using...
}
```

The first time a polynomial is evaluated, the `WriteCode()` function writes the code out to the file and compiles it. It then uses `Assembly.LoadFrom()` to load the assembly and `Activator.CreateInstance()` to create an instance of the class. The instance and the type are then stored away for later use.

When it's time to call the function, the value for `x` is put into an array, and `Type.InvokeMember()` is used to locate and call the function.

When this version is called, the following results are generated:

METHOD	C=1	C=7	C=50
Simple	18,000,000	6,400,000	1,600,000
Custom	43,000	43,000	41,000

Not exactly the results we were looking for. The problem is that `Type.MethodInvoke()` is a very general function and has a lot to do. It needs to locate the function based on the name and parameters and perform other operations, and it does this every time the function is called.

What's needed is a way to perform the call without the overhead—in other words, a way to define the way a method will look without defining what class the method is in. That's a perfect description of an interface.

A Fast Custom C# Class

Rather than calling the evaluate function directly like in the previous example, we'll change our code so that the custom class implements the interface. After the assembly is loaded and an instance of the class is created, it will be cast to the interface, and that interface will be returned to the driver program.

This approach has two benefits. First, we'll be calling directly through the interface, so the overhead of `Type.InvokeMember()` is avoided. Second, instead of the driver calling the class evaluation function, which then called the custom function, the driver will call the custom function directly.

When we try this example, we get the following results:

METHOD	C=1	C=7	C=50
Simple	18,000,000	6,400,000	1,600,000
Custom	43,000	43,000	41,000
Custom Fast	51,000,000	9,600,000	1,500,000

That gives a very nice performance increase for small polynomials. For very large ones, however, it turns out that the function is so big that it doesn't fit into the cache and therefore gets slower than the simple method.

There is a problem, however. There's approximately half a second of overhead to write the file, compile it, and read in the resulting assembly. That's fine if each polynomial is evaluated many times, but not if each one is only evaluated a few times.

Also, because this technique involves C# code, the compiler must be present on the system on which the code executes. Depending on where the application will run, this may be a problem.

What is needed is a way to get rid of the overhead and the dependency on the C# compiler.

A CodeDOM Implementation

A trip through the Frameworks documentation shows a set of classes referred to as the "CodeDOM." The CodeDOM is used by the Visual Studio.NET designers to write the code for Windows Forms and WebForms.

A similar technique can be used to generate a custom class for our example:

```
using System;
using System.IO;
using System.Diagnostics;
using System.Reflection;
using PolyInterface;
using System.CodeDom;
using System.CodeDom.Compiler;
using Microsoft.CSharp;

class PolyCodeDom: Polynomial
{
    public PolyCodeDom(params double[] coefficients): base(coefficients)
    {
    }

    void WriteCode()
    {
        string timeString = polyNumber.ToString();
        polyNumber++;

        string filename = "PSCD_" + timeString;
        Stream s = File.Open(filename + ".cs", FileMode.Create);
        StreamWriter t = new StreamWriter(s);
```

```
    // Generate code in C#
CSharpCodeProvider provider = new CSharpCodeProvider();
ICodeGenerator cg = provider.CreateGenerator(t);
CodeGeneratorOptions op = new CodeGeneratorOptions();

    // Generate the comments at the beginning of the function
CodeCommentStatement comment =
       new CodeCommentStatement("Polynomial evaluator");
cg.GenerateCodeFromStatement(comment, t, op);

string[] terms = new string[coefficients.Length];
terms[0] = coefficients[0].ToString();

for (int i = 1; i < coefficients.Length; i++)
    terms[i] = String.Format("{0} X^{1}", coefficients[i], i);

comment = new CodeCommentStatement(
        "Evaluating Y = " + String.Join(" + ", terms));
cg.GenerateCodeFromStatement(comment, t, op);

    // The class is named with a unique name
string className = "Poly_" + timeString;
CodeTypeDeclaration polyClass = new CodeTypeDeclaration(className);
    // The class implements IPolynomial
polyClass.BaseTypes.Add("PolyInterface.IPolynomial");

    // Set up the Eval function
CodeParameterDeclarationExpression param1 =
    new CodeParameterDeclarationExpression("double", "x");
CodeMemberMethod eval = new CodeMemberMethod();
eval.Name = "Evaluate";
eval.Parameters.Add(param1);

    // workaround for bug below...
eval.ReturnType = new CodeTypeReference("public double");
    // BUG: This doesn't generate "public", it just leaves
    // the attribute off of the member...
eval.Attributes |= MemberAttributes.Public;
```

```
    // Create the expression to do the evaluation of the
    // polynomail. To do this, we chain together binary
    // operators to get the desired expression
    // a0 + x * (a1 + x * (a2 + x * (a3)));
    //
    // This is very much like building a parse tree for
    // an expression.

CodeBinaryOperatorExpression plus = new CodeBinaryOperatorExpression();
plus.Left = new CodePrimitiveExpression(coefficients[0]);
plus.Operator = CodeBinaryOperatorType.Add;

CodeBinaryOperatorExpression current = plus;

for (int i = 1; i < coefficients.Length; i++)
{
    CodeBinaryOperatorExpression multiply =
        new CodeBinaryOperatorExpression();
    current.Right = multiply;
    multiply.Left = new CodeSnippetExpression("x");
    multiply.Operator = CodeBinaryOperatorType.Multiply;

    CodeBinaryOperatorExpression add = new CodeBinaryOperatorExpression();
    multiply.Right = add;
    add.Operator = CodeBinaryOperatorType.Add;
    add.Left = new CodePrimitiveExpression(coefficients[i]);
    current = add;
}
current.Right = new CodePrimitiveExpression(0.0);

    // return the expression...
eval.Statements.Add(new CodeMethodReturnStatement(plus));
polyClass.Members.Add(eval);
cg.GenerateCodeFromType(polyClass, t, op);

t.Close();
s.Close();
```

```
        // Build the file
    ProcessStartInfo psi = new ProcessStartInfo();
    psi.FileName = "cmd.exe";
    psi.Arguments = String.Format(
        "/c csc /o+ /r:polynomial.exe /target:library {0}.cs > compile.out",
        filename);
    psi.WindowStyle = ProcessWindowStyle.Minimized;

    Process proc = Process.Start(psi);
    proc.WaitForExit();

        // Open the file, create the instance, and cast it
        // to the assembly
    Assembly a = Assembly.LoadFrom(filename + ".dll");
    polynomial = (IPolynomial) a.CreateInstance(className);

    File.Delete(filename + ".cs");
}

public override IPolynomial GetEvaluate()
{
    if (polynomial == null)
        WriteCode();

    return((IPolynomial) polynomial);
}

public override double Evaluate(double value)
{
    return(0.0);        // not used
}

IPolynomial polynomial = null;
static int polyNumber = 1000;
}
```

Because the approach is the same, this technique yields similar performance.

A Reflection.Emit Implementation

A bit more digging in the documentation, and we come across the `Reflection.Emit` namespace. Using the classes in this namespace, it's possible to create classes in memory and write the IL for the functions directly.

Using `Reflection.Emit` is fairly challenging because functions are written in the IL language rather than in C#. IL is roughly as difficult to develop in as assembly language, though the .NET IL is quite a bit simpler than x86 assembly language. The IL reference guide that ships with the SDK will be a useful reference.[1]

The easiest way to determine what IL to generate is to write the class in C#, compile it, and then use ILDASM to figure out what IL to generate. To evaluate the polynomial expression, the C# compiler uses a very regular pattern, so generating the IL was straightforward.

Here's the class that does it:

```
using System;
using System.IO;
using System.Diagnostics;
using System.Reflection;
using System.Reflection.Emit;
using System.Threading;
using PolyInterface;

class PolyEmit: Polynomial
{
    Type    theType = null;
    object    theObject = null;
    IPolynomial poly = null;

    public PolyEmit(params double[] coefficients): base(coefficients)
    {
    }
        /// <summary>
        /// Create an assembly that will evaluate the polynomial.
        /// </summary>
```

1. Look in `C:\Program Files\Microsoft.Net\FrameworkSDK\Tool Developers Guide`.

```
private Assembly EmitAssembly()
{
        //
        // Create an assembly name
        //
    AssemblyName assemblyName = new AssemblyName();
    assemblyName.Name = "PolynomialAssembly";

        //
        // Create a new assembly with one module
        //
    AssemblyBuilder newAssembly =
        Thread.GetDomain().DefineDynamicAssembly(
                assemblyName, AssemblyBuilderAccess.Run);
    ModuleBuilder newModule = newAssembly.DefineDynamicModule("Evaluate");

        //
        //  Define a public class named "PolyEvaluate" in the assembly.
        //
    TypeBuilder myType =
        newModule.DefineType("PolyEvaluate", TypeAttributes.Public);

        //
        // Mark the class as implementing IPolynomial. This is
        // the first step in that process.
        //
    myType.AddInterfaceImplementation(typeof(IPolynomial));

        // Add a constructor
    ConstructorBuilder constructor =
        myType.DefineDefaultConstructor(MethodAttributes.Public);

        //
        // Define a method on the type to call. We pass an
        // array that defines the types of the parameters,
        // the type of the return type, the name of the method,
        // and the method attributes.
        //
```

```
Type[] paramTypes = new Type[] {typeof(double)};
Type returnType = typeof(double);
MethodBuilder simpleMethod =
    myType.DefineMethod("Evaluate",
                    MethodAttributes.Public | MethodAttributes.Virtual,
                    returnType,
                    paramTypes);

    //
    // From the method, get an ILGenerator. This is used to
    // emit the IL that we want.
    //
ILGenerator il = simpleMethod.GetILGenerator();

    //
    // Emit the IL. This is a hand-coded version of what
    // you'd get if you compiled the code example and then ran
    // ILDASM on the output.
    //

    //
    // This first section repeated loads the coefficients
    // x value on the stack for evaluation.
    //
for (int index = 0; index < coefficients.Length - 1;index++)
{
    il.Emit(OpCodes.Ldc_R8, coefficients[index]);
    il.Emit(OpCodes.Ldarg_1);
}

    // load the last coefficient
il.Emit(OpCodes.Ldc_R8, coefficients[coefficients.Length - 1]);

    // Emit the remainder of the code. This is a repeated
    // section of multiplying the terms together and
    // accumulating them.
for (int loop = 0; loop < coefficients.Length - 1; loop++)
{
    il.Emit(OpCodes.Mul);
    il.Emit(OpCodes.Add);
}
```

```
            // return the value
        il.Emit(OpCodes.Ret);

            //
            // Finish the process.
            // Create the type.
            //
        //myType.CreateType();

            //
            // Hook up the interface member to the member function
            // that implements that member.
            // 1) Get the interface member.
            // 2) Hook the method to the interface member.
            //
        MethodInfo methodInterfaceEval = typeof(IPolynomial).GetMethod("Evaluate");

        myType.DefineMethodOverride(simpleMethod, methodInterfaceEval);
        myType.CreateType();

          return newAssembly;
    }

    public void Setup()
    {
            // Create the assembly, create an instance of the
            // evalution class, and save away an interface
            // reference to it.
        Assembly ass = EmitAssembly();

        theObject = ass.CreateInstance("PolyEvaluate");
        theType = theObject.GetType();

        poly = (IPolynomial) theObject;
    }
```

```
    public override IPolynomial GetEvaluate()
    {
        if (theType == null)
            Setup();

        return((IPolynomial) poly);
    }

    public override double Evaluate(double value)
    {
        return(0.0f);
    }
}
```

The best way to understand this code is to look at the ILDASM for the previous example, walk through the code, look up the classes in the documentation, and read the comments.

The implementation using `Reflection.Emit` has nearly identical performance to the other fast techniques but less overhead (about 0.25 seconds for the first polynomial, and no measurable overhead for later ones). The final results are shown in the following table:

METHOD	C=1	C=7	C=50
Simple	18,000,000	6,400,000	1,600,000
Custom	43,000	43,000	41,000
Custom Fast	51,000,000	9,600,000	1,500,000
CodeDOM	51,000,000	9,600,000	1,500,000
Reflection.Emit	51,000,000	9,600,000	1,500,000

Summary

Generating C# code and compiling it or using `Reflection.Emit` are valid techniques, but they should probably be the last resort in your performance improvement arsenal. The simple example is much easier to write, debug, and maintain.

Techniques such as these are used in the .NET Frameworks; the regular expression class in the `System.Text.RegularExpressions` namespace uses `Reflection.Emit` to generate a custom-matching engine when a regular expression is compiled.

CHAPTER 31
Interop

ONE OF THE IMPORTANT CAPABILITIES of C# is being able to interoperate with existing code, whether it is COM-based or in a native DLL. This chapter provides a brief overview of how interop works.

Using COM Objects

To call a COM object, the first step is to define a proxy (or "wrapper") class that defines the functions in the COM object, along with additional information. This is a fair amount of work, which can be avoided in most cases by using the `tlbimp` utility. This utility reads the COM typelib information and then creates the proxy class automatically. This will work in many situations, but if more control is needed over marshalling, the proxy class may need to be written by hand. In this case, attributes are used to specify how marshalling should be performed.

Once the proxy class is written, it is used like any other .NET class, and the runtime handles the ugly stuff.

Being Used by COM Objects

The runtime also lets .NET objects be used in place of COM objects. The `tlbexp` utility is used to create a typelib that describes the COM objects so that other COM-based programs can determine the object's interface, and the `regasm` utility is used to register an assembly so that it can be accessed through COM. When COM accesses a .NET class, the runtime creates the .NET object, fabricating whatever COM interfaces are required and marshalling the data between the .NET world and the COM world.

Calling Native DLL Functions

C# can call C functions written in native code through a runtime feature known as "platform invoke." The file that the function is located in is specified by the `DllImport` attribute, which can also be used to specify the default character marshalling. In many cases, that attribute is all that is needed, but if a value is passed by reference, `ref` or `out` may be specified to tell the marshaller how to pass the value. Here's an example:

```
using System.Runtime.InteropServices;
class Test
{
    [DllImport("user32.dll")]
    public static extern int MessageBox(int h, string m,
        string c, int type);
    public static void Main()
    {
        int retval = MessageBox(0, "Hello", "Caption", 0);
    }
}
```

When this code runs, a message box will appear. Note that the code uses `MessageBox()` rather than the ASCII- or Unicode-specific versions; the runtime will automatically use the appropriate function (`MessageBoxA()` or `MessageBoxW()`) based on the platform.

C# cannot use C++ classes directly; to use such objects, they must be exposed in a .NET-compliant way either using the Managed Extensions to C++ or as COM objects.

Pointers and Declarative Pinning

It's common for C-style functions to take pointers as their parameters. Since C# supports pointers in an unsafe context, it's straightforward to use such functions. This example calls `ReadFile()` from `kernel32.dll`:

```
// file=ReadFileUnsafe.cs
// compile with: csc /unsafe ReadFileUnsafe.cs
using System;
using System.Runtime.InteropServices;
using System.Text;

class FileRead
{
    const uint GENERIC_READ = 0x80000000;
    const uint OPEN_EXISTING = 3;
    int handle;
```

```
    public FileRead(string filename)
    {
        // opens the existing file...
        handle = CreateFile(    filename,
                GENERIC_READ,
                0,
                0,
                OPEN_EXISTING,
                0,
                0);
    }

    [DllImport("kernel32", SetLastError=true)]
    static extern int CreateFile(
        string filename,
        uint desiredAccess,
        uint shareMode,
        uint attributes,        // really SecurityAttributes pointer
        uint creationDisposition,
        uint flagsAndAttributes,
        uint templateFile);

    [DllImport("kernel32", SetLastError=true)]
    static extern unsafe bool ReadFile(
        int hFile,
        void* lpBuffer,
        int nBytesToRead,
        int* nBytesRead,
        int overlapped);

    public unsafe int Read(byte[] buffer, int count)
    {
        int n = 0;
        fixed (byte* p = buffer)
        {
            ReadFile(handle, p, count, &n, 0);
        }
        return n;
    }
}
```

```
class Test
{
    public static void Main(string[] args)
    {
        FileRead fr = new FileRead(args[0]);

        byte[] buffer = new byte[128];
        ASCIIEncoding e = new ASCIIEncoding();

            // loop through, read until done...
        Console.WriteLine("Contents");
        while (fr.Read(buffer, 128) != 0)
        {
            Console.Write("{0}", e.GetString(buffer));
        }
    }
}
```

In this example, the `FileRead` class encapsulates the code to read from the file. It declares the functions to import and the `unsafe` read function.

Calling the `ReadFile()` function presents a dilemma. The `byte[]` array buffer is a managed variable, which means the garbage collector can move it at any time. But `ReadFile()` expects that the buffer pointer passed to it will not move during the call to `ReadFile()`.

The `fixed` statement is used as a bridge between the two worlds. It "pins" the `byte[]` buffer by setting a flag on the object so that the garbage collector won't move the object if a collection occurs inside the `fixed` block. This makes it safe to pass the pointer to the buffer to `ReadFile()`. After the call, the flag is cleared and execution continues.

This approach is nice in that it has very low overhead—unless a garbage collection occurs while the code is inside the `fixed` block, which is unlikely.

This sample works fine, but the class is subject to the usual constraints on code written with `unsafe`. See the section on `unsafe` in Chapter 36, "Deeper into C#."

A Safe Version

Since pointer support isn't required for .NET languages, other languages need to be able to call functions like `ReadFile()` without using pointers. The runtime provides a considerable amount of support to make the marshalling from managed to unmanaged types (including pointer types) transparent.

The previous example can be rewritten without using `unsafe`. All that is required is to change the extern declaration for `ReadFile()` and the `Read()` function:

```
[DllImport("kernel32", SetLastError=true)]
static extern bool ReadFile(
    int hFile,
    byte[] buffer,
    int nBytesToRead,
    ref int nBytesRead,
    int overlapped);

public int Read(byte[] buffer, int count)
{
    int n = 0;
    ReadFile(handle, buffer, count, ref n, 0);
    return n;
}
```

The pointer parameter for the buffer has been changed to a `byte[]`, and the number of characters read is defined as a `ref int` instead of a `int*`.

In this version, the runtime will do the pinning of the buffer automatically rather than it having to be explicit, and because `unsafe` isn't required, this version isn't subject to the same restrictions as the previous example.

Structure Layout

The runtime allows a structure to specify the layout of its data members, using the `StructLayout` attribute. By default, the layout of a structure is automatic, which means the runtime is free to rearrange the fields. When using interop to call into native or COM code, better control may be required.

When specifying the `StructLayout` attribute, three kinds of layout can be specified using the `LayoutKind` enum:

- `Auto`, where the runtime chooses the appropriate way to layout the members.

- `Sequential`, where all fields are in declaration order. For sequential layout, the Pack property can be used to specify the type of packing.

- `Explicit`, where every field has a specified offset. In explicit layout, the `StructOffset` attribute must be used on every member, to specify the offset in bytes of the element.

Additionally, the `CharSet` property can be specified to set the default marshalling for string data members.

By default, the Beta 2 C# Compiler sets sequential layout for all structs.

Calling a Function with a Structure Parameter

To call a function with a structure parameter, the structure is defined with the appropriate parameters. This example shows how to call `GetWindowPlacement()`:

```
using System;
using System.Runtime.InteropServices;

struct Point
{
    public int x;
    public int y;

    public override string ToString()
    {
        return(String.Format("({0}, {1})", x, y));
    }
}

struct Rect
{
    public int left;
    public int top;
    public int right;
    public int bottom;

    public override string ToString()
    {
        return(String.Format("({0}, {1})\n    ({2}, {3})",
                    left, top, right, bottom));
    }
}

struct WindowPlacement
{
    public uint length;
    public uint flags;
    public uint showCmd;
    public Point minPosition;
    public Point maxPosition;
    public Rect normalPosition;
```

```
    public override string ToString()
    {
        return(String.Format("min, max, normal:\n{0}\n{1}\n{2}",
            minPosition, maxPosition, normalPosition));
    }
}

class Window
{
    [DllImport("user32")]
    static extern int GetForegroundWindow();

    [DllImport("user32")]
    static extern bool GetWindowPlacement(int handle, ref WindowPlacement wp);

    public static void Main()
    {
        int window = GetForegroundWindow();

        WindowPlacement wp = new WindowPlacement();
        wp.length = (uint) Marshal.SizeOf(wp);

        bool result = GetWindowPlacement(window, ref wp);

        if (result)
        {
            Console.WriteLine(wp);
        }
    }
}
```

Hooking Up to a Windows Callback

The Win32 API sometimes uses callback functions to pass information back to the caller asynchronously. The closest analogy to a callback function in C# (and in the Common Language Runtime) is a delegate, so the runtime interop layer can map a delegate to a callback. Here's an example that does so for the `SetConsoleHandler()` API (the one used to catch Ctrl-C):

```
using System;
using System.Threading;
using System.Runtime.InteropServices;
```

```
class ConsoleCtrl
{
    public enum ConsoleEvent
    {
        CTRL_C = 0,         // From wincom.h
        CTRL_BREAK = 1,
        CTRL_CLOSE = 2,
        CTRL_LOGOFF = 5,
        CTRL_SHUTDOWN = 6
    }

    public delegate void ControlEventHandler(ConsoleEvent consoleEvent);

    public event ControlEventHandler ControlEvent;

        // save delegate so the GC doesn't collect it.
    ControlEventHandler eventHandler;

    public ConsoleCtrl()
    {
            // save this to a private var so the GC doesn't collect it...
        eventHandler = new ControlEventHandler(Handler);
        SetConsoleCtrlHandler(eventHandler, true);
    }

    private void Handler(ConsoleEvent consoleEvent)
    {
        if (ControlEvent != null)
            ControlEvent(consoleEvent);
    }

    [DllImport("kernel32.dll")]
    static extern bool SetConsoleCtrlHandler(ControlEventHandler e, bool add);
}

class Test
{
    public static void MyHandler(ConsoleCtrl.ConsoleEvent consoleEvent)
    {
        Console.WriteLine("Event: {0}", consoleEvent);
    }
```

```
    public static void Main()
    {
        ConsoleCtrl cc = new ConsoleCtrl();
        cc.ControlEvent += new ConsoleCtrl.ControlEventHandler(MyHandler);

        Console.WriteLine("Enter 'E' to exit");

        Thread.Sleep(15000);              // sleep 15 seconds
    }
}
```

The ConsoleCtrl class encapsulates the API function. It defines a delegate that matches the signature of the Win32 callback function, and then uses that as the type passed to the Win32 function. It exposes an event that other classes can hook up to.

The one subtlety of this example has to do with the following line:

```
ControlEventHandler eventHandler;
```

This line is required because the interop layer will pass a pointer to the delegate to the Win32 function, but there's no way for the garbage collector to know that pointer exists. If the delegate weren't stored in a place the garbage collector could find, it would be collected the next time the garbage collector runs, which would be bad.

Design Guidelines

There are a few guidelines that can be used to decide what method of interop to use and how to use it.

C# or C++?

The two options for doing interop with existing C libraries are calling functions directly from C# using platform invoke and using the Managed Extensions to C++ to encapsulate the C functions in a nice managed class written in C++.

Which is the better choice depends upon the interface being called. It's easy to tell by how much effort it takes to get it working. If it's straightforward, then doing it in C# is easy. If you find yourself asking, "How do I do that in C#?" several times, or you start using a lot of unsafe code, then it's likely that doing it using the Managed Extensions is a better choice. This is especially true for complex interfaces, where a structure contains pointers to other structures or the sizes of a structure aren't fixed.

In such cases, you'll need to do a translation from the C-style way of doing things to the .NET-managed way of doing things. This might involve grabbing a value out of a union or walking through a structure of variable size and then putting the values into the appropriate variable on collection class. Doing such an operation is a lot easier in C++ than it is in C#, and you likely already have working C++ code on which you can base your C# code.

Marshalling in C#

When defining functions in C#, consider the following guidelines:

- In general, the data marshalling layer does the right thing. Choose the type that's closest to the type you want.
- For opaque types (like pointers) where all you really care about is the size of the variable, just use an `int`.
- To control data marshalling, use the `MarshalAs` attribute. This is most often used to control string marshalling.
- Rather than using a pointer type for a parameter, define it using `ref`.
- Read the "Data Marshalling Specification" in the .NET Framework Developer Specifications.
- If things get ugly, switch to using the Managed Extensions.

CHAPTER 32

.NET Frameworks Overview

THE .NET FRAMEWORKS CONTAINS many functions normally found in language-specific runtime libraries, and it is therefore important to understand what classes are available in the Frameworks.

Numeric Formatting

Numeric types are formatted through the `Format()` member function of that data type. This can be called directly, through `String.Format()`, which calls the `Format()` function of each data type, or through `Console.WriteLine()`, which calls `String.Format()`.

Adding formatting to a user-defined object is discussed in the "Custom Object Formatting" section later in this chapter. This section discusses how formatting is done with the built-in types.

There are two methods of specifying numeric formatting. A standard format string can be used to convert a numeric type to a specific string representation. If further control over the output is desired, a custom format string can be used.

Standard Format Strings

A standard format string consists of a character specifying the format, followed by a sequence of digits specifying the precision. The following formats are supported:

FORMAT CHARACTER	DESCRIPTION
C, c	Currency
D, d	Decimal
E, e	Scientific (exponential)
F, f	Fixed-point
G, g	General
N, n	Number
R, r	Roundtrip
X, x	Hexadecimal

Currency

The currency format string converts the numerical value to a string containing a locale-specific currency amount. By default, the format information is determined by the current locale, but this may be changed by passing a `NumberFormatInfo` object. This example:

```
using System;
class Test
{
    public static void Main()
    {
        Console.WriteLine("{0:C}", 33345.8977);
        Console.WriteLine("{0:C}", -33345.8977);
    }
}
```

gives the following output:

```
$33,345.90
($33,345.90)
```

An integer following the `c` specifies the number of decimal places to use; two places are used if the integer is omitted.

Decimal

The decimal format string converts the numerical value to an integer. The minimum number of digits is determined by the precision specifier. The result is left-padded with zeroes to obtain the required number of digits. This example:

```
using System;
class Test
{
    public static void Main()
    {
        Console.WriteLine("{0:D}", 33345);
        Console.WriteLine("{0:D7}", 33345);
    }
}
```

gives the following output:

```
33345
0033345
```

Scientific (Exponential)

The scientific (exponential) format string converts the value to a string in the following form:

```
m.dddE+xxx
```

One digit always precedes the decimal point, and the number of decimal places is specified by the precision specifier, with six places used as the default. The format specifier controls whether `E` or `e` appears in the output. This example:

```
using System;
class Test
{
    public static void Main()
    {
        Console.WriteLine("{0:E}", 33345.8977);
        Console.WriteLine("{0:E10}", 33345.8977);
        Console.WriteLine("{0:e4}", 33345.8977);
    }
}
```

gives the following output:

```
3.334590E+004
3.3345897700E+004
3.3346e+004
```

Fixed-Point

The fixed-point format string converts the value to a string, with the number of places after the decimal point specified by the precision specifier. Two places are used if the precision specifier is omitted. This example:

```
using System;
class Test
{
    public static void Main()
    {
        Console.WriteLine("{0:F}", 33345.8977);
        Console.WriteLine("{0:F0}", 33345.8977);
        Console.WriteLine("{0:F5}", 33345.8977);
    }
}
```

gives the following output:

```
33345.90
33346
33345.89770
```

General

The general format string converts the value to either a fixed-point or scientific format, whichever one gives a more compact format. This example:

```
using System;
class Test
{
    public static void Main()
    {
        Console.WriteLine("{0:G}", 33345.8977);
        Console.WriteLine("{0:G7}", 33345.8977);
        Console.WriteLine("{0:G4}", 33345.8977);
    }
}
```

gives the following output:

```
33345.8977
33345.9
3.335E4
```

Number

The number format string converts the value to a number that has embedded commas, such as:

```
12,345.11
```

By default, the number is formatted with two digits to the right of the decimal point. This can be controlled by specifying the number of digits after the format specifier. This example:

```
using System;
class Test
{
    public static void Main()
    {
        Console.WriteLine("{0:N}", 33345.8977);
        Console.WriteLine("{0:N4}", 33345.8977);
    }
}
```

gives the following output:

```
33,345.90
33,345.8977
```

It's possible to control the character used for the decimal point by passing a `NumberFormatInfo` object to the `Format()` function.

Roundtrip

Using the roundtrip format ensures that a value represented as a string can be parsed back into the same value. This is especially useful for floating-point types, where extra digits are sometimes required to read a number back in with the identical value.

Hexadecimal

The hexadecimal format string converts the value to hexadecimal format. The minimum number of digits is set by the precision specifier; the number will be zero-padded to that width.

Using `X` will result in uppercase letters in the converted value; `x` will result in lowercase letters. This example:

```
using System;
class Test
{
    public static void Main()
    {
        Console.WriteLine("{0:X}", 255);
        Console.WriteLine("{0:x8}", 1456);
    }
}
```

gives the following output:

```
FF
000005b0
```

NumberFormatInfo

The `NumberFormatInfo` class is used to control the formatting of numbers. By setting the properties in this class, the programmer can control the currency symbol, decimal separator, and other formatting properties.

Custom Format Strings

Custom format strings are used to obtain more control over the conversion than is available through the standard format strings. In custom format strings, special characters form a template that the number is formatted into. Any characters that do not have a special meaning in the format string are copied verbatim to the output. The following table describes the custom strings available:

CHARACTER	DESCRIPTION	RESULT
0	Display zero placeholder	Displays leading zero if a number has fewer digits than there are zeroes in the format
#	Display digit placeholder	Replaces # with the digit only for significant digits
.	Decimal point	Displays the decimal point
,	Group separator and multiplier	Separates number groups, such as 1,000. When used after a number, divides it by 1,000
%	Display % notation	Displays the percent character
;	Section separator	Uses different formats for positive, negative, and zero values

Digit or Zero Placeholder

The zero (0) character is used as a digit or zero placeholder. If the numeric value has a digit in the position at which the 0 appears in the format string, the digit will appear in the result. If not, a zero appears in that position. This example:

```
using System;
class Test
{
    public static void Main()
    {
        Console.WriteLine("{0:000}", 55);
        Console.WriteLine("{0:000}", 1456);
    }
}
```

gives the following output:

```
055
1456
```

Digit or Space Placeholder

The pound (`#`) character is used as the digit or space placeholder. It works exactly the same as the `0` placeholder, except that the character is omitted if there is no digit in that position. This example:

```
using System;
class Test
{
    public static void Main()
    {
        Console.WriteLine("{0:#####}", 255);
        Console.WriteLine("{0:#####}", 1456);
        Console.WriteLine("{0:###}", 32767);
    }
}
```

gives the following output:

```
255
1456
32767
```

Decimal Point

The first period (`.`) character that appears in the format string determines the location of the decimal separator in the result. The character used as the decimal separator in the formatted string is controlled by a `NumberFormatInfo` instance. This example:

```
using System;
class Test
{
    public static void Main()
    {
        Console.WriteLine("{0:#####.000}", 75928.3);
        Console.WriteLine("{0:##.000}", 1456.456456);
    }
}
```

gives the following output:

```
75928.300
1456.456
```

Group Separator

The comma (,) character is used as a group separator. If a comma appears in the middle of a display digit placeholder and to the left of the decimal point (if present), a group separator will be inserted in the string. The character used in the formatted string and the number of numbers to group together is controlled by a `NumberFormatInfo` instance. This example:

```
using System;
class Test
{
    public static void Main()
    {
        Console.WriteLine("{0:##,###}", 2555634323);
        Console.WriteLine("{0:##,000.000}", 14563553.593993);
        Console.WriteLine("{0:#,#.000}", 14563553.593993);
    }
}
```

gives the following output:

```
2,555,634,323
14,563,553.594
14,563,553.594
```

Number Prescaler

The comma (,) character can also be used to indicate that the number should be prescaled. In this usage, the comma must come directly before the decimal point or at the end of the format string.

For each comma present in this location, the number is divided by 1,000 before it is formatted. This example:

```
using System;
class Test
{
    public static void Main()
    {
        Console.WriteLine("{0:000,.##}", 158847);
        Console.WriteLine("{0:000,,,.###}", 1593833);
    }
}
```

gives the following output:

```
158.85
000.002
```

Percent Notation

The percent (%) character is used to indicate that the number to be displayed should be displayed as a percentage. The number is multiplied by 100 before it is formatted. This example:

```
using System;
class Test
{
    public static void Main()
    {
        Console.WriteLine("{0:##.000%}", 0.89144);
        Console.WriteLine("{0:00%}", 0.01285);
    }
}
```

gives the following output:

```
89.144%
01%
```

Exponential Notation

When `E+0`, `E-0`, `e+0`, or `e-0` appear in the format string directly after a `#` or `0` placeholder, the number will be formatted in exponential notation. The number of digits in the exponent is controlled by the number of `0` placeholders that appear in the exponent specifier. The `E` or `e` is copied directly into the formatted string, and a

+ means that there will be a plus or minus sign in that position, while a minus sign means there is a character there only if the number is negative. This example:

```
using System;
class Test
{
    public static void Main()
    {
        Console.WriteLine("{0:###.000E-00}", 3.1415533E+04);
        Console.WriteLine("{0:#.0000000E+000}", 2.553939939E+101);
    }
}
```

gives the following output:

```
314.155E-02
2.5539399E+101
```

Section Separator

The semicolon (;) character is used to specify different format strings for a number, depending on whether the number is positive, negative, or zero. If there are only two sections, the first section applies to positive and zero values, and the second applies to negative values. If there are three sections, they apply to positive values, negative values, and the zero value. This example:

```
using System;
class Test
{
    public static void Main()
    {
        Console.WriteLine("{0:###.00;0;(###.00)}", -456.55);
        Console.WriteLine("{0:###.00;0;(###.00)}", 0);
        Console.WriteLine("{0:###.00;0;(###.00)}", 456.55);
    }
}
```

gives the following output:

```
457
(.00)
456.55
```

Escapes and Literals

The slash (\) character can be used to escape characters so they aren't interpreted as formatting characters. Because the slash already has meaning within C# literals, it will be easier to specify the string using the verbatim literal syntax; otherwise, a double slash (\\) is required to generate a single slash in the output string.

A string of uninterpreted characters can be specified by enclosing them in single quotes; this may be more convenient than using the slash character. This example:

```
using System;
class Test
{
    public static void Main()
    {
        Console.WriteLine("{0:###\\#}", 255);
        Console.WriteLine(@"{0:###\#}", 255);
        Console.WriteLine("{0:###'#0%;'}", 1456);
    }
}
```

gives the following output:

```
255#
255#
1456#0%;
```

Date and Time Formatting

The `DateTime` class provides flexible formatting options. Several single-character formats can be specified, and custom formatting is also supported. The following table specifies the standard `DateTime` formats:

CHARACTER	PATTERN	DESCRIPTION
d	MM/dd/yyyy	ShortDatePattern
D	dddd, MMMM dd, yyy	LongDatePattern
f	dddd, MMMM dd, YYYY HH:mm	Full (long date + short time)
F	dddd, MMMM dd, yyyy HH:mm:ss	FullDateTimePattern (long date + long time)

CHARACTER	PATTERN	DESCRIPTION
g	MM/dd/yyyy HH:mm	General (short date + short time)
G	MM/dd/yyyy HH:mm:ss	General (short date + long time)
m, M	MMMM dd	MonthDayPattern
r, R	ddd, dd MMM yy HH':'mm':'ss 'GMT'	RFC1123Pattern
s	yyyy-MM-dd HH:mm:ss	SortableDateTimePattern (ISO 8601)
S	YYYY-mm-DD hh:MM:SS GMT	Sortable with time zone information
t	HH:mm	ShortTimePattern
T	HH:mm:ss	LongTimePattern
u	yyyy-MM-dd HH:mm:ss	Same as s, but with universal instead of local time
U	dddd, MMMM dd, yyyy HH:mm:ss	UniversalSortableDateTimePattern

Custom DateTime Format

The following patterns can be used to build a custom format:

PATTERN	DESCRIPTION
d	Day of month as digits with no leading zero for single-digit days
dd	Day of month as digits with leading zero for single-digit days
ddd	Day of week as a three-letter abbreviation
dddd	Day of week as its full name
M	Month as digits with no leading zero for single-digit months
MM	Month as digits with leading zero
MMM	Month as three-letter abbreviation
MMMM	Month as its full name
y	Year as last two digits, no leading zero
yy	Year as last two digits, with leading zero
yyyy	Year represented by four digits

The day and month names are determined by the appropriate field in the `DateTimeFormatInfo` class.

Custom Object Formatting

Earlier examples have overridden the `ToString()` function to provide a string representation of a function. An object can supply different formats by defining the `IFormattable` interface and then changing the representation based upon the string of the function.

For example, an `employee` class could add additional information with a different format string. This example:

```
using System;
class Employee: IFormattable
{
    public Employee(int id, string firstName, string lastName)
    {
        this.id = id;
        this.firstName = firstName;
        this.lastName = lastName;
    }
     public string ToString (string format, IFormatProvider fp)
    {
        if ((format != null) && (format.Equals("F")))
            return(String.Format("{0}: {1}, {2}",
                id, lastName, firstName));
        else
            return(id.ToString(format, fp));
    }
    int    id;
    string    firstName;
    string    lastName;
}
class Test
{
    public static void Main()
    {
        Employee fred = new Employee(123, "Fred", "Morthwaite");
        Console.WriteLine("No format: {0}", fred);
        Console.WriteLine("Full format: {0:F}", fred);
    }
}
```

produces the following output:

```
No format: 123
Full format: 123: Morthwaite, Fred
```

The `Format()` function looks for the `F` format. If it finds it, it writes out the full information. If it doesn't find it, it uses the default format for the object.

The `Main()` function passes the format flag in the second `WriteLine()` call.

Numeric Parsing

Numbers are parsed using the `Parse()` method provided by the numeric data types. Flags from the `NumberStyles` class can be passed to specify which styles are allowed, and a `NumberFormatInfo` instance can be passed to control parsing.

A numeric string produced by any of the standard format specifiers (excluding hexadecimal) is guaranteed to be correctly parsed if the `NumberStyles.Any` style is specified. This example:

```
using System;
class Test
{
    public static void Main()
    {
        int value = Int32.Parse("99953");
        double dval = Double.Parse("1.3433E+35");
        Console.WriteLine("{0}", value);
        Console.WriteLine("{0}", dval);
    }
}
```

produces the following output.

```
99953
1.3433E35
```

Using XML in C#

Although C# does support XML documentation (see the "XML Documentation" section in Chapter 36, "Deeper into C#"), C# doesn't provide any specific language support for using XML.

That's OK, however, because the Common Language Runtime provides extensive support for XML. Some areas of interest are the `System.Data.Xml` and `System.Xml` namespaces.

InputOutput

The .NET Common Language Runtime provides I/O functions in the `System.IO` namespace. This namespace contains classes for doing I/O and for other I/O-related functions, such as directory traversal, file watching, and so on.

Reading and writing is done using the `Stream` class, which merely describes how bytes can be read and written to some sort of backing store. `Stream` is an abstract class, so in practice classes derived from `Stream` will be used. The following classes are available:

CLASS	DESCRIPTION
`FileStream`	A stream on a disk file
`MemoryStream`	A stream that is stored in memory
`NetworkStream`	A stream on a network connection
`BufferedStream`	Implements a buffer on top of another stream

With the exception of `BufferedStream`, which sits on top of another stream, each stream defines where the written data will go.

The `Stream` class provides raw functions to read and write at a byte level, both synchronously and asynchronously. Usually, however, it's nice to have a higher-level interface on top of a stream, and there are several supplied ones that can be selected depending on what final format is desired.

Binary

The `BinaryReader` and `BinaryWriter` classes are used to read and write values in binary (or raw) format. For example, a `BinaryWriter` can be used to write an `int`, followed by a `float`, followed by another `int`. These classes operate on a stream.

Text

The TextReader and TextWriter abstract classes define how text is read and written. They allow operations on characters, lines, blocks, and so on. There are two different implementations of TextReader available.

The somewhat strangely named StreamWriter class is the one used for "normal" I/O (open a file, read the lines out) and operates on a Stream.

The StringReader and StringWriter classes can be used to read and write from a string.

XML

The XmlTextReader and XmlTextWriter classes are used to read and write XML. They are similar to TextReader and TextWriter in design, but they do not derive from those classes because they deal with XML entities rather than text. They are low-level classes used to create or decode XML from scratch.

Reading and Writing Files

There are two ways to get streams that connect to files. The first is to use the FileStream class, which provides full control over file access, including access mode, sharing, and buffering:

```
using System;
using System.IO;

class Test
{
    public static void Main()
    {
        FileStream f = new FileStream("output.txt", FileMode.Create);
        StreamWriter s = new StreamWriter(f);

        s.WriteLine("{0} {1}", "test", 55);
        s.Close();
        f.Close();
    }
}
```

It is also possible to use the functions in the `File` class to get a stream to a file. This is most useful if there is already a `File` object with the file information available, as in the `PrintFile()` function in the next example.

Traversing Directories

This example shows how to traverse a directory structure. It defines both a `DirectoryWalker` class that takes delegates to be called for each directory and file and a path to traverse:

```
using System;
using System.IO;

public class DirectoryWalker
{
    public delegate void ProcessDirCallback(DirectoryInfo dir, int level, object
obj);
    public delegate void ProcessFileCallback(FileInfo file, int level, object obj);

    public DirectoryWalker(    ProcessDirCallback dirCallback,
                ProcessFileCallback fileCallback)
    {
        this.dirCallback = dirCallback;
        this.fileCallback = fileCallback;
    }

    public void Walk(string rootDir, object obj)
    {
        DoWalk(new DirectoryInfo(rootDir), 0, obj);
    }
    void DoWalk(DirectoryInfo dir, int level, object obj)
    {
        foreach (FileInfo f in dir.GetFiles())
        {
            if (fileCallback != null)
                fileCallback(f, level, obj);
        }
```

```
        foreach (DirectoryInfo d in dir.GetDirectories())
        {
            if (dirCallback != null)
                dirCallback(d, level, obj);
            DoWalk(d, level + 1, obj);
        }
    }

    ProcessDirCallback    dirCallback;
    ProcessFileCallback    fileCallback;
}

class Test
{
    public static void PrintDir(DirectoryInfo d, int level, object obj)
    {
        WriteSpaces(level * 2);
        Console.WriteLine("Dir: {0}", d.FullName);
    }
    public static void PrintFile(FileInfo f, int level, object obj)
    {
        WriteSpaces(level * 2);
        Console.WriteLine("File: {0}", f.FullName);
    }
    public static void WriteSpaces(int spaces)
    {
        for (int i = 0; i < spaces; i++)
            Console.Write(" ");

    }
    public static void Main(string[] args)
    {
        DirectoryWalker dw = new DirectoryWalker(
            new DirectoryWalker.ProcessDirCallback(PrintDir),
            new DirectoryWalker.ProcessFileCallback(PrintFile));

        string root = ".";
        if (args.Length == 1)
            root = args[0];
        dw.Walk(root, "Passed string object");
    }
}
```

Starting Processes

The .NET Frameworks provides the `Process` class, which is used to start processes. The following examples shows how to start Notepad:

```
// file=process.cs
// compile with csc process.cs
using System.Diagnostics;
class Test
{
    public static void Main()
    {
        ProcessStartInfo startInfo = new ProcessStartInfo();
        startInfo.FileName = "notepad.exe";
        startInfo.Arguments = "process.cs";

        Process.Start(startInfo);
    }
}
```

The arguments used in starting the process are contained in the `ProcessStartInfo` object.

Redirecting Process Output

Sometimes it's useful to get the output from a process. This can be done in the following way:

```
using System;
using System.Diagnostics;
class Test
{
    public static void Main()
    {
        Process p = new Process();
        p.StartInfo.FileName = "cmd.exe";
        p.StartInfo.Arguments = "/c dir *.cs";
        p.StartInfo.UseShellExecute = false;
        p.StartInfo.RedirectStandardOutput = true;
        p.Start();

        string output = p.StandardOutput.ReadToEnd();

        Console.WriteLine("Output:");
        Console.WriteLine(output);    }
}
```

Detecting Process Completion

It's also possible to detect when a process exits:

```
// file=process3.cs
// compile with csc process3.cs
using System;
using System.Diagnostics;
class Test
{
    static void ProcessDone(object sender, EventArgs e)
    {
        Console.WriteLine("Process Exited");
    }

    public static void Main()
    {
        Process p = new Process();
        p.StartInfo.FileName = "notepad.exe";
        p.StartInfo.Arguments = "process3.cs";
        p.EnableRaisingEvents = true;
        p.Exited += new EventHandler(ProcessDone);
        p.Start();
        p.WaitForExit();
        Console.WriteLine("Back from WaitForExit()");
    }
}
```

This example shows two different ways of detecting process completion. The `ProcessDone()` function is called when the `Exited` event is fired, and the `WaitForExit()` function also returns when the process is done.

Serialization

Serialization is the process used by the runtime to persist objects in some sort of storage or to transfer them from one location to another.

The metadata information on an object contains sufficient information for the runtime to serialize the fields, but the runtime needs a little help to do the right thing.

This help is provided through two attributes. The `[Serializable]` attribute is used to mark an object as okay to serialize. The `[NonSerialized]` attribute can be applied to a field or property to indicate that it shouldn't be serialized. This is useful if it is a cache or derived value.

The following example has a container class named `MyRow` that has elements of the `MyElement` class. The `cacheValue` field in `MyElement` is marked with the `[NonSerialized]` attribute to prevent it from being serialized.

In this example, the `MyRow` object is serialized and deserialized to a binary format and then to an XML format:

```
// file=serial.cs
// compile with: csc serial.cs
using System;
using System.IO;
using System.Collections;
using System.Runtime.Serialization;
using System.Runtime.Serialization.Formatters.Binary;
using System.Runtime.Serialization.Formatters.Soap;

[Serializable]
public class MyElement
{
    public MyElement(string name)
    {
        this.name = name;
        this.cacheValue = 15;
    }
    public override string ToString()
    {
        return(String.Format("{0}: {1}", name, cacheValue));
    }
    string name;
        // this field isn't persisted.
    [NonSerialized]
    int cacheValue;
}
[Serializable]
public class MyRow
{
    public void Add(MyElement my)
    {
        row.Add(my);
    }
```

```
    public override string ToString()
    {
        string temp = null;
        foreach (MyElement my in row)
            temp += my.ToString() + "\n";
        return(temp);
    }

    ArrayList row = new ArrayList();
}

class Test
{
    public static void Main()
    {
        MyRow row = new MyRow();
        row.Add(new MyElement("Gumby"));
        row.Add(new MyElement("Pokey"));

        Console.WriteLine("Initial value");
        Console.WriteLine("{0}", row);

            // write to binary, read it back
        Stream streamWrite = File.Create("MyRow.bin");
        BinaryFormatter binaryWrite = new BinaryFormatter();
        binaryWrite.Serialize(streamWrite, row);
        streamWrite.Close();

        Stream streamRead = File.OpenRead("MyRow.bin");
        BinaryFormatter binaryRead = new BinaryFormatter();
        MyRow rowBinary = (MyRow) binaryRead.Deserialize(streamRead);
        streamRead.Close();

        Console.WriteLine("Values after binary serialization");
        Console.WriteLine("{0}", rowBinary);

            // write to SOAP (XML), read it back
        streamWrite = File.Create("MyRow.xml");
        SoapFormatter soapWrite = new SoapFormatter();
        soapWrite.Serialize(streamWrite, row);
        streamWrite.Close();
```

```
            streamRead = File.OpenRead("MyRow.xml");
            SoapFormatter soapRead = new SoapFormatter();
            MyRow rowSoap = (MyRow) soapRead.Deserialize(streamRead);
            streamRead.Close();

            Console.WriteLine("Values after SOAP serialization");
            Console.WriteLine("{0}", rowSoap);
        }
}
```

The example produces the following output:

```
Initial value
Gumby: 15
Pokey: 15

Values after binary serialization
Gumby: 0
Pokey: 0

Values after SOAP serialization
Gumby: 0
Pokey: 0
```

The field `cacheValue` is not preserved since it was marked as `[NonSerialized]`. The file `MyRow.Bin` will contain the binary serialization, and the file `MyRow.xml` will contain the XML version.

The XML encoding is in SOAP, which is a textual dump of the objects, in an (almost) human-readable form. To produce a specific XML encoding, use the `XmlSerializer` class.

Custom Serialization

If the standard serialization doesn't do exactly what is desired or doesn't give sufficient control, a class can define exactly how it wants to be serialized,[1] like in this example:

1. If you're familiar with how MFC serialization worked in Visual C++, this approach will seem fairly familiar.

```
using System;
using System.IO;
using System.Runtime.Serialization;
using System.Runtime.Serialization.Formatters.Soap;

class Employee: ISerializable
{
    int id;
    string name;
    string address;

    public Employee(int id, string name, string address)
    {
        this.id = id;
        this.name = name;
        this.address = address;
    }

    public override string ToString()
    {
        return(String.Format("{0} {1} {2}", id, name, address));
    }

    Employee(SerializationInfo info, StreamingContext content)
    {
        id = info.GetInt32("id");
        name = info.GetString("name");
        address = info.GetString("address");
    }

        // called to save the object data...
    public void GetObjectData(SerializationInfo info, StreamingContext content)
    {
        info.AddValue("id", id);
        info.AddValue("name", name);
        info.AddValue("address", address);
    }
}
```

```
class Test
{
    public static void Serialize(Employee employee, string filename)
    {
        Stream streamWrite = File.Create(filename);
        IFormatter writer = new SoapFormatter();
        writer.Serialize(streamWrite, employee);
        streamWrite.Close();
    }

    public static Employee Deserialize(string filename)
    {
        Stream streamRead = File.OpenRead(filename);
        IFormatter reader = new SoapFormatter();
        Employee employee = (Employee) reader.Deserialize(streamRead);
        streamRead.Close();
        return(employee);
    }

    public static void Main()
    {
        Employee employee = new Employee(15, "Fred", "Bedrock");

        Serialize(employee, "emp.dat");
        employee = Deserialize("emp.dat");
        Console.WriteLine("Employee: {0}", employee);
    }
}
```

To do customer serialization, an object must implement the `ISerializable` interface. The `GetObjectData()` method is the only method on that interface. The implementation of that method stores each value by calling `AddValue()` on each value and passing in a name for the field and the field value.

To deserialize an object, the runtime relies on a special constructor. This constructor will call the appropriate get function to fetch a value based on the name.

Although this approach does take some extra space to store the names—and a bit of time to look them up—it versions very well, allowing new values to be added without invalidating existing stored files.

Reading Web Pages

The following example demonstrates how to write a "screen scraper" using C#. The following bit of code will take a stock symbol, format a URL to fetch a quote from Microsoft's Money Central site, and then extract the quote out of the HTML page using a regular expression:

```
using System;
using System.Net;
using System.IO;
using System.Text;
using System.Text.RegularExpressions;

class QuoteFetch
{
    public QuoteFetch(string symbol)
    {
        this.symbol = symbol;
    }

    public string Last
    {
        get
        {
            string url = "http://moneycentral.msn.com/scripts/
webquote.dll?ipage=qd&Symbol=";
            url += symbol;

            ExtractQuote(ReadUrl(url));
            return(last);
        }
    }
    string ReadUrl(string url)
    {
        Uri uri = new Uri(url);

            //Create the request object

        WebRequest req = WebRequest.Create(uri);
        WebResponse resp = req.GetResponse();
        Stream stream = resp.GetResponseStream();
        StreamReader sr = new StreamReader(stream);

        string s = sr.ReadToEnd();

        return(s);

    }
```

```
    void ExtractQuote(string s)
    {
        // Line like: "Last</TD><TD ALIGN=RIGHT NOWRAP><B> 78 3/16"

        Regex lastmatch = new Regex(@"Last\D+(?<last>.+)<\/B>");
        last = lastmatch.Match(s).Groups[1].ToString();
    }
    string    symbol;
    string    last;
}

class Test
{
    public static void Main(string[] args)
    {
        if (args.Length != 1)
            Console.WriteLine("Quote <symbol>");
        else
        {
            // GlobalProxySelection.Select = new DefaultControlObject("proxy", 80);
            QuoteFetch q = new QuoteFetch(args[0]);
            Console.WriteLine("{0} = {1}", args[0], q.Last);
        }
    }
}
```

NOTE *When working from behind a firewall, it may be necessary to set a proxy. This can be done with the commented out code in* `Main()`.

Accessing Environment Settings

The `System.Environment` class can be used to obtain information about the machine and environment, as the following example demonstrates:

```
using System;
using System.Collections;

class Test
{
    public static void Main()
    {
        Console.WriteLine("Command Line: {0}", Environment.CommandLine);
        Console.WriteLine("Current Directory: {0}", Environment.CurrentDirectory);
        Console.WriteLine("Machine Name: {0}", Environment.MachineName);
        Console.WriteLine("OS Version: {0}", Environment.OSVersion);
        Console.WriteLine("Stack Trace: {0}", Environment.StackTrace);
        Console.WriteLine("System Configuration File: {0}",
                                Environment.SystemConfigurationFile);
        Console.WriteLine("System Directory: {0}", Environment.SystemDirectory);
        Console.WriteLine("Tick Count: {0}", Environment.TickCount);
        Console.WriteLine("Version: {0}", Environment.Version);
        Console.WriteLine("Working Set: {0}", Environment.WorkingSet);

        Console.WriteLine("Environment Variables");
        foreach (DictionaryEntry var in Environment.GetEnvironmentVariables())
            Console.WriteLine("    {0}={1}", var.Key, var.Value);

        Console.WriteLine("Logical Drives");
        foreach (string drive in Environment.GetLogicalDrives())
            Console.WriteLine("    {0}", drive);
    }
}
```

When this is run on my machine, it generates the following output:

```
Command Line: envtest
Current Directory: D:\booknew
Machine Name: ERICGUT
OS Version: Microsoft Windows NT 5.0.2195.0
Stack Trace:    at System.Environment.GetStackTrace(Exception e)
   at System.Environment.GetStackTrace(Exception e)
   at System.Environment.get_StackTrace()
   at Test.Main()
System Configuration File: C:\WINNT\Microsoft.NET\Framework\v1.0.2702\config\mac
hine.config
System Directory: C:\WINNT\System32
Tick Count: 140411180
Version: 1.0.2702.0
```

```
Working Set: 7290880
Environment Variables
    SystemDrive=C:
    USERPROFILE=C:\Documents and Settings\ericgu
    INCLUDE=C:\Program Files\Microsoft.Net\FrameworkSDK\include\
    Path=D:\Perl\bin\;C:\Program Files\Microsoft.Net\FrameworkSDK\Bin\;C:\WINNT\
Microsoft.NET\Framework\v1.0.2702\;C:\Perl\bin\;C:\WINNT\system32;C:\WINNT;C:\WI
NNT\System32\Wbem
    CommonProgramFiles=C:\Program Files\Common Files
    Os2LibPath=C:\WINNT\system32\os2\dll;
    LOGONSERVER=\\ERICGUT
    PROCESSOR_ARCHITECTURE=x86
    ProgramFiles=C:\Program Files
    NUMBER_OF_PROCESSORS=1
    NetSamplePath=C:\Program Files\Microsoft.Net\FrameworkSDK\Samples\
    TMP=C:\DOCUME~1\ericgu\LOCALS~1\Temp
    APPDATA=C:\Documents and Settings\ericgu\Application Data
    ComSpec=C:\WINNT\system32\cmd.exe
    PROCESSOR_IDENTIFIER=x86 Family 6 Model 8 Stepping 3, GenuineIntel
    HOMEDRIVE=C:
    COMPUTERNAME=ERICGUT
    OANOCACHE=1
    PROCESSOR_LEVEL=6
    OS=Windows_NT
    VSCOMNTOOLS="D:\Program Files\Microsoft Visual Studio.NET\Common7\Tools\"
    SystemRoot=C:\WINNT
    USERDNSDOMAIN=redmond.corp.microsoft.com
    windir=C:\WINNT
    SMS_LOCAL_DIR=C:\WINNT
    ALLUSERSPROFILE=C:\Documents and Settings\All Users
    USERNAME=ericgu
    PATHEXT=.COM;.EXE;.BAT;.CMD;.VBS;.VBE;.JS;.JSE;.WSF;.WSH
    USERDOMAIN=REDMOND
    HOMEPATH=\
    PROMPT=$P$G
    TEMP=C:\DOCUME~1\ericgu\LOCALS~1\Temp
    LIB=C:\Program Files\Microsoft.Net\FrameworkSDK\Lib\
    PROCESSOR_REVISION=0803
Logical Drives
    A:\
    C:\
    D:\
    E:\
    I:\
```

CHAPTER 33

Windows Forms

Windows Forms (previously known as WinForms) is the section of the .NET Frameworks used to write "rich-client" applications (otherwise known as Windows Applications).

This chapter will cover the initial steps of developing an application in Windows Forms. The application will be expanded in later chapters.

> **NOTE** *I've written the chapters that describe this application at the same time as writing the application itself in order to present the process of application development. I've tried to be reasonably honest about any refactoring[1] that was required along the way, and I've tried to explain my rationale for choosing specific approaches.*

Our Application

To best understand how to write a Windows Forms applications, it is useful to develop a real application.

Recently, one of my test machines was running out of space on its C: drive. To try to find out what was happening, I spent some time looking in likely directories, but it wasn't an easy task. What I really wanted was a way to see what had changed, so I'd know exactly where the disk space went.

The solution is an application named DiskDiff. Not only will it show a tree view of the space used on a system, it can compare the space used at two different time periods.

Getting Started

The first task is to create a default Windows Forms application. This is done by creating a new C# project and choosing Windows Application as the template. The name is set as DiskDiff, as shown in Figure 33-1.

1. Refactoring is process of making changes to your code based on what you learn while writing the application.

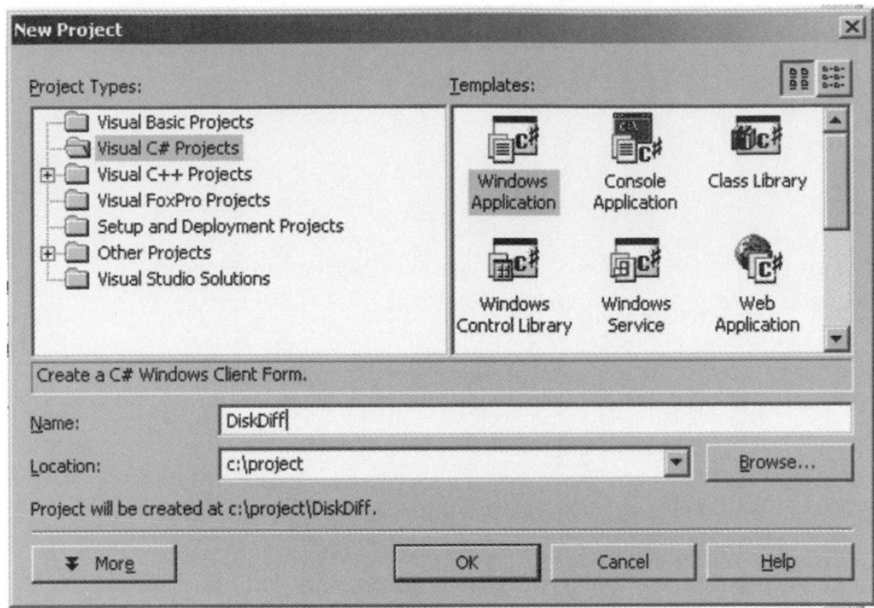

Figure 33-1. Creating a Windows Application Project

The VS.NET environment will create the initial project and show the initial form. In Windows Forms projects, a form is simply a class derived from `System.Windows.Forms.Form`. These forms are listed under a project in the Solution Explorer with a special form icon.

There are two different ways a form class can be viewed. The code of the form can be viewed by right-clicking on the form and choosing View Code. By double-clicking on the form (or by right-clicking and choosing View Designer), the form can be viewed in the form designer (more about that in a bit).

The Windows Form architecture differs from other approaches in that the layout and controls for a form are implemented in the code of the form class, rather than some sort of resource storage.

The initial class for our project looks like this (with XML comments removed for clarity):

```
namespace DiskDiff
{
    using System;
    using System.Drawing;
    using System.Collections;
    using System.ComponentModel;
    using System.Windows.Forms;
    using System.Data;
```

```
    public class Form1 : System.Windows.Forms.Form
    {
        private System.ComponentModel.Container components;

        public Form1()
        {
            //
            // Required for Windows Form Designer support
            //
            InitializeComponent();

            //
            // TODO: Add any constructor code after InitializeComponent call
            //
        }

        public override void Dispose()
        {
            base.Dispose();
            components.Dispose();
        }

        private void InitializeComponent()
        {
            this.components = new System.ComponentModel.Container();
            this.Size = new System.Drawing.Size(300,300);
            this.Text = "Form1";
        }

        public static void Main(string[] args)
        {
            Application.Run(new Form1());
        }
    }
}
```

This class is fairly simple. The constructor for the class calls `InitializeComponent()`, which is the member that the class designer will deal with. Initially, all it has is a container for the other items on the form and lines to set the size and text of the form. There's a `Dispose()` member that will clean up the form when it's closed.[2]

---

2. Forms use system resources that the garbage collector can't track, so the `Dispose()` method can be called to clean these up before the garbage collector gets around to the next collection.

Finally, there's the `Main()` function for the whole application, which creates an instance of the form class, and then calls `Application.Run()`, passing the form. This will execute the standard Windows message loop to get messages and dispatch them to the appropriate objects.

The Form Designer

The VS.NET environment makes laying out forms easy. The Toolbox can be viewed by clicking on the Toolbox tab along the left side of the development environment. Selecting Windows Forms will show all the controls that can be placed on a form.

The directories that we want to show make the `TreeView` a good choice, so we'll drag one onto our form. The designer will show us the `TreeView` object and add the following code to the `InitializeComponent()` method:

```
this.treeView1 = new System.Windows.Forms.TreeView ();
treeView1.Location = new System.Drawing.Point (200, 112);
treeView1.Size = new System.Drawing.Size (121, 97);
treeView1.TabIndex = 0;
```

The commented fields are used by the designer for information that isn't required by the application.

We'd like the `TreeView` control to take up all the space in the form. This could be done by resizing the control when the size of the form is changed, but the Windows Forms architecture can do this for us. If the tree view object is selected, the `Anchor` property can be set in the property window. Initially, the object is anchored to the top-left; by setting the anchor to all four sides, the tree view will be resized whenever the form is resized. Anchoring is used in this case, but since there is only a single object in this form, the same effect could be achieved by setting the `Dock` property on the `TreeView` to `DockStyle.Fill`.

Now that the basic framework of the application is ready, it's time to move onto some disk operations.

Finding Directory Sizes

The base of DiskDiff is the code that can traverse a directory tree and figure out the sizes of the files there.

A quick look in the `System.IO` namespace shows there's a `DirectoryInfo` class that will work. We'll encapsulate it in a class of our own so we can store the list of files and the list of directories in each directory. The class will look like this:

```
public class DirectoryNode
{
    string root;
    ArrayList files = new ArrayList();
    ArrayList dirs = new ArrayList();
    DirectoryInfo directoryInfo;    // this directory

    public DirectoryNode(string root)
    {
        this.root = root;
        directoryInfo = new DirectoryInfo(root);
    }
    public DirectoryNode(DirectoryInfo directoryInfo)
    {
        this.directory = directoryInfo;
    }
    public void Populate()
    {
        foreach (FileInfo f in directoryInfo.GetFiles())
        {
            FileNode fileNode = new FileNode(f);
            this.files.Add(f);
        }

        foreach (DirectoryInfo d in directory.GetDirectories())
        {
            DirectoryNode dirNode = new DirectoryNode(d.FullName);
            dirs.Add(dirNode);
            dirNode.Populate();
        }
    }
    public void PrintTree(int level)
    {
        for (int i = 0; i < level; i++)
        {
            Console.Write("  ");
        }
        Console.WriteLine("{0}", this.root);
        foreach (DirectoryNode dirNode in dirs)
        {
            dirNode.PrintTree(level + 1);
        }
    }
}
```

There are two constructors for `DirectoryNode`. The first is used to create the top-level directory, and the other is used to create a `DirectoryNode` from a `DirectoryInfo` object.

The `Populate()` function is the heart of the class. It uses the `DirectoryInfo` object that is encapsulated, calling `GetFiles()` to get the list of files in the directory and `GetDirectories()` to get the list of directories. It then recurses for each subdirectory, so the directory tree can be fully traversed.

The `PrintTree()` function is used for testing, along with a little test program:

```
class Test
{
    public static void Main()
    {
        DirectoryNode directoryNode = new DirectoryNode(@"c:\project\diskdiff");
        directoryNode.Populate();
        directoryNode.PrintTree(0);
    }
}
```

On my system, this gives the following output:

```
c:\project\diskdiff
  c:\project\diskdiff\bin
    c:\project\diskdiff\bin\Debug
  c:\project\diskdiff\obj
    c:\project\diskdiff\obj\Debug
      c:\project\diskdiff\obj\Debug\temp
      c:\project\diskdiff\obj\Debug\TempPE
```

Calculating Sizes

Now that we have the directory code, we need to sum the sizes of the files for a directory and then pass that size up to the parent directories. We'll want to be able to fetch both the size of this directory and the size of this directory and the subdirectories under it. For this, we'll add two properties:

```
long size = -1;             // size of dir in bytes
long sizeTree = -1;         // size of dir and subdirs
public long Size
{
    get
    {
        if (size == -1)
        {
            size = 0;
            foreach (FileNode f in files)
            {
                size += f.fileInfo.Length;
            }
        }
        return(size);
    }
}
public long SizeTree
{
    get
    {
        if (sizeTree == -1)
        {
            sizeTree = 0;
            sizeTree += Size;
            foreach (DirectoryNode dirNode in dirs)
            {
                sizeTree += dirNode.SizeTree;
            }
        }
        return(sizeTree);
    }
}
```

The `Size` property simply walks through all the files in the current node and adds up their sizes. This total size is then stored in the `size` variable so it doesn't need to be recalculated.

The `SizeTree` property adds the size of all the subdirectories to the current size. Because `SizeTree` recourses down the tree, getting the value of the property at the root will cause the sizes to be calculated all the way down the tree.

Although this is a nice way to use properties, it may turn out that calculating the sizes during the call to `Populate()` is a better choice.

The `PrintTree()` is renamed to `PrintSizes()`, and now prints out the values of `Tree` and `TreeSize` next to the name of the directory. Running the code produces the following output:

```
c:\project\diskdiff 32632 119672
  c:\project\diskdiff\bin 0 43520
    c:\project\diskdiff\bin\Debug 43520 43520
  c:\project\diskdiff\obj 0 43520
    c:\project\diskdiff\obj\Debug 43520 43520
      c:\project\diskdiff\obj\Debug\temp 0 0
      c:\project\diskdiff\obj\Debug\TempPE 0 0
```

Now it's time to integrate the directory traversal code into the `treeview` class.

A Debugging Suggestion

Though there's a separate `DirectoryNode.cs` file as part of the examples, the class was written in the main project. For testing purposes, I wanted to print the traversal of a big directory, but since `DiskDiff` is a Windows Forms project, it doesn't have a console window.

However, there's no reason a Windows Form project can't have a console window. By right-clicking on the project in the Solution Explorer and choosing Properties, the output type of the project can be changed to `Console Application`.

This does mean that you will have to dismiss the console window when exiting the application, but that's fine for debugging. When you're finished, just change the output type of the project back and the console window will go away.

Displaying the Directory Tree and Sizes

A decision must now be made on how to interface the form and the `DirectoryNode` classes so that the tree can be populated. One option is to have `DirectoryNode` expose enough of its internals (perhaps through an indexer) so that the form can iterate over it. Another option is to pass the `TreeView` control to a function in `DirectoryNode` and have it populate the control.

There's a tradeoff between having `DirectoryNode` expose a more complex interface, and having `DirectoryNode` be more tightly coupled to the form. In this case, I'm going to choose the first option, but the second option can sometimes be better, especially if the processing to be done is very complex.

Because a directory can be thought of as an array of files, an indexer is a reasonable choice. However, we need to differentiate between directories and files, so doing what the Directory class does, with GetFiles() and GetDirectories() members, is a better choice.

The code for these functions is the following:

```
public DirectoryNode[] GetDirectories()
{
    DirectoryNode[] array = new DirectoryNode[dirs.Count];

    for (int index = 0; index < dirs.Count; index++)
    {
        array[index] = (DirectoryNode) dirs[index];
    }
    return(array);
}

public FileNode[] GetFiles()
{
    FileNode[] array = new FileNode[files.Count];

    for (int index = 0; index < files.Count; index++)
    {
        array[index] = (FileNode) files[index];
    }
    return(array);
}
```

These functions merely transfer the DirectoryNode and FileNode objects from the ArrayList objects that they live in to arrays. The functions could have just returned the ArrayList objects, but that would have required the caller to cast them to the proper type, so I chose this so I could return a strongly typed array.[3] This also means that I don't have to worry about the caller messing up my collections.[4]

This is a good example of how garbage collection can simplify interaction between different objects; in C++, the question of who owned the objects in the returned array would have to have been carefully considered.

---

3. This is a case where having generics would be a real benefit; DirectoryNode would simply store an ArrayList of the real type (instead of object), and that could be returned. Alas, generics aren't present in the initial release of VS.NET, but they may be in later releases.

4. Though the caller could still mess up the objects in the array.

The code to populate the TreeView object is only a few lines:

```
public void PopulateTree(TreeNodeCollection treeNodeCollection,
DirectoryNode directoryNode)
{
    TreeNode treeNode = new TreeNode(directoryNode.NameSize);
    treeNodeCollection.Add(treeNode);

    foreach (DirectoryNode subdir in directoryNode.GetDirectories())
    {
        PopulateTree(treeNode.Nodes, subdir);
    }

    foreach (FileNode fileNode in directoryNode.GetFiles())
    {
        TreeNode treeFileNode = new TreeNode(fileNode.NameSize);
        treeNode.Nodes.Add(treeFileNode);
    }
}
```

This is a recursive function. It adds a TreeNode instance to the collection for the current level and then recourses to add all the subdirectories under this directory as children of this directory.

It then adds entries for all the FileNode objects in this directory. The FileNode object was added to encapsulate functions dealing with files, primarily the NameSize property that returns the properly formatted string for this file.

When this code is run, it generates the window (after expanding all the nodes) shown in Figure 33-2.

Setting the Directory

Our application will be a bit more useful if the directory can be changed from the current hard-coded one (c:\project\diskdiff). This will require adding a menu bar with a pick to set bring up a dialog to set the directory and a bit of modification of the main form to store the directory.

Adding the menu bar is easy. Simply drag a MainMenu object from the toolbar onto the form, add a File menu and an Options menu, and then add a Configure pick under Options. Double-click on Configure, and the designers will add an event handler for this pick.

Next, we'll need to create the dialog box, which will be a separate form class. We do this by right-clicking on the project, and adding a Windows Form as a new item. The class will be called DialogConfigure.

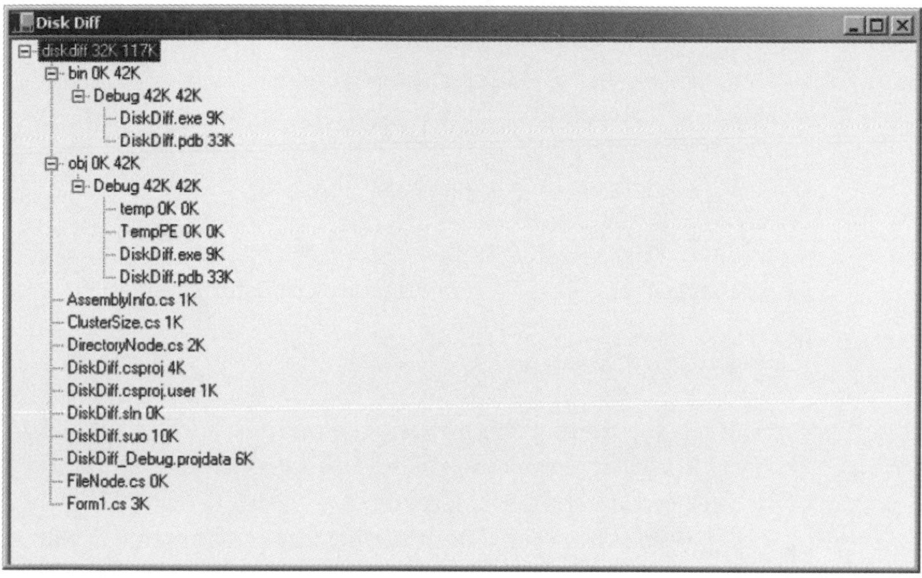

Figure 33-2. DiskDiff view of a directory tree

Dragging a label, a text box, and two buttons onto the form results in the dialog box shown in Figure 33-3.

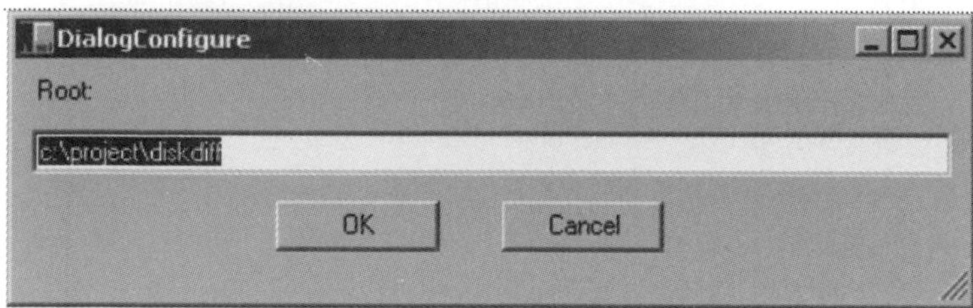

Figure 33-3. Configure Dialogire

To make things simpler, the `DialogResult` property is set for the OK and Cancel buttons so that they will automatically close the dialog. A `Root` property is added to the dialog class to make it easy to get and set the value in the textbox.

The following function is added as a click-event handler for the `Configure` menu item:

```
protected void Configure_Click (object sender, System.EventArgs e)
{
    DialogConfigure dialog = new DialogConfigure();
    dialog.Root = rootDirectory;
    dialog.ShowDialog();
    if (dialog.DialogResult == DialogResult.OK)
    {
        rootDirectory = dialog.Root;
        DoTree();
    }
}
```

It creates the dialog, sets the root directory, and runs the dialog. When the dialog is finished, it checks to see if the result was OK, and if so, gets the new string and re-populates the treeview with the new information.

There's a slight problem, however. If the root directory `c:\` is entered, it will take the code quite a while to fetch all the information, and the program will appear to hang. That's bad.

Tracking Our Progress

The first step will be to indicate to the user that something is happening. One option would be to add a `ProgressBar` control to the program. The problem with doing this is that we don't know how many files we'll need to process, so it's difficult to know what the endpoint of the process should mean.

This means that either the progress bar would complete many times, or it would never complete, which would be misleading to the user.

Another option is to indicate some directory or file information in the status bar. To start, a `StatusBar` control is dragged from the toolbox to the form, and the initial text of the status bar is set to an empty string so that there isn't any text displayed to start.

The next thing to do is to figure out how to update the `StatusBar` control when the directories are being scanned. There are two ways this could be done. The first would be to change the `DirectoryNode.Populate()` member so that it would take a `StatusBar` as a parameter and have it change the text in the `StatusBar` directly.

That would work fine, but it would mean that the `DirectoryNode` class would need to know how the program wanted to handle updating information. It wouldn't be a very general implementation.

The second option would be to have the `DirectoryNode` class support an event that is fired whenever a file or directory is scanned. Since that's a bit nicer, that's what we'll do. Note that a downside of this approach is that we'll have to have two event fields in each DirectoryNode object, even though only the root will ever have events hooked to it.[5]

The first step is to define a class that will carry the event information:

```
public class ScannedItemEventArgs: EventArgs
    {
        string name;
        public ScannedItemEventArgs(string name)
        {
            this.name = name;
        }

        public string Name
        {
            get
            {
                return name;
            }
        }
    }
```

By convention, EventArgs is used as a base class for any class passing information for an event.

The next step is to add a delegate to DirectoryNode:

```
public delegate void ScannedEventHandler(object sender, ScannedItemEventArgs e);
```

Then, we'll declare two events: one for a directory being scanned and one for a file being scanned.

```
public event ScannedEventHandler DirectoryScanned;
public event ScannedEventHandler FileScanned;
```

Finally, we'll add functions to fire the events. Having separate functions for these isn't strictly necessary, but they make the class a bit easier to use and easier to derive from.

The event framework is now ready. The next step will be to modify the code in Populate() so that it fires the events. There's an interesting subtlety here. The class that uses the events will hook up to the events declared in the root directory node, but since the Populate() function is recursive, it can't fire the events using its own events. Instead, it needs to use the root's events.

5. If necessary, this overhead could be overcome using the advanced event syntax.

This will be done by writing a private version of `Populate()` that takes a `DirectoryNode` as a parameter and passing the root object as a parameter during recursive calls. The public version will then be modified to call the private version.

To hook up the events, we need to declare the functions to be called when the event is fired, as part of the main form class:

```
void myFileScanned(object sender, ScannedItemEventArgs e)
{
    statusBar1.Text = "File: " + e.Name;
}

void myDirectoryScanned(object sender, ScannedItemEventArgs e)
{
    statusBar1.Text = "Directory: " + e.Name;
}
```

These functions merely update the status bar with the name of the file. We'll also need to hook those to the events in the `DirectoryNode` object. Here's the relevant code:

```
try
{
            DirectoryNode newNode = new DirectoryNode(rootDirectory);

      directoryNode = newNode;
      directoryNode.DirectoryScanned +=
                  new DirectoryNode.ScannedEventHandler(myDirectoryScanned);
            directoryNode.FileScanned +=
                  new DirectoryNode.ScannedEventHandler(myFileScanned);
            directoryNode.Populate(null);

            treeView1.Nodes.Clear();
            PopulateTree(treeView1.Nodes, directoryNode);
         }
         catch (DirectoryNotFoundException e)
         {
            // don't do anything; happens on some system directories.
         }
```

The `try` block in this code is used to handle an invalid entry for the root directory; in that case, the `catch` block will be executed, and the tree will still be valid.

After the new `DirectoryNode` instance is created, the event handlers are added to it, the directory is populated, and then the tree view is refreshed with the new data.

When this code is run, it will update the status bar as it walks through the specified directory tree. It's a bit distracting to see an update on every file (not to mention a bit wasteful to fire an event for every file), so we'll need to figure out a way to update less often. My initial idea was to merely update the status bar for directories, but this meant there was no change for a few seconds with really big directories, and too many updates for small directories. What is needed is an update based on time rather than on the item that's being scanned.

Two items are added to the `DirectoryNode` class:

```
TimeSpan scanUpdateMinimum = new TimeSpan(0, 0, 0, 0, 200);
DateTime lastUpdateTime;
```

The `scanUpdateMinimum` field defines the time period for which there should be no update. The constructor call sets this period to 200 milliseconds. The `lastUpdateTime` field is used to store the time of the last update.

Two lines of code are then added to the event firing functions `OnDirectory-Scanned` and `OnFileScanned`:

```
if ((DateTime.Now - this.lastUpdateTime) < scanUpdateMinimum)
    return;
```

This code calculates how long it has been since the last update was sent, and doesn't send the update if there was a recent update.

It's now obvious that the application isn't hung, but there's no way to interrupt the application in the middle of a scan. We'll tackle that in Chapter 34, "DiskDiff: More Sophistication."

CHAPTER 34

DiskDiff: More Sophistication

NOW THAT THE BASIC OUTLINE of our DiskDiff application is done, it's time to make it better.

Populating on a Thread

To make our application behave, we need to do the scan on a different thread so the user-interface thread can continue operating. We'll use the `Thread` object from the `System.Threading` namespace. Starting the thread is easy:

```
public void Populate()
{
    Thread t = new Thread(new ThreadStart(DoPopulate));
    t.Start();
}
```

The function that will be called at the start of the thread is `DoPopulate()`. To create a new thread, a `ThreadStart` delegate must be created on the function we want called and passed to the thread. Then, the `Start()` member on the thread is called, and the thread starts and runs on its merry way.

That gets the process working, but our app is now broken. When the `DoTree()` function in the form calls `Populate()`, it will start the thread and return immediately, and then try to repaint the tree form. This is *bad*, because the information isn't ready to paint yet.

To fix this, we'll add a new event to the `DirectoryNode` object for when the populate function is done:

```
void DoPopulate()
{
    Console.WriteLine("Thread start");
    DoPopulate(this);
    OnPopulateComplete();
}
```

Finally, we'll add a function to the form to repaint the tree when the population is done:

```
void DoTreeDone(object sender, EventArgs e)
{
    Console.WriteLine("DoTreeDone");
    statusBar1.Text = "";

    treeView1.Nodes.Clear();

    PopulateTree(treeView1.Nodes, directoryNode);
}
```

And, to finish, we'll hook this function up to the event.

Now, the user interface is still active while the population is happening, so you can move the application around and have it paint correctly.

At least, that's what we'd hope would happen, but there's a little problem. The thread doing the population isn't allowed to do anything that updates the control, and adding a node to the node collection automatically updates the tree view. When you try to do this, the system throws an exception that tells you the update can't be done on the current thread.

Very nicely, however, the exception that's thrown tells you exactly what to do; you need to use `Control.Invoke()` to pass a delegate to the function you want to call, and `Control.Invoke()` will find the control and arrange to have the function called on the proper thread.

This is actually pretty easy to set up. The first step is to declare a delegate to the function we want to call:

```
delegate int AddDelegate(TreeNode treeNode);
```

This delegate matches the signature of the function we want to call. The next step is to modify the call. Instead of:

```
treeNodeCollection.Add(treeNode);
```

we need the following:

```
AddDelegate addDelegate = new AddDelegate(treeNodeCollection.Add);
treeView1.Invoke(addDelegate, new object[] {treeNode});
```

The first line sets up the pointer to the function, and the second one passes it off to the control to be called, along with an array of parameters to pass to the function.

With that change, the program starts working again, but if you point it at a big drive, it might take a *long* time to complete, and there's no way to interrupt it.

Interrupting a Thread

We'll modify the `DirectoryNode` class to add a `CancelPopulate()` member function. This function will set an internal flag that the populate code will poll, and the code will terminate if it finds that the flag is set.

When doing polling, there's usually a tradeoff related to how often you poll. If the polling is done too often, it can take up more time than the processing. Conversely, if the polling is done rarely, it can make the cancel appear to have no effect. In this case, the polling is done before processing each file in a directory.

Another option would be for the DirectoryNode to store the thread instance, and then stop the thread directly, by calling the `Abort()` method. This would have less overhead since there would be no polling, but it would make the code a bit less obvious,[1] and it also could make cleanup a bit more complex since the object could be left in a bad state when the thread was stopped. To properly do the cleanup, the processing loop would want to catch the `ThreadAbortException` that will be thrown when `Abort()` is called.

`The modification to Populate()` is very simple; the file-processing loop simply tests the flag and aborts the thread if the flag is set:

```
foreach (FileInfo f in directory.GetFiles())
{
    if (rootDirectoryNode.cancelled)
    {
        Thread.CurrentThread.Abort();
    }
    rootDirectoryNode.OnFileScanned(f.Name);
    this.files.Add(new FileNode(f));
}
```

This will interrupt the processing, but unfortunately the user interface never finds out the operation was interrupted,[2] so it doesn't have the opportunity to clear the status bar. This is easily fixed by a slight modification to the `PopulateComplete` event so that the delegate takes a success parameter (so that the user interface can do different things in the success and cancel cases), and the call when the processing is cancelled becomes:

```
rootDirectoryNode.OnPopulateComplete(false);
Thread.CurrentThread.Abort();
```

1. Polling makes it clear that an operation can be interrupted.
2. The user interface may have generated the event, but it could also have come from somewhere else.

A Cancel Button

To keep things simple, a button will be used to cancel the processing. Using the designer, a Cancel button is added at the lower-left corner of the form on top of the tree view. So that it isn't in the way, the visibility is set to false.

When processing is started, the visibility is set to true, and the button is now visible and pickable. The populate complete event handler will set the visibility back to false when the processing is completed or aborted.

Figure 34-1 shows a view of the application while processing a big directory tree.

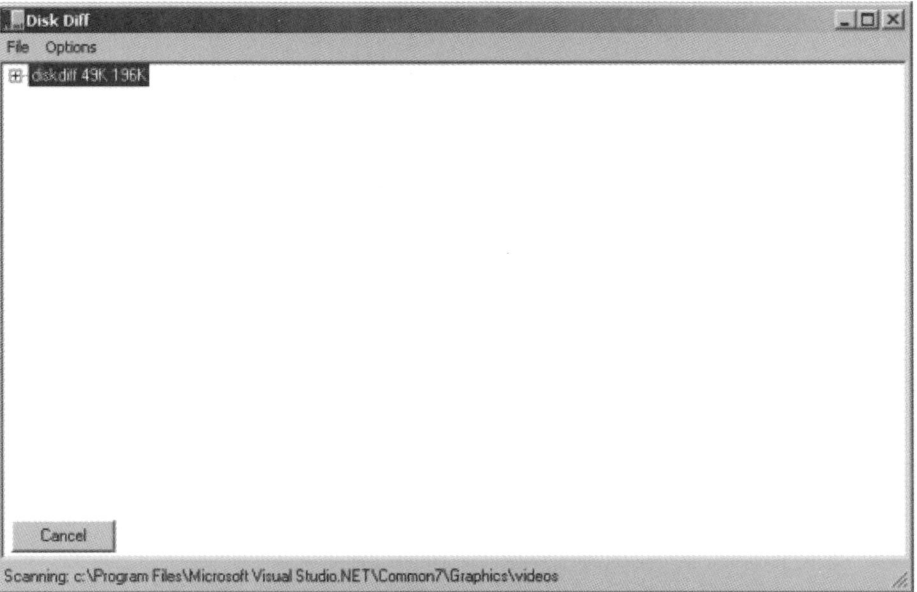

Figure 34-1. DiskDiff with Cancel button

We now have an application that can be interrupted. In this case, using threads was a simple way to get what we wanted. Another way to do this would be to use the asynchronous call mechanism in the .NET Common Language Runtime (see Chapter 29, "Threading and Asynchronous Operations").

Decorating the TreeView

Our application displays the sizes well, but it's fairly difficult to tell where the disk space is used based upon the numbers. What is needed is a graphical representation of the amount of space used by each directory and file.

The TreeView control can put bitmaps in front of each item. To do this, an ImageList that contains all the bitmaps is attached to the TreeView, and then the index of the desired bitmap is set for each item in the tree.

To get started, we need to add an ImageList to our form and then populate it with images. First, an ImageList object is dragged from the toolbox to the form. Images can then be added through the Collections property in the property browser. The images for this project were drawn using Paint Shop Pro.

To hook up the ImageList to the TreeView, set the ImageList property in the TreeView control to the name of the ImageList in the form.

The next task is to figure out which image to present for each item in the list. The bitmaps are pie charts representing the percentage of the total space an item used. The index can therefore be determined by multiplying the percentage of space used by the number of images (8) to get the index. That requires modifying the population function to the following:

```
public void PopulateTree(TreeNodeCollection treeNodeCollection,
                                         DirectoryNode directoryNode,
                                         float fractionUsed)
{
    TreeNode treeNode = new TreeNode(directoryNode.NameSize);
    treeNode.ImageIndex = FractionToIndex(fractionUsed);
    treeNodeCollection.Add(treeNode);

        // As we walk though the tree, we need to figure out the
        // percentages for each item. We do that based upon the
        // full size of this directory.
    float dirSize = directoryNode.SizeTree;
    foreach (DirectoryNode subdir in directoryNode.GetDirectories())
    {
        PopulateTree(treeNode.Nodes, subdir, subdir.SizeTree / dirSize);
    }

    foreach (FileNode fileNode in directoryNode.GetFiles())
    {
        TreeNode treeFileNode = new TreeNode(fileNode.NameSize);
        treeFileNode.ImageIndex =
                            FractionToIndex(fileNode.Size / dirSize);
        treeNode.Nodes.Add(treeFileNode);
    }
}
```

The percentage is passed into the PopulateTree() function because each directory creates its own node. The top node is passed in the value 1.0, since it obviously contains all of the size in the tree. The fraction of each element is computed based on the size of that element and the size of the directory it's in, and the index for that fraction is obtained from the `FractionToIndex()` function.

Figure 34-2 shows how a tree looks with all the nodes expanded.

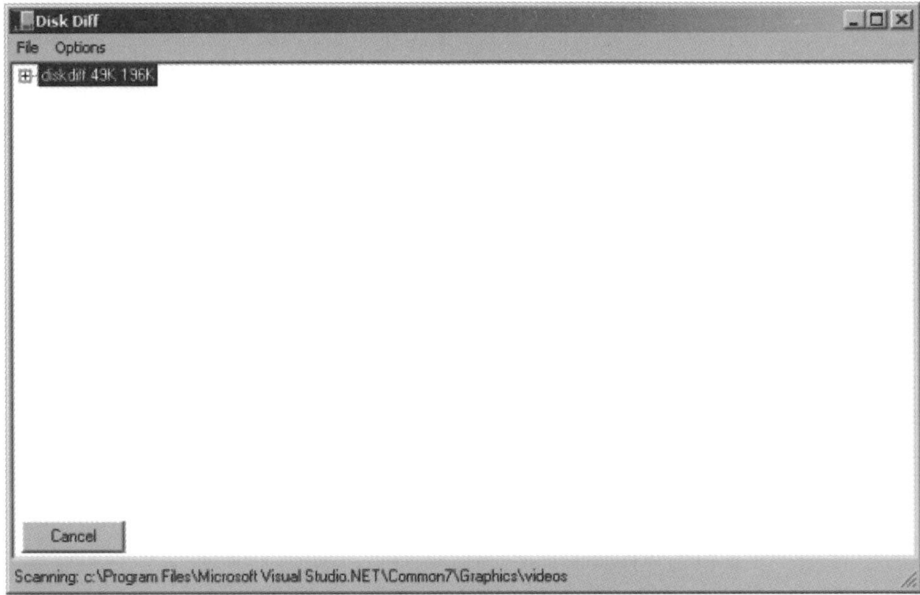

Figure 34-2. TreeView with size icons

Our program is starting to get useful, but there are still a few problems. One is that populating the `TreeView` object with all the nodes of the directory tree can take a long time—and use lots of memory—if the directory tree is large.

Expand-o-Matic

Instead of populating the whole tree, we'll only populate the currently visible portion of the tree initially. When a user clicks on the plus sign to expand a directory, we'll populate the newly visible section.

Hooking up to the `BeforeExpand` event is fairly easy. When this event occurs, a `TreeViewCancelEventArgs` is passed, and that class contains the node that is expanding. The event code will merely need to figure out what `DirectoryNode` object corresponds to the node passed with the event.

When dealing with a tree view control in the MFC framework or directly in Win32, a value could be stored with each tree node, and this value was used to point back to the object that corresponded to the tree node.

WinForms doesn't provide access to this, so we'll need to use another approach. One approach would be to change `DirectoryNode` and `FileNode` so that they are derived from `TreeNode` and then store those directly. That would work fine, but would complicate those classes, since they'd now be dependent on the `WinForms` classes.

Another approach is to define a class derived from `TreeNode` that has a reference to the `DirectoryNode` or `FileNode` object for that node. That class is very simple and looks like this:

```
public class MyTreeNode: TreeNode
{
    object node;    // DirectoryNode or TreeNode

    public MyTreeNode(string text, object node): base(text)
    {
        this.node = node;
    }

    public object Node
    {
        get
        {
            return(node);
        }
    }
}
```

The `MyTreeNode` stores the additional information in an `object` variable. For a little nicer type-checking, I could have added a base class for both `DirectoryNode` and `TreeNode` so that `MyTreeNode` could store a class rather than just `object`.

After this node is defined, the form's `PopulateTree()` function merely needs to have a few lines changed to create `MyTreeNode` instances rather than `TreeNode` instances.

At first glance, it may appear there's an extra object for each node now, but in actuality, we've merely replaced the `TreeNode` instances with `MyTreeNode` instances, and the added overhead is merely the extra `object` field.

Populate on Demand

The next task is to change the population code so that it only populates a single level. To do this, the recursion will need to be removed from the `Populate()` function. There's a bit of a subtlety involved; our goal is to get rid of the extra nodes below all the directories, but if we get rid of the extra nodes, there won't be any plus signs on the directories to click on.

We get around this by putting a single blank node under each directory that has files in it, and setting the `Node` of that entry to null. This enables the plus signs on the directory. Our populate code now looks like this:

```
public void PopulateTreeNode(TreeNodeCollection treeNodeCollection,
            DirectoryNode directoryNode,
            float fractionUsed)
{
    TreeNode treeNode = new MyTreeNode(directoryNode.NameSize, directoryNode);
    treeNode.ImageIndex = FractionToIndex(fractionUsed);
    treeNode.SelectedImageIndex = treeNode.ImageIndex;
    treeNodeCollection.Add(treeNode);

    if (directoryNode.SizeTree != 0)
    {
        // Add a fake entry to this node so that there will be
        // a + sign in front of it.
        treeNode.Nodes.Add(new MyTreeNode("", null));
    }
}
```

Next, we'll need to write the function that populates the nodes below a directory when it's clicked on. It looks like this:

```
public void ExpandTreeNode(MyTreeNode treeNode)
{
        // look at the first child of this tree. If the node
        // associated with it isn't null, then we've already
        // done the expansion before.
    MyTreeNode childTreeNode = (MyTreeNode) treeNode.Nodes[0];
    if (childTreeNode.Node != null)
        return;

    treeNode.Nodes.Clear();         // get rid of null entry
    DirectoryNode directoryNode = (DirectoryNode) treeNode.Node;

        // As we walk though the tree, we need to figure out the
        // percentages for each item. We do that based upon the
        // full size of this directory.
    float dirSize = directoryNode.SizeTree;
    foreach (DirectoryNode subdir in directoryNode.GetDirectories())
    {
        PopulateTreeNode(treeNode.Nodes, subdir, subdir.SizeTree / dirSize);
    }
```

```
        foreach (FileNode fileNode in directoryNode.GetFiles())
        {
            TreeNode treeFileNode = new MyTreeNode(fileNode.NameSize, fileNode);
            treeFileNode.ImageIndex = FractionToIndex(fileNode.Size / dirSize);
            treeFileNode.SelectedImageIndex = treeFileNode.ImageIndex;
            treeNode.Nodes.Add(treeFileNode);
        }
    }
```

The code at the beginning of the function checks to see if the first entry in the node list has a null node. If it isn't null, then this node has been expanded before, and the tree is already up-to-date. If it is null, we delete the blank node and then add all the nodes for this directory.

Finally, we need to hook this up to the expand event. We add a handler for the `BeforeExpand` event in the forms designer and then write the code. It's really only one line of code:

```
protected void treeView1_BeforeExpand (
            object sender, System.WinForms.TreeViewCancelEventArgs e)
{
    ExpandTreeNode((MyTreeNode) e.node);
}
```

Sorting the Files

While using the application at this point, I noticed it's tough to find the biggest files in the directory. It would be nice to sort the files so that they are listed in order from largest to smallest.

A few chapters ago, we added a `GetFiles()` function to the `DirectoryNode` class. This function returns an array of `FileNode` objects, so we can just sort the array before `GetFiles()` returns it, and that should give us the proper ordering. Nicely, the `System.Array` class has a `Sort()` member that we can call to do sorting.

For `Sort()` to work, it has to be able to figure out how to order the `FileNode` members. In the .NET Frameworks, this is done by implementing the `IComparable` interface on `FileNode`. `IComparable` has a single member to compare two objects, and returns integer values based on the ordering of the objects. The function for `FileNode` looks like this:

```
public int CompareTo(object obj2)
{
    FileNode node2 = (FileNode) obj2;

    if (this.Size < node2.Size)
        return(1);
    else if (this.Size > node2.Size)
        return(-1);
    else
        return(0);
}
```

Since `CompareTo()` takes an `object` as a parameter, it has to be cast to the proper type. The remainder of the function compares the appropriate fields of the `FileNode` objects and returns the integer value. In this case, the `CompareTo()` function uses the `Size` property of the `FileNode` class; this simplifies the class a bit, though it does add a small bit of overhead due to the code in the `get` accessor of the property.

The call to `Array.Sort()` is then added in the `GetFiles()` function before the array is returned. That's it! It was so simple that I added similar code to the `DirectoryNode` class so that the directories are also sorted based on size.

One enhancement that could be added would be to allow the user to sort the files and directories either by directory or by file. This is covered in the section on `IComparable` in Chapter 28, "System.Array and the Collection Classes."

Saving and Restoring

One of the points of DiskDiff is to be able to compare the current state of a directory tree to a previous state. It's therefore important to be able to store and retrieve that state.

The logical way to do this in the .NET Frameworks is to use serialization. This is one of the areas that a managed environment really shines; the runtime already has enough information in the metadata associated with a class to be able to do the serialization. We must only write the serialization code and define how we want our classes to be serialized.

The .NET Frameworks support serialization either to SOAP format (the same XML format used by Web Services) or to a binary format. For this example, I've decided to use SOAP formatting since it's easy to look at the resulting file and see what's happening.[3]

3. This will become important in a few paragraphs.

After adding `Save` and `Open` menu items on the `File` menu, I added the following code in the save event handler:

```
protected void FileSave_Click (object sender, System.EventArgs e)
{
    SaveFileDialog dialog = new SaveFileDialog();
    dialog.Filter = "DiskDiff files (*.diskdiff)|*.diskdiff|All files (*.*)|*.*";
    dialog.ShowDialog();

    Stream streamWrite = File.Create(dialog.FileName);
    SoapFormatter soapWrite = new SoapFormatter();
    soapWrite.Serialize(streamWrite, directoryNode);
    streamWrite.Close();
}
```

`SaveFileDialog` is a class that comes with the system, and the `Filter` property is used to control which files are shown. Once a filename is obtained from the dialog, it's simply a matter of creating a file with that name, creating a new `SoapFormatter`, and calling the `Serialize()` function.

The open event handler is only a bit more complicated:

```
protected void FileOpen_Click (object sender, System.EventArgs e)
{
    OpenFileDialog dialog = new OpenFileDialog();
    dialog.Filter = "DiskDiff files (*.diskdiff)|*.diskdiff|All files
(*.*)|*.*";
    dialog.ShowDialog();

    try
    {
        Stream streamRead = File.OpenRead(dialog.FileName);
        SoapFormatter soapRead = new SoapFormatter();
        directoryNode = (DirectoryNode) soapRead.Deserialize(streamRead);
        streamRead.Close();
        rootDirectory = directoryNode.Root;
        treeView1.Nodes.Clear();

        PopulateTreeNode(treeView1.Nodes, directoryNode, 1.0f);
    }
    catch (Exception exception)
    {
        MessageBox.Show(exception.ToString());
    }
}
```

In this handler, the `Deserialize()` call is used to reconstruct the objects in the stream passed to it. If everything goes correctly in this code, the `rootDirectory` field of the form is set to the top-level directory that was deserialized, and the `TreeView` object is populated.

Controlling Serialization

Serialization is covered in detail in Chapter 32, ".Net Frameworks Overview." The behavior of the `Serializers` is controlled by two attributes:

```
[Serializable]
[NonSerialized]
```

The `Serializable` attribute is placed on classes that should be serialized, and the `NonSerialized` attribute is placed on class members that shouldn't be serialized. When doing serialization, a class is serialized only if it has the `Serialized` attribute, and each member in that class is serialized if it doesn't have the `NonSerialized` attribute.[4]

We'll be serializing a `DirectoryNode` object, which can contain `FileNode` objects, so we'll have to annotate both of those classes. This is simple; just look through the definition of the object, and figure out which members shouldn't be saved. `DirectoryNode` looks like this:

```
[Serializable]
public class DirectoryNode: IComparable
{
    string root;
    ArrayList files = new ArrayList();
    ArrayList dirs = new ArrayList();
    Directory directory;    // this directory

    long size = -1;         // size of dir in bytes
    long sizeTree = -1;         // size of dir and subdirs]
    [NonSerialized]
    bool cancelled = false;
}
```

The `cancelled` field is set as `NonSerialized` since we don't need to save it.

When I first wrote this code, the serialization worked fine, but the objects wouldn't deserialize successfully. I brought up the serialized file in the editor and started looking at the SOAP format. Here's a sample of how it looks:

4. In the Beta 1 release of the Frameworks, `Serialized` wasn't checked for on classes and therefore wasn't required.

```
<a1:DirectoryNode id="ref-1">
<root id="ref-3">c:\project</root>
<files href="#ref-4"/>
<dirs href="#ref-5"/>
<directory href="#ref-6"/>
<size>4744</size>
<sizeTree>4717281</sizeTree>
<cancelled>false</cancelled>
</a1:DirectoryNode>
<a3:ArrayList id="ref-4">
<_items href="#ref-7"/>
<_size>3</_size>
<_version>3</_version>
</a3:ArrayList>
<a3:ArrayList id="ref-5">
<_items href="#ref-8"/>
<_size>19</_size>
<_version>19</_version>
</a3:ArrayList>
<a4:Directory id="ref-6">
<_data>
<fileAttributes>0</fileAttributes>
<ftCreationTimeLow>0</ftCreationTimeLow>
<ftCreationTimeHigh>0</ftCreationTimeHigh>
<ftLastAccessTimeLow>0</ftLastAccessTimeLow>
<ftLastAccessTimeHigh>0</ftLastAccessTimeHigh>
<ftLastWriteTimeLow>0</ftLastWriteTimeLow>
<ftLastWriteTimeHigh>0</ftLastWriteTimeHigh>
<fileSizeHigh>0</fileSizeHigh>
<fileSizeLow>0</fileSizeLow>
</_data>
<_dataInitialised>-1</_dataInitialised>
<FullPath id="ref-9">c:\project</FullPath>
<FileSystemEntry_0x2b_FullPath href="#ref-9"/>
</a4:Directory>
```

When decoding SOAP, there are two things to look for. Tags that have an `id` attribute can be referenced by another tag using an `href` attribute. For example, the `files` variable has a reference to `ref-4`, which is an `ArrayList` that holds the files, and the `ArrayList` has a reference to the items in the list (not shown). Similarly, the `directory` member has a reference to `ref-6`, which is the definition for the `Directory` object and holds the data for it.

After a few minutes of looking at the SOAP file, it became clear that something strange was happening; there were lots of form objects saved as part of the file.

This included the top-level form for the application, which meant that most of the user interface was being serialized (and wasn't happy being deserialized).

After a bit more investigation, I found that this was happening when the event members of the `DirectoryNode` were being serialized, a bug that has since been fixed. After putting the `NonSerialized` attribute on all the event members of the object, it was then possible to serialize and deserialize the `DirectoryNode` object.

Serialization Performance

As mentioned earlier, using SOAP as a format makes debugging easy because it is stored as text. From a performance standpoint, however, storing data in text has a fair amount of overhead.

On my system, loading the directory tree for my Windows directory (`C:\winnt`) takes 45 seconds, and the file is 8.6MB in size.

To switch to another format is easy because of the design of the runtime, by simply replacing the `SoapFormatter` class with the `BinaryFormatter` class. This reduces the above time to 15 seconds, and the file to 1.6MB.

This is better, but it's still not great. A look at the SOAP output shows that we're storing a considerable amount of information for each `FileNode` and `DirectoryNode` object. We'll attack that next.

Finer Control of Serialization

For the `FileNode` object, the minimal amount of information to save is the full path to the file.[5] But the full path is stored in the `FileInfo` object that is part of the FileNode object, and there's no way to change how `FileInfo` serializes.

One option would be to have the full filename stored along with the `File` object, and not serialize the file object, but that would result in a duplication of data. Not only would that be wasteful, but we'd have to keep the two variables in sync.

The Common Language Runtime serialization code provides a way for our object to take over how serialization occurs. This is done by implementing the `ISerializable` interface on our object.[6] The routines that are added to `FileNode` are as follows:

5. It may be possible to save just the filename and build up the full name based on the directory structure, but that would take a fair amount of code that I don't want to write right now.
6. If you've used serialization in MFC, the approach used by the runtime will be quite familiar.

```
        // Routines to handle serialization
        // The full name and size are the only items that need
        // to be serialized.
    FileNode(SerializationInfo info, StreamingContext content)
    {
        file = new FileInfo(info.GetString("N"));
        size = info.GetInt64("S");
    }

    public void GetObjectData(SerializationInfo info, StreamingContext content)
    {
        info.AddValue("N", file.FullName);
        info.AddValue("S", this.size);
    }
```

The first change was to have the FileNode object store the size itself, rather than use the Length property on the File object.[7] The GetObjectData() function is implemented for the ISerializable interface, and it is called with each object during serialization. The function saves out the values for the full name of the file and the size of the file.

To deserialize an object, the runtime creates a new instance of an object and then calls the special constructor listed above. It extracts the two fields out of the object and creates the contained File object.

Incidentally, the constructor isn't part of the ISerializable interface because constructors can't be members of interfaces. Adding this constructor is something that you need to remember to do, or you'll get an exception when you try to deserialize your object.

The code changes to the DirectoryNode class are similar:

```
        // Routines to handle serialization
        // The full name and size are the only items that need
        // to be serialized.
    DirectoryNode(SerializationInfo info, StreamingContext content)
    {
        root = info.GetString("R");
        directory = new Directory(root);
        files = (ArrayList) info.GetValue("F", typeof(ArrayList));
        dirs = (ArrayList) info.GetValue("D", typeof(ArrayList));
        size = info.GetInt64("S");
        sizeTree = info.GetInt64("ST");
    }
```

7. Length is read-only, so there would be no way to set it.

```
public void GetObjectData(SerializationInfo info, StreamingContext content)
{
    info.AddValue("R", root);
    info.AddValue("F", files);
    info.AddValue("D", dirs);
    info.AddValue("S", size);
    info.AddValue("ST", sizeTree);
}
```

The `ArrayList` members `dirs` and `files` are stored in a simple manner, but they must be retrieved by type in the constructor.

After these changes, the SOAP version of the `WINNT` directory tree is shrunk from 8MB to 1.8 MB and will now load in 13 seconds rather than 45 seconds. The binary version shrinks from 1.6MB to only 740K and loads in about 8 seconds rather than 15 seconds. That's a nice improvement and probably OK for now.

One possible to further reduce the file size would be not to serialize the `FileNode` objects at all, but to save the names and sizes of files from within the `DirectoryNode` serialization code. This would require naming the fields `File1`, `Size1`, `File2`, `Size2`, and so on.

CHAPTER 35

DiskDiff: Making It Useful

AFTER A LONG TRIP, we've finally arrived at the point of getting something useful done with DiskDiff. In this chapter, we'll start hooking up more useful functions.

Comparing Directories

Since the state of a directory tree can now be saved and retrieved, it will be possible to compare the saved state of a directory tree with the current state.

To do this, code is added to the file-loading code so that it will load the tree to a separate structure, scan the directories to get the current state of that tree, and then perform a comparison between the two trees. The code in the open handler is as follows:

```
    // deserialize the save version, and read in the new version
this.statusBar1.Text = "Opening...";
directoryNodeBaseline = DirectoryNode.Deserialize(dialog.FileName);
directoryNode = directoryNodeBaseline;
rootDirectory = directoryNodeBaseline.Root;
DoTree();
```

The `directoryNodeBaseline` variable holds the baseline version, and `DoTree()` is called to get the current state of that directory. The `DoTreeDone()` function is then modified to call a comparison function.

The comparison function `CompareTrees()` is added to the `DirectoryNode` class. This function matches file and directory entries in the current and baseline trees. For each match, it computes the ratio of the space used in the trees and stores the ratio as part of the object. The ratio is then displayed as part of the file and directory entries, and the icon displayed for an entry is coded red if the entry is bigger than the baseline entry.

The DiskDiff application now looks like Figure 35-1.

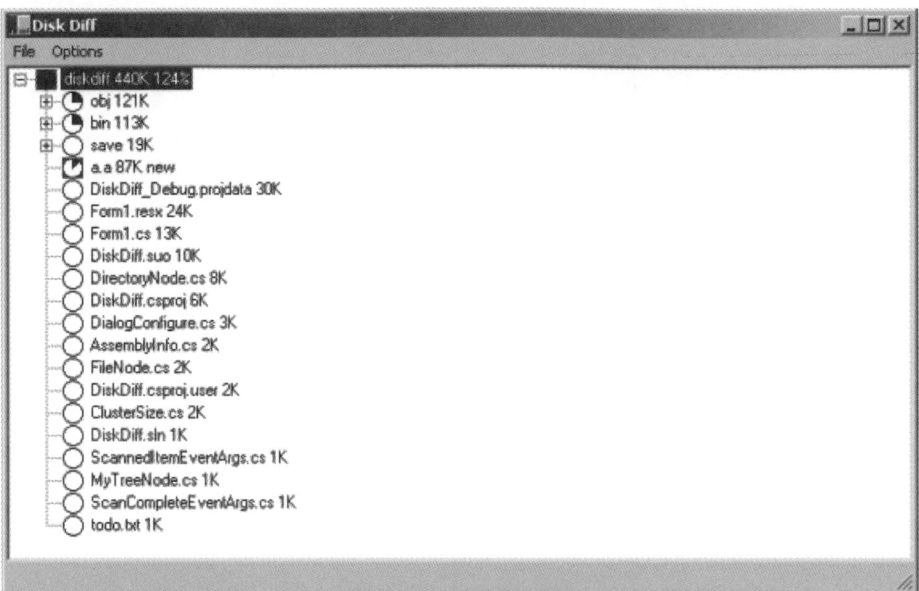

Figure 35-1. Directory tree with differences flagged

This baseline view is of the project directory. I then added the `a.a` file to the directory and loaded the baseline, creating this view. Note that `a.a` is flagged as a new file and is presented using an icon with a red background. The root level shows the increase in size of the entire tree and is also presented with a red background.

DiskDiff can now be used for its intended use: to identify which directories have increased usage. In the current version, however, there is no way to perform the file operations to clean up the issues.

File Manipulation

To be able to clean up the extra junk on a drive, we need to be able to delete files from our interface. The usual user interface to use in this situation is a context menu.

Adding a context menu to a `TreeView` is very simple. Drag a context menu control from the toolbox to the form. Then, select the `TreeView` object, go to the property browser, and set the `ContextMenu` property to the context menu you just added.

Next, we'll need to set up the contents of the menu. This will be done in the form constructor after the call to `InitializeComponent()`. In this case, we add a helper function to add items to the menu, since all the menu items have the same handler:

```
void AddContextMenuItem(string itemString)
{
    MenuItem menuItem;
    menuItem = new MenuItem(itemString,
                new EventHandler(treeContextMenuClick));
    treeContextMenu.MenuItems.Add(menuItem);
}
```

Next, add the following lines to the constructor for the form:

```
AddContextMenuItem("Filename");
AddContextMenuItem("Delete");
AddContextMenuItem("Delete Contents");
AddContextMenuItem("-");
AddContextMenuItem("View in Notepad");
AddContextMenuItem("Launch");
```

The fourth line gives us a divider in the menu. We also define some constants so we know what the index of the menu items are:

```
const int menuIndexFilename = 0;
const int menuIndexDelete = 1;
const int menuIndexDeleteContents = 2;
const int menuIndexViewInNotepad = 4;
const int menuIndexLaunch = 5;
```

That gets the initial plumbing hooked up.

A Context-Menu Bug

In of the Beta 1 version of Windows Forms, there is a bug in the context-menu code. If you set the `ContextMenu` property of the `TreeView`, the context menu will come up when the right button is clicked, but the `SelectedNode` property will not be updated with the node that was clicked upon. To work around this, a `MouseUp` handler can be written that works properly:

```
protected void treeView1_MouseUp (
                    object sender, System.WinForms.MouseEventArgs e)
{
    if (e.Button == MouseButtons.Right)
    {
        treeView1.SelectedNode = treeView1.GetNodeAt(e.X, e.Y);
        treeContextMenu_Popup(sender, new EventArgs());
        treeContextMenu.Show(this, new Point(e.X, e.Y));
    }
}
```

If the mouse button was the right one, the selected node is set, the popup event handler is called, and the context menu is then shown in the correct location.

Now it's time to write some code to customize the menu before it pops up. In this case, we want to add the name of the file or directory as the first entry of the menu, and enable/disable the menu items based on the item that was selected. Here's the code that I wrote initially:

```
protected void treeContextMenu_Popup (object sender, System.EventArgs e)
{
    MyTreeNode treeNode = (MyTreeNode) treeView1.SelectedNode;

    string filename = null;
    bool deleteContents = false;
    bool viewInNotepad = false;
    bool launch = false;
    if (treeNode.Node is DirectoryNode)
    {
        DirectoryNode directoryNode = (DirectoryNode) treeNode.Node;
        filename = directoryNode.Name;
        deleteContents = true;
        viewInNotepad = false;
    }

    if (treeNode.Node is FileNode)
    {
        FileNode fileNode = (FileNode) treeNode.Node;
        filename = fileNode.Name;
        deleteContents = false;
        viewInNotepad = true;
    }
```

```
        treeContextMenu.MenuItems[menuIndexFilename].Text = filename;
        treeContextMenu.MenuItems[menuIndexDeleteContents].Enabled =
                        deleteContents;
        treeContextMenu.MenuItems[menuIndexViewInNotepad].Enabled =
                        viewInNotepad;
    }
```

This code works, but the two `if` blocks are a good example of a poor design choice. The code for `DirectoryNode` and `FileNode` is essentially identical, but we still have to write separate code for each type of entry.

Now is a good time to define an abstract class for the properties that are shared. It will be called `BaseNode` and will have abstract properties for the properties that `DirectoryNode` and `FileNode` share. It turns out there are quite a few of them, which is another good indication that this is a good change to make:

```
public abstract class BaseNode
{
    public abstract long Size { get; }
    public abstract string Name  { get; }
    public abstract string FullName {get; }
    public abstract string NameSize { get; }
    public abstract bool FlagRed { get; }
    public abstract bool EnableDeleteContents { get; }
    public abstract bool EnableViewInNotepad { get; }
}
```

The `FileNode` and `DirectoryNode` classes are modified to override these properties. The code in the handler is reduced from 18 lines to only four:

```
protected void treeContextMenu_Popup (object sender, System.EventArgs e)
{
    BaseNode baseNode = ((MyTreeNode)treeView1.SelectedNode).Node;

    treeContextMenu.MenuItems[menuIndexFilename].Text =
        baseNode.Name;
    treeContextMenu.MenuItems[menuIndexDeleteContents].Enabled =
        baseNode.EnableDeleteContents;
    treeContextMenu.MenuItems[menuIndexViewInNotepad].Enabled =
        baseNode.EnableViewInNotepad;
}
```

File and Directory Operations

Now it's time to actually implement the file and directory operation. This is done in the event handler for the context-menu items. Here's the initial version:

```
protected void treeContextMenuClick(object sender, EventArgs e)
{
    MenuItem menuItem = (MenuItem) sender;
    BaseNode baseNode = ((MyTreeNode) treeView1.SelectedNode).Node;

    switch (menuItem.Index)
    {
        case menuIndexDelete:
            baseNode.Delete();
            break;
        case menuIndexDeleteContents:
            ((DirectoryNode)baseNode).DeleteContents();
            break;
        case menuIndexViewInNotepad:
            ProcessStartInfo processStartInfo = new ProcessStartInfo();
            processStartInfo.FileName = "notepad";
            processStartInfo.Arguments = baseNode.FullName;
            Process.Start(processStartInfo);
            break;
        case menuIndexLaunch:
            try
            {
                processStartInfo = new ProcessStartInfo();
                processStartInfo.FileName = baseNode.FullName;
                Process.Start(processStartInfo);
            }
            catch (Exception exc)
            {
                MessageBox.Show(exc.ToString());
            }
            break;
    }
}
```

Let's cover each menu item in a little more detail in the following sections.

Delete

The delete case calls a virtual function in the `FileNode` and `DirectoryNode` classes to delete the file or directory. This virtual function will call either `File.Delete()` or `Directory.Delete()`.

Delete Contents

The delete contents case is done by a function in the `DirectoryNode` class.

View in Notepad and Launch

These two cases are both handled by starting a separate process. The process is started by using the `Process` class in the `System.Diagnostics` namespace, as discussed in Chapter 32, ".NET Frameworks Overview."

Updating the User Interface

When either of the delete options are used, they work correctly, but the `TreeView` object does not correctly reflect the updated structure nor does our internal structure.

We will attack these separately, handling the internal structure first (for reasons that will soon become apparent). To delete a file or directory from our internal structure, we need to find the parent of that item and then delete the node from the parent's file or directory list (as appropriate).

Our internal structure doesn't have any back reference, so if we were to do the delete only based on that structure, we'd have to search for the node from the root. Luckily, the `TreeNode` objects do have such links, so we'll merely get the parent of the selected node and then tell the parent `DirectoryNode` to delete the selected node.

Deleting the contents of a directory is easier; the `DeleteContents()` method on `DirectoryNode` is merely modified to clear the `files` and `dirs` arrays.

That finishes the update the nodes of our internal structure, but now that the nodes have been removed, the cached sizes along the modified path (from the deleted nodes up to the root) are now incorrect. To update these, I had originally planned on traversing the modified path and modifying the sizes based on the changed values. After a bit of reflection, however, I decided to do the brute force method and added the `ClearSizeCache()` to the `DirectoryNode` class; this method merely resets the sizes on all the directories to `-1`, forcing them to be recalculated when they are requested through the properties.

We are now ready to update the tree so that it reflects the new state. Removing a node from the `TreeView` is as simple as calling the `Remove()` function.

Finally, the sizes on the displayed nodes need to be updated. This is done in the `UpdateTreeNodes()` member on the form. This member takes a collection of nodes and updates the text for each of them (which will indirectly cause the sizes to be recalculated).

That's it; we now can delete files from our structure and have the `TreeView` always show us the proper information.

However, if we load an existing baseline and then delete files, we notice that our comparison is no longer correct.

A Bit of Refactoring

My initial view of the display of ratios (and the color-coding) of directories and files was that they would be static, which was why the `DirectoryNode` stored the ratio rather than calculating it when needed. In retrospect, this was a poor decision, since I knew I'd be wanting to delete files later. Mea culpa.[1]

After exploring updating the ratio when necessary (an ugly task), I decided to have the `DirectoryNode` store a reference to the corresponding baseline `DirectoryNode` and then calculate the ratio when it was requested.[2]

The change to the `DirectoryNode` class simplifies the code elsewhere, and the percentages are now updated correctly. Another problem appears, however; the "pie chart" coding of the icons does not get updated correctly when a file is deleted. A look at the current code shows that the fraction is calculated by the form when the tree is populated. Adding code to update this—and to get it right—seems to be decidedly non-trivial.

An alternate approach is to have a files or directory calculate the fraction directly, based on the parent's size. To do this will require that files and directories be able to easily get to their parents, and the easiest way to do that is to add a `Parent` property to the `BaseNode` class. This enables calculating the fraction on the fly and finally allows us to get the behavior that we want. It also allows a directory or file to be able to delete itself from the parent directory, which eliminates the code that walked the tree to do this.

Cleaning Up for the Parents

Although you may not mind if your friends see a big mess, you'd prefer that things are nicer for your parents. In this chapter, will add a few things to make our application nicer.

1. Literally, "my bad."
2. This works because there is no way to add files in our interface, which would require re-walking the baseline tree to check for a corresponding baseline file (or directory).

Keyboard Accelerators

Accelerators are quite easy to add to an application, by putting an & in front of whatever character is the accelerator key in the text.

Most Recently Used List

The MRU list is a nice way to access recently used documents. On the File menu, entries are added (typically four in number) to hold the last four documents used and then these can be used to open those documents.

The user interface side of this will be done as any other menu item is done, but to store the items themselves, we'll need to use the Windows Registry. We'll encapsulate this access in the following class:

```
public class MRU
{
    ArrayList entries = new ArrayList();
    string keyRoot = @"Software\Sample\DiskDiff";

    public MRU()
    {
        RegistryKey ourKey;
        ourKey = Registry.CurrentUser.CreateSubKey(keyRoot);

        for (int index = 0; index < 4; index++)
        {
            string keyName = "MRU_" + index;
            string value = (string) ourKey.GetValue(keyName);
            if (value != null)
            {
                entries.Insert(index, value);
                Console.WriteLine("{0} {1}", index, value);
            }
        }
        ourKey.Close();
    }
```

```
    public string this[int index]
    {
        get
        {
            if (index >= entries.Count)
                return("");
            else
                return((string) entries[index]);
        }
    }

    public void AddEntry(string entry)
    {
        entries.Insert(0, entry);
        if (entries.Count > 4)
        {
            entries.RemoveAt(4);
        }

        Save();
    }

    void Save()
    {
        RegistryKey ourKey;
        ourKey = Registry.CurrentUser.CreateSubKey(keyRoot);

        for (int index = 0; index < entries.Count; index++)
        {
            string keyName = "MRU_" + index;
            ourKey.SetValue(keyName, entries[index]);
        }
        ourKey.Close();
    }
}
```

The Registry can be thought of as a hierarchical database in which a program can store values. We're storing our information in the `Software\Sample\DiskDiff` key off of the `HKEY_CURRENT_USER` root (which stores per-user customization).[3]

To access information in the Registry, one must first open up a key at the specific level. In the constructor, the key is open and then each of the keys is looked up. To

3. The typical pattern is `Software/<Company>/<Program>`, but I don't have a company to use here.

save the data to the Registry, the process is reduced. The indexer is used to retrieve the current values of the list, and the `AddEntry()` function is used to add an entry to the first entry of the list.

This class is then hooked into the rest of the application. The code to save an item now adds an entry to the MRU list, and a menu item handler is added to open the file when one of the items is chosen.

Using the Registry is the traditional way of storing such information, but the Frameworks provide a new method, using a config file. More details on the config file can be found in the .NET Frameworks documentation.[4]

Tooltips

Having tooltips makes your user-interface much easier to figure out and reduces the need for help. Adding them is very easy in a WinForms application. Dragging a tooltip object from the toolbox to the form adds a tooltip property to the property page of each item on the form. Merely set the tooltip text for each property, and you're done.

Increased Accuracy

There's still one problem with our code. Our goal is to keep track of disk space usage, but our program is tracking the size of the files, not the disk space used by those files. The difference has to do with the way file systems work.

Each disk on your computer has what is known as the "cluster size," which is the unit of allocation for the files on that disk. When space for a file is allocated, a sufficient number of clusters are allocated to hold the contents of the file.[5] This means that if I have a disk with a cluster size of 4,096 bytes, a file with a single byte in it still occupies a full 4,096 bytes of space.[6]

For the purposes of our application, the effect of this can be considerable. If I have a file that has 1,000 300-byte files, our current implementation would total 300,000 bytes. Depending on the cluster size, however, the usage could be quite a bit more. The current cluster size on my system is 512 bytes, so the actual usage is 512,000 bytes. This cluster size is pretty small; a more typical cluster size on an NTFS system is 4KB. That would mean we would be using 4MB of space to store 300K bytes.

---

4. I hope. I wasn't there when this example was written, which is why it uses the Registry.
5. Incidentally, this is where file fragmentation comes from. If the files system cannot find enough contiguous clusters for a file, it will have to put the file on non-contiguous clusters. As files are added and deleted, the situation gets worse, and the file system slows down.
6. This is the simplified view. Additional space is used to track the file, but it's not relevant to this discussion.

It can get worse than this if you're running the FAT16 file system. In a FAT16 system, there can only be 64KB clusters on a disk, so if your disk size is 2GB, your cluster size is 32KB. In the previous example, this means you'd be using 32MB of space to store 300KB bytes of file.[7]

It would therefore be useful to use the cluster size to determine the actual amount of space used by the files in a directory. The first thing to do is to figure out how to get the cluster size for a disk.

The cluster size for a disk can be accessed by using the `GetDiskFreeSpace()` function. This is a Win32 function, so we'll need to use platform invoke to call it. It's nicest if we encapsulate this function in a class, which is listed below:

```
public class ClusterSize
{
    private ClusterSize() {}

    public static int GetClusterSize(string root)
    {
        int sectorsPerCluster = 0;
        int bytesPerSector = 0;
        int numberOfFreeClusters = 0;
        int totalNumberOfClusters = 0;
        Console.WriteLine("GetFreeSpace: {0}", root);
        bool result = GetDiskFreeSpace(
            root,
            ref sectorsPerCluster,
            ref bytesPerSector,
            ref numberOfFreeClusters,
            ref totalNumberOfClusters);

                return(sectorsPerCluster * bytesPerSector);
    }

    [DllImport("kernel32.dll", SetLastError=true)]
    static extern bool GetDiskFreeSpace(
        string rootPathName,
        ref int sectorsPerCluster,
        ref int bytesPerSector,
        ref int numberOfFreeClusters,
        ref int totalNumberOfClusters);
}
```

7. You may think this would be a rare occurrence, but I recently came across a case where I had 16,000 small files on such a FAT16 disk.

The declaration for the function is at the end of the class, and it follows the usual `PInvoke` format. The function to get the cluster size of a disk and returns the value.

This function works, but it has a few problems. The first one is that it would be nicer to pass in a full directory rather than a disk name. The second one is that it would be convenient for every directory to call and get this function, but we don't want to call the function every time. In other words, we need to cache the value. This is done by keeping a static hash table that stores the cluster sizes for disks and then checking it calling the function. The following lines are added to the `GetClusterSize()` function:

```
string diskName = root.Substring(0, 1) + @":\";
object lookup;
lookup = sizeCache[diskName];

if (lookup != null)
    return((int) lookup);
```

Switching to Use Cluster Size

Now that there's a way to get the cluster size for a disk, the main program can be modified to use this function. The code will be written to support both the allocated and used sizes so that there will be the option of (somehow) displaying both.

The first change will be to the `FileNode` class. It will now store both sizes and determine their values in the constructor:

```
this.sizeUsed = file.Length;
long clusterSize = ClusterSize.GetClusterSize(file.FullName);
this.size = ((sizeUsed + clusterSize - 1) / clusterSize) * clusterSize;
```

A bit of explanation is probably in order. To figure out the allocated size of this file, the size needs to be rounded to the next multiple of the cluster size. The first step is to determine the number of clusters, which is done by adding one less than the cluster size to the size and then dividing it (an integer division) to get the number of clusters.

Whether this works is easy to determine by considering the boundary conditions. Assuming a cluster size of 512, a file that is 1 byte long will occupy 512 bytes:

```
((1 + 511) / 512) * 512
```

Similarly, a file that is 512 bytes will occupy 512 bytes:

```
((512 + 511) / 512) * 512
```

while a file of size 513 bytes will occupy 1024 bytes:

```
((513 + 511) / 512) * 512
```

Now that the `FileNode` object has been updated, the `DirectoryNode` class can also be updated. A `SizeUsed` property is added, and the `UpdateTreeSizes()` member is added to update both values when necessary. I also took this opportunity to remove some of the code that tried to calculate these values during the file scan; it turned out to be hassle than it was worth maintaining the code in both places.

CHAPTER 36

Deeper into C#

THIS CHAPTER WILL DELVE deeper into some issues you might encounter using C#. It covers some topics of interest to the library/framework author, such as style guidelines and XML documentation, and it also discusses how to write unsafe code and how the .NET Runtime's garbage collector works.

C# Style

Most languages develop an expected idiom for expression. When dealing with C character strings, for example, the usual idiom involves pointer arithmetic rather than array references. C# hasn't been around long enough for programmers to have lots of experience in this area, but there are some guidelines from the .NET Common Language Runtime that should be considered.

These guidelines are detailed in "Class Library Design Guidelines" in the .NET documentation and are especially important for framework or library authors.

The examples in this book conform to the guidelines, so they should be fairly familiar already. The .NET Common Language Runtime classes and samples also have many examples.

Naming

There are two naming conventions that are used.

- PascalCasing capitalizes the first character of the first word.
- camelCasing is the same as PascalCasing, except the first character of the first word isn't capitalized.

In general, PascalCasing is used for anything that would be visible externally from a class, such as classes, enums, methods, etc. The exception to this is method parameters, which are defined using camelCasing.

Private members of classes, such as fields, are defined using camelCasing.

There are a few other conventions in naming:

- Avoid common keywords in naming, to decrease the chance of collisions in other languages.
- Event classes should end with `EventArgs`.
- Exception classes should end with `Exception`.
- Interfaces should start with `I`.
- Attribute classes should end in `Attribute`.

Hungarian naming (prefixing the name of the variable with the type of the variable) is discouraged for C# code because the added information about the variable isn't as important as making the code easier to read. For example, `strEmployeeName` is tougher to read than `employeeName`, and pointer use is rare in C#.

Conventions such as adding "m_" or "_" at the beginning of fields to denote that the field belongs to an instance is a matter of personal taste, though the usual convention in sample code is to use simple names without prefixes for fields.

Encapsulation

In general, classes should be heavily encapsulated. In other words, a class should expose as little of its internal architecture as possible.

In practice, this means using properties rather than fields, to allow for future change.

Guidelines for the Library Author

The following guidelines are useful to programmers who are writing libraries that will be used by others.

CLS Compliance

When writing software that will be consumed by other developers, it makes sense to comply with the Common Language Specification. This specification details what features a language should support to be a .NET-compliant language, and can be found in the "What is the Common Language Specification" section of the .NET SDK documentation.

The C# compiler will check code for compliance if the `ClsCompliant` assembly attribute is placed in one of the source files:

To be CLS compliant, there are the following restrictions:

- Unsigned types can't be exposed as part of the public interface of a class. They can be freely used in the private part of a class.
- Unsafe (for example, pointer) types can't be exposed in the public interface of the class. As with unsigned types, they can be used in the private parts of the class.
- Identifiers (such as class names or member names) can't differ only in case.

For example, compiling the following will produce an error:

```
// error
using System;

[CLSCompliant(true)]

class Test
{
    public uint Process() {return(0);}
}
```

Class Naming

To help prevent collisions between namespaces and classes provided by different companies, namespaces should be named using the `CompanyName.TechnologyName` convention. For example, the full name of a class to control an X-ray laser would be something like:

```
AppliedEnergy.XRayLaser.Controller
```

Unsafe Context

There are many benefits of code verification in the .NET runtime. Being able to verify that code is type-safe not only enables download scenarios, it also prevents many common programming errors.

When dealing with binary structures or talking to COM objects that take structures containing pointers, or when performance is critical, more control is needed. In these situations, unsafe code can be used.

Unsafe means that the runtime cannot verify that the code is safe to execute. It therefore can only be executed if the assembly has full trust, which means it cannot be used in download scenarios, preventing abuse of unsafe code for malicious purposes.

The following is an example of using unsafe code to copy arrays of structures quickly. The structure being copied is a point structure consisting of x and y values.

There are three versions of the function that clones arrays of points. `ClonePointArray()` is written without using unsafe features, and merely copies the array entries over. The second version, `ClonePointArrayUnsafe()`, uses pointers to iterate through the memory and copy it over. The final version, `ClonePointArrayMemcpy()`, calls the system function `CopyMemory()` to perform the copy.

To give some time comparisons, the following code is instrumented.

```
// file=unsafe.cs
// compile with: csc /unsafe /o+ unsafe.cs
using System;
using System.Diagnostics;
using System.Runtime.InteropServices;
class Counter
{
    public static long Frequency
    {
        get
        {
            long freq = 0;
            QueryPerformanceFrequency(ref freq);
            return freq;
        }
    }
    public static long Value
    {
        get
        {
            long count = 0;
            QueryPerformanceCounter(ref count);
            return count;
        }
    }
```

```
    [System.Runtime.InteropServices.DllImport("KERNEL32",
    CharSet=System.Runtime.InteropServices.CharSet.Auto)]
    private static extern bool QueryPerformanceCounter(
        ref long lpPerformanceCount);

    [System.Runtime.InteropServices.DllImport("KERNEL32",
    CharSet=System.Runtime.InteropServices.CharSet.Auto)]
    private static extern bool QueryPerformanceFrequency( ref long lpFrequency);
}

public struct Point
{
    public Point(int x, int y)
    {
        this.x = x;
        this.y = y;
    }

        // safe version
    public static Point[] ClonePointArray(Point[] a)
    {
        Point[] ret = new Point[a.Length];

        for (int index = 0; index < a.Length; index++)
            ret[index] = a[index];

        return(ret);
    }

        // unsafe version using pointer arithmetic
    unsafe public static Point[] ClonePointArrayUnsafe(Point[] a)
    {
        Point[] ret = new Point[a.Length];

            // a and ret are pinned; they cannot be moved by
            // the garbage collector inside the fixed block.
        fixed (Point* src = a, dest = ret)
        {
            Point*    pSrc = src;
            Point*    pDest = dest;
```

```
                for (int index = 0; index < a.Length; index++)
                {
                    *pDest = *pSrc;
                    pSrc++;
                    pDest++;
                }
            }

            return(ret);
        }
            // import CopyMemory from kernel32
        [DllImport("kernel32.dll")]
        unsafe public static extern void
        CopyMemory(void* dest, void* src, int length);

        // unsafe version calling CopyMemory()
        unsafe public static Point[] ClonePointArrayMemcpy(Point[] a)
        {
            Point[] ret = new Point[a.Length];

            fixed (Point* src = a, dest = ret)
            {
                CopyMemory(dest, src, a.Length * sizeof(Point));
            }

            return(ret);
        }

        public override string ToString()
        {
            return(String.Format("({0}, {1})", x, y));
        }

        int x;
        int y;
    }

    class Test
    {
        const int iterations = 20000;    // # to do copy
        const int points = 1000;         // # of points in array
        const int retryCount = 5;        // # of times to retry
```

```
    public delegate Point[] CloneFunction(Point[] a);

    public static void TimeFunction(Point[] arr,
        CloneFunction func, string label)
    {
        Point[]    arrCopy = null;
        long start;
        long delta;
        double min = 5000.0d;     // big number;

            // do the whole copy retryCount times, find fastest time
        for (int retry = 0; retry < retryCount; retry++)
        {
            start = Counter.Value;
            for (int iterate = 0; iterate < iterations; iterate++)
                arrCopy = func(arr);
            delta = Counter.Value - start;
            double result = (double) delta / Counter.Frequency;
            if (result < min)
                min = result;
        }
        Console.WriteLine("{0}: {1:F3} seconds", label, min);
    }

    public static void Main()
    {
        Console.WriteLine("Points, Iterations: {0} {1}", points, iterations);
        Point[] arr = new Point[points];
        for (int index = 0; index < points; index++)
            arr[index] = new Point(3, 5);

        TimeFunction(arr,
            new CloneFunction(Point.ClonePointArrayMemcpy), "Memcpy");
        TimeFunction(arr,
            new CloneFunction(Point.ClonePointArrayUnsafe), "Unsafe");
        TimeFunction(arr,
            new CloneFunction(Point.ClonePointArray), "Baseline");
    }
}
```

The timer function uses a delegate to describe the clone function, so that it can use any of the clone functions. It uses a `Counter` class, which provides access to the system timers. The accuracy of this class will vary based upon the version of Windows that is being used.

As with any benchmarking, the initial state of memory is very important. To help control for this, `TimeFunction()` does each method 5 times and only prints out the shortest time. Typically, the first iteration is slower, because the CPU cache isn't ready yet, and subsequent times get faster. For those interested, these times were generated on a 600 MHz Pentium III laptop running Windows 2000 Professional, but they were generated with beta software, so the performance probably isn't indicative of the performance of the final product.

The program was run with several different values for `points` and `iterations`. The results are summarized below:

METHOD	P=10, I=2,000,000	P=1,000, I=20,000	P=100,000, I=200
Baseline	0.775	0.506	2.266
Unsafe	0.754	0.431	2.266
Memcpy	1.101	0.315	2.121

For small arrays, the unsafe code is fastest, and for very large arrays, the system call is the fastest. The system call loses on smaller arrays because of the overhead of calling into the native function. The interesting part here is that the unsafe code isn't a clear win over the baseline code.

The lesson in all this is that unsafe code doesn't automatically mean faster code, and that it's important to benchmark when doing performance work.

XML Documentation

Keeping documentation synchronized with the actual implementation is always a challenge. One way of keeping it up to date is to write the documentation as part of the source and then extract it into a separate file.

C# supports an XML-based documentation format. It can verify that the XML is well-formed, do some context-based validation, add in some information that only a compiler can get consistently correct, and write it out to a separate file.

C# XML support can be divided into two sections: compiler support and documentation convention. In the compiler support section, there are tags that are specially processed by the compiler, for verification of contents or symbol lookup. The remaining tags define the .NET documentation convention and are passed through unchanged by the compiler.

Compiler Support Tags

The compiler-support tags are a good example of compiler magic; they are processed using information that is only known to the compiler. The following example illustrates the use of the support tags:

```
// file: employee.cs
using System;
namespace Payroll
{

/// <summary>
/// The Employee class holds data about an employee.
/// This class class contains a <see cref="String">string</see>
/// </summary>
public class Employee
{
    /// <summary>
    /// Constructor for an Employee instance. Note that
    /// <paramref name="name">name2</paramref> is a string.
    /// </summary>
    /// <param name="id">Employee id number</param>
    /// <param name="name">Employee Name</param>
    public Employee(int id, string name)
    {
        this.id = id;
        this.name = name;
    }

    /// <summary>
    /// Parameterless constructor for an employee instance
    /// </summary>
    /// <remarks>
    /// <seealso cref="Employee(int, string)">Employee(int, string)</seealso>
    /// </remarks>
    public Employee()
    {
        id = -1;
        name = null;
    }
    int id;
    string name;
}
}
```

The compiler performs special processing on four of the documentation tags. For the `param` and `paramref` tags, it validates that the name referred to inside the tag is the name of a parameter to the function.

For the `see` and `seealso` tags, it takes the name passed in the `cref` attribute and looks it up using the identifier lookup rules so that the name can be resolved to a fully qualified name. It then places a code at the front of the name to tell what the name refers to. For example,

```
<see cref="String">
```

becomes

```
<see cref="T:System.String">
```

`String` resolved to the `System.String` class, and `T:` means that it's a type.

The `seealso` tag is handled in a similar manner:

```
<seealso cref="Employee(int, string)">
```

becomes

```
<seealso cref="M:Payroll.Employee.#ctor(System.Int32,System.String)">
```

The reference was to a constructor method that had an `int` as the first parameter and a `string` as the second parameter.

In addition to the preceding translations, the compiler wraps the XML information about each code element in a `member` tag that specifies the name of the member using the same encoding. This allows a post-processing tool to easily match up members and references to members.

The generated XML file from the preceding example is as follows (with a few word wraps):

```
<?xml version="1.0"?>
<doc>
    <assembly>
        <name>employee</name>
    </assembly>
    <members>
        <member name="T:Payroll.Employee">
            <summary>
            The Employee class holds data about an employee.
            This class class contains a <see cref="T:System.String">string</see>
            </summary>
        </member>
```

```
        <member name="M:Payroll.Employee.#ctor(System.Int32,System.String)">
            <summary>
            Constructor for an Employee instance. Note that
            <paramref name="name2">name</paramref> is a string.
            </summary>
            <param name="id">Employee id number</param>
            <param name="name">Employee Name</param>
        </member>
        <member name="M:Payroll.Employee.#ctor">
            <summary>
            Parameterless constructor for an employee instance
            </summary>
            <remarks>
            <seealso cref="M:Payroll.Employee.#ctor(System.Int32,System.String)"
>Employee(int, string)</seealso>
            </remarks>
        </member>
    </members>
</doc>
```

The post-processing on a file can be quite simple; an XSL file that specifies how the XML should be rendered can be added, which would lead to the display shown in Figure 36-1 in a browser that supports XSL.

Note that XML documentation isn't designed to be a full solution to generating documentation. The final documentation should be generated by a tool that uses reflection to examine a class and combines the information from XML documentation to the information from reflection to produce the final documentation.

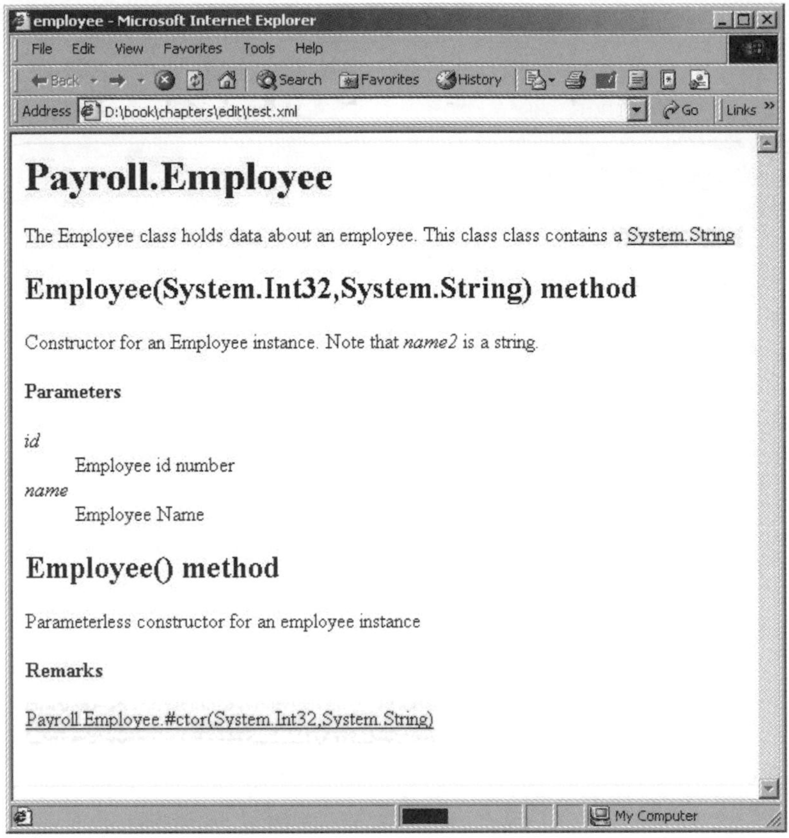

Figure 36-1. XML file in Internet Explorer with formatting specified by an XSL file

XML Documentation Tags

The remainder of the XML documentation tags describe the .NET documentation convention. They can be extended, modified, or ignored if necessary for a specific project.

TAG	DESCRIPTION
`<Summary>`	A short description of the item
`<Remarks>`	A long description of an item
`<c>`	Format characters as code within other text
`<code>`	Multiline section of code—usually used in an <example> section

(Continued)

TAG	DESCRIPTION
<example>	An example of using a class or method
<exception>	The exceptions a class throws
<list>	A list of items
<param>	Describes a parameter to a member function
<paramref>	A reference to a parameter in other text
<permission>	The permission applied to a member
<returns>	The return value of a function
<see cref="member">	A link to a member or field in the current compilation environment
<seealso cref="member">	A link in the "see also" section of the documentation
<value>	Describes the value of a property

XML Include Files

In a project that has a separate technical-writing team, it may be more convenient to keep the XML text outside of the code. To support this, C# provides an include syntax for XML documentation. Instead of having all the documentation before a function, the following include statement can be used:

```
/// <include file='Foo.csx' path='doc/member[@name="Foo.Comp"]' />
```

This will open the Foo.csx file and look for a <doc> tag. Inside the doc section, it will then look for a <member> tag that has the name Foo.Comp specified as an attribute. In other words, something like this:

```
<doc>
    <member name="Foo.Comp">
        <summary>A description of the routine</summary>
       <param name="obj1">the first object</param>
    </member>
    ...
</doc>
```

Once the compiler has identified the matching section from the include file, it proceeds as if the XML was contained in the source file.

Garbage Collection in the .NET Runtime

Garbage collection has a bad reputation in a few areas of the software world. Some programmers feel that they can do a better job at memory allocation than a garbage collector (GC) can.

They're correct; they can do a better job, but only with a custom allocator for each program, and possibly for each class. Also, custom allocators are a lot of work to write, to understand, and to maintain.

In the vast majority of cases, a well-tuned garbage collector will give similar or better performance to an unmanaged heap allocator.

This section will explain a bit about how the garbage collector works, how it can be controlled, and what can't be controlled in a garbage-collected world. The information presented here describes the situation for platforms such as the PC. Systems with more constrained resources are likely to have simpler GC systems.

Note also that there are optimizations performed for multiproc and server machines.

Allocation

Heap allocation in the .NET Runtime world is very fast; all the system has to do is make sure that there's enough room in the managed heap for the requested object, return a pointer to that memory, and increment the pointer to the end of the object.

Garbage collectors trade simplicity at allocation time for complexity at cleanup time. Allocations are really, really fast in most cases, though if there isn't enough room, a garbage collection might be required to obtain enough room for object allocation.

Of course, to make sure that there's enough room, the system might have to perform a garbage collection.

To improve performance, large objects (>20K) are allocated from a large object heap.

Mark and Compact

The .NET garbage collector uses a "Mark and Compact" algorithm. When a collection is performed, the garbage collector starts at root objects (including globals, statics, locals, and CPU registers), and finds all the objects that are referenced from those root objects. This collection of objects denotes the objects that are in use at the time of the collection, and therefore all other objects in the system are no longer needed.

To finish the collection process, all the referenced objects are copied down in the managed heap, and the pointers to those objects are all fixed up. Then, the pointer for the next available spot is moved to the end of the referenced objects.

Since the garbage collector is moving objects and object references, there can't be any other operations going on in the system. In other words, all useful work must be stopped while the GC takes place.

Generations

It's costly to walk through all the objects that are currently referenced. Much of the work in doing this will be wasted work, since the older an object is, the more likely it is to stay around. Conversely, the younger an object is, the more likely it is to be unreferenced.

The runtime capitalizes on this behavior by implementing generations in the garbage collector. It divides the objects in the heap into three generations:

Generation 0 objects are newly allocated objects that have never been considered for collection. Generation 1 objects have survived a single garbage collection, and generation 2 objects have survived multiple garbage collections. In design terms, generation 2 tends to contain long-lived objects, such as applications, generation 1 tends to contain objects with medium lifetimes, such as forms or lists, and generation 0 tends to contain short-lived objects, such as local variables.

When the runtime needs to perform a collection, it first performs a generation 0 collection. This generation contains the largest percentage of unreferenced objects, and will therefore yield the most memory for the least work. If collecting that generation doesn't generate enough memory, generation 1 will then be collected, and finally, if required, generation 2.

Figure 36-2 illustrates some objects allocated on the heap before a garbage collection takes place. The numerical suffix indicates the generation of the object; initially, all objects will be of generation 0. Active objects are the only ones shown on the heap, though there is space for additional objects to be allocated.

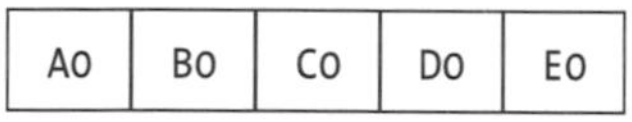

A0	B0	C0	D0	E0

Figure 36-2. Initial memory state before any garbage collection

At the time of the first garbage collection, B and D are the only objects that are still in use. The heap looks like Figure 36-3 after collection.

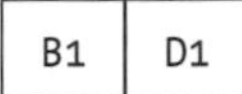

Figure 36-3. Memory state after first garbage collection

Since B and D survived a collection, their generation is incremented to 1. New objects are then allocated, as shown in Figure 36-4.

B1	D1	F0	G0	H0	J0

Figure 36-4. New objects are allocated

Time passes. When another garbage collection occurs, D, G, and H are the live objects. The garbage collector tries a generation 0 collection, which leads to the layout shown in Figure 36-5.

B1	D1	G1	H1

Figure 36-5. Memory state after a generation 0 collection

Even though B is no longer live, it doesn't get collected because the collection was only for generation 0. After a few new objects are allocated, the heap looks like Figure 36-6.

B1	D1	G1	H1	K0	L0	M0	N0

Figure 36-6. More new objects are allocated

Time passes, and the live objects are D, G, and L. The next garbage collection does both generation 0 and generation 1, and leads to the layout shown in Figure 36-7.

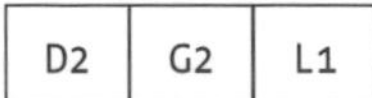

Figure 36-7. Memory state after a generation 0 and generation 1 garbage collection

Finalization

The garbage collector supports a concept known as finalization, which is somewhat analogous to destructors in C++. In C#, they are known as destructors and are declared with the same syntax as C++ destructors, but from the runtime perspective, they are known as finalizers.

Finalizers allow the opportunity to perform some cleanup before an object is collected, but they have considerable limitations, and therefore really shouldn't be used much.

Before discussing their limitations, it's useful to understand how they work. When an object with a finalizer is allocated, the runtime adds the object reference to a list of objects that will need finalization. When a garbage collection occurs, if an object has no references but is contained on the finalization list, it is marked as ready for finalization.

After the garbage collection has completed, the finalizer thread wakes up and calls the finalizer for all objects that are ready for finalization. After the finalizer is called for an object, it is removed from the list of objects that need finalizers, which will make it available for collection the next time garbage collection occurs.

This scheme results in the following limitations regarding finalizers:

- Objects that have finalizers have more overhead in the system, and they hang around longer.
- Finalization takes place on a separate thread from execution.
- There is no guaranteed order for finalization. If object `a` has a reference to object `b`, and both objects have finalizers, the object `b` finalizer might run before the object `a` finalizer, and therefore object `a` might not have a valid object `b` to use during finalization.
- Finalizers aren't called on normal program exit, to speed up exit. This can be controlled, but is discouraged.

All of these limitations are why doing work in destructors is discouraged.

Controlling GC Behavior

At times, it may be useful to control the GC behavior. This should be done in moderation; the whole point of a managed environment is that it controls what's going on, and controlling it tightly can lead to problems elsewhere.

Forcing a Collection

The function `System.GC.Collect()` can be called to force a collection. This is useful for the times where the behavior of a program won't be obvious to the runtime. If, for example, the program has just finished a bunch of processing and is getting rid of a considerable number of objects, it might make sense to do a collection at that point.

Finalization on Exit

The runtime will ensure that all finalizers are run when an application is shut down.

Suppressing Finalization

As mentioned earlier, an instance of an object is placed on the finalization list when it is created. If it turns out that an object doesn't need to be finalized (because the cleanup function has been called, for example), the `System.GC.SupressFinalize()` function can be used to remove the object from the finalization list.

Deeper Reflection

Examples in the attributes section showed how to use reflection to determine the attributes that were attached to a class. Reflection can also be used to find all the types in an assembly or dynamically locate and call functions in an assembly. It can even be used to emit the .NET intermediate language on the fly, to generate code that can be executed directly.

The documentation for the .NET Common Language Runtime contains more details on using reflection.

Listing All the Types in an Assembly

This example looks through an assembly and locates all the types in that assembly.

```
using System;
using System.Reflection;
enum MyEnum
{
    Val1,
    Val2,
    Val3
}
```

```
class MyClass
{
}
struct MyStruct
{
}
class Test
{
    public static void Main(String[] args)
    {
            // list all types in the assembly that is passed
            // in as a parameter
        Assembly a = Assembly.LoadFrom (args[0]);
        Type[] types = a.GetTypes();

            // look through each type, and write out some information
            // about them.
        foreach (Type t in types)
        {
            Console.WriteLine ("Name: {0}", t.FullName);
            Console.WriteLine ("Namespace: {0}", t.Namespace);
            Console.WriteLine ("Base Class: {0}", t.BaseType.FullName);
        }
    }
}
```

If this example is run, passing the name of the .exe in, it will generate the following output:

```
Name: MyEnum
Namespace:
Base Class: System.Enum
Name: MyClass
Namespace:
Base Class: System.Object
Name: MyStruct
Namespace:
Base Class: System.ValueType
Name: Test
Namespace:
Base Class: System.Object
```

Finding Members

This example will list the members of a type.

```
using System;
using System.Reflection;
class MyClass
{
    MyClass() {}
    static void Process()
    {
    }
    public int DoThatThing(int i, Decimal d, string[] args)
    {
        return(55);
    }
    public int         value = 0;
    public float        log = 1.0f;
    public static int    value2 = 44;
}
class Test
{
    public static void Main(String[] args)
    {
            // Iterate through the fields of the class
        Console.WriteLine("Fields of MyClass");
        type t = typeof (MyClass);
        foreach (MemberInfo m in t.GetFields())
        {
            Console.WriteLine("{0}", m);
        }

            // and iterate through the methods of the class
        Console.WriteLine("Methods of MyClass");
        foreach (MethodInfo m in t.GetMethods())
        {
            Console.WriteLine("{0}", m);
            foreach (ParameterInfo p in m.GetParameters())
            {
                Console.WriteLine("  Param: {0} {1}",
                    p.ParameterType, p.Name);
            }
        }
    }
}
```

This example produces the following output:

```
Fields of MyClass
Int32 value
Single log
Int32 value2
Methods of MyClass
Void Finalize ()
Int32 GetHashCode ()
Boolean Equals (System.Object)
  Param: System.Object obj
System.String ToString ()
Void Process ()
Int32 DoThatThing (Int32, System.Decimal, System.String[])
  Param: Int32 i
  Param: System.Decimal d
  Param: System.String[] args
System.Type GetType ()
System.Object MemberwiseClone ()
```

For information on how to reflect over an enum, see Chapter 20, "Enumerations."

When iterating over the methods in `MyClass`, the standard methods from `object` also show up.

Invoking Functions

In this example, reflection will be used to open the names of all the assemblies on the command lines, to search for the classes in them that implement a specific interface, and then to create an instance of those classes and invoke a function on the instance.

This is useful to provide a very late-bound architecture, where a component can be integrated with other components' runtime.

This example consists of four files. The first one defines the `IProcess` interface that will be searched for. The second and third files contain classes that implement this interface, and each is compiled to a separate assembly. The last file is the driver file; it opens the assemblies passed on the command line and searches for classes that implement `IProcess`. When it finds one, it instantiates an instance of the class and calls the `Process()` function.

IProcess.cs

`IProcess` defines that interface that we'll search for.

```
// file=IProcess.cs
namespace MamaSoft
{
    interface IProcess
    {
        string Process(int param);
    }
}
```

Process1.cs

```
// file=process1.cs
// compile with: csc /target:library process1.cs iprocess.cs
using System;
namespace MamaSoft
{
    class Processor1: IProcess
    {
        Processor1() {}

        public string Process(int param)
        {
            Console.WriteLine("In Processor1.Process(): {0}", param);
            return("Raise the mainsail! ");
        }
    }
}
```

This should be compiled with

```
csc /target:library process1.cs iprocess.cs
```

Process2.cs

```
// file=process2.cs
// compile with: csc /target:library process2.cs iprocess.cs
using System;
namespace MamaSoft
{
    class Processor2: IProcess
    {
        Processor2() {}

        public string Process(int param)
        {
            Console.WriteLine("In Processor2.Process(): {0}", param);
            return("Shiver me timbers! ");
        }
    }
}
class Unrelated
{
}
```

This should be compiled with

```
csc /target:library process2.cs iprocess.cs
```

Driver.cs

```
// file=driver.cs
// compile with: csc driver.cs iprocess.cs
using System;
using System.Reflection;
using MamaSoft;
class Test
{
    public static void ProcessAssembly(string aname)
    {
        Console.WriteLine("Loading: {0}", aname);
        Assembly a = Assembly.LoadFrom (aname);
```

```
        // walk through each type in the assembly
        foreach (Type t in a.GetTypes())
        {
            // if it's a class, it might be one that we want.
            if (t.IsClass)
            {
                Console.WriteLine("  Found Class: {0}", t.FullName);

                // check to see if it implements IProcess
                if (t.GetInterface("IProcess") == null)
                    continue;

                // it implements IProcess. Create an instance
                  // of the object.
                object o = Activator.CreateInstance(t);

                // create the parameter list, call it,
                // and print out the return value.
                Console.WriteLine("    Calling Process() on {0}",
                        t.FullName);
                object[] args = new object[] {55};
                object result;
                result = t.InvokeMember("Process",
                    BindingFlags.Default |
                    BindingFlags.InvokeMethod,
                    null, o, args);
                Console.WriteLine("    Result: {0}", result);
            }
        }
    }
    public static void Main(String[] args)
    {
        foreach (string arg in args)
            ProcessAssembly(arg);
    }
}
```

After this sample has been compiled, it can be run with

```
process process1.dll process2.dll
```

which will generate the following output:

```
Loading: process1.dll
  Found Class: MamaSoft.Processor1
    Calling Process() on MamaSoft.Processor1
In Processor1.Process(): 55
    Result: Raise the mainsail!
Loading: process2.dll
  Found Class: MamaSoft.Processor2
    Calling Process() on MamaSoft.Processor2
In Processor2.Process(): 55
    Result: Shiver me timbers!
  Found Class: MamaSoft.Unrelated
```

For more information on generating code at execution time, see Chapter 30, "Execution-Time Code Generation."

When calling functions with `MemberInvoke()`, any exceptions thrown will be wrapped in a `TargetInvocationException`, so the actual exception is accessed through the inner exception.

Optimizations

The following optimizations are performed by the C# compiler when the `/optimize+` flag is used:

- Local variables that are never read are eliminated, even if they are assigned to
- Unreachable code (code after a `return`, for example) is eliminated
- A `try-catch` with an empty `try` block is eliminated
- A `try-finally` with an empty `try` is converted to normal code
- A `try-finally` with an empty `finally` is converted to normal code
- Branch optimization is performed

Additionally, when optimization is turned on, it enables optimizations by the JIT compiler.

CHAPTER 37

Defensive Programming

THE .NET RUNTIME PROVIDES a few facilities to make programming less dangerous. Conditional methods and tracing can be used to add checks and log code to an application, to catch errors during development, and to diagnose errors in released code.

Conditional Methods

Conditional methods are typically used to write code that only performs operations when compiled in a certain way. This is often used to add code that is only called when a debug build is made, and not called in other builds, usually because the additional check is too slow.

In C++, this would be done by using a macro in the `include` file that changed a function call to nothing if the debug symbol wasn't defined. This doesn't work in C#, however, because there is no `include` file or macro.

In C#, a method can be marked with the `conditional` attribute, which indicates when calls to it should be generated. For example:

```
using System;
using System.Diagnostics;

class MyClass
{
    public MyClass(int i)
    {
        this.i = i;
    }

    [Conditional("DEBUG")]
    public void VerifyState()
    {
        if (i != 0)
            Console.WriteLine("Bad State");
    }

    int i = 0;
}
```

```
class Test
{
    public static void Main()
    {
        MyClass c = new MyClass(1);

        c.VerifyState();
    }
}
```

The `VerifyState()` function has the `Conditional` attribute applied to it, with "`DEBUG`" as the conditional string. When the compiler comes across a function call to such a function, it looks to see if the conditional string has been defined. If it hasn't been defined, the call to the function is eliminated.

If this code is compiled using "`/D:DEBUG`" on the command line, it will print out "`Bad State`" when it is run. If compiled without `DEBUG` defined, the function won't be called, and there will be no output.

Debug and Trace Classes

The .NET Runtime has generalized this concept by providing the `Debug` and `Trace` classes in the `System.Diagnostics` namespace. These classes implement the same functionality but have slightly different uses. Code that uses the `Trace` classes is intended to be present in released software, and therefore it's important not to overuse it, as it could affect performance.

`Debug`, on the other hand, isn't going to be present in the released software, and therefore can be used more liberally.

Calls to `Debug` are conditional on `DEBUG` being defined, and calls to `Trace` are conditional on `TRACE` being defined. By default, the VS IDE will define `TRACE` on both debug and retail builds, and `DEBUG` only on debug builds. When compiling from the command line, the appropriate option is required.

In the remainder of this chapter, examples that use `Debug` also work with `Trace`.

Asserts

An assert is simply a statement of a condition that should be true, followed by some text to output if it is false. The preceding code example would be written better as this:

```
// compile with: csc /r:system.dll file_1.cs
using System;
using System.Diagnostics;
```

```
class MyClass
{
    public MyClass(int i)
    {
        this.i = i;
    }

    [Conditional("DEBUG")]
    public void VerifyState()
    {
        Debug.Assert(i == 0, "Bad State");
    }

    int i = 0;
}

class Test
{
    public static void Main()
    {
        Debug.Listeners.Clear();
        Debug.Listeners.Add(new TextWriterTraceListener(Console.Out));
        MyClass c = new MyClass(1);

        c.VerifyState();
    }
}
```

By default, asserts and other debug output are sent to all the listeners in the `Debug.Listeners` collection. Since the default behavior is to bring up a dialog box, the code in `Main()` clears the `Listeners` collection and then adds a new listener that is hooked to `Console.Out`. This results in the output going to the console.

Asserts are hugely useful in complex projects, to ensure that expected conditions are true.

Debug and Trace Output

In addition to asserts, the `Debug` and `Trace` classes can be used to send useful information to the current debug or trace listeners. This is a useful adjunct to running in the debugger, in that it is less intrusive and can be enabled in released builds to generate log files.

The `Write()` and `WriteLine()` functions send output to the current listeners. These are useful in debugging, but not really useful in released software, since it's rare to want to log something all the time.

The `WriteIf()` and `WriteLineIf()` functions send output only if the first parameter is true. This allows the behavior to be controlled by a static variable in the class, which could be changed at runtime to control the amount of logging that is performed.

```
// compile with: csc /r:system.dll file_1.cs
using System;
using System.Diagnostics;
class MyClass
{
    public MyClass(int i)
    {
        this.i = i;
    }

    [Conditional("DEBUG")]
    public void VerifyState()
    {
        Debug.WriteLineIf(debugOutput, "In VerifyState");
        Debug.Assert(i == 0, "Bad State");
    }

    static public bool DebugOutput
    {
        get
        {
            return(debugOutput);
        }
        set
        {
            debugOutput = value;
        }
    }

    int i = 0;
    static bool debugOutput = false;
}
```

```
class Test
{
    public static void Main()
    {
        Debug.Listeners.Clear();
        Debug.Listeners.Add(new TextWriterTraceListener(Console.Out));
        MyClass c = new MyClass(1);

        c.VerifyState();
        MyClass.DebugOutput = true;
        c.VerifyState();
    }
}
```

This code produces the following output:

```
Fail: Bad State
In VerifyState
Fail: Bad State
```

Using Switches to Control Debug and Trace

The last example showed how to control logging based upon a `bool` variable. The drawback of this approach is that there must be a way to set that variable within the program. What would be more useful is a way to set the value of such a variable externally.

The `BooleanSwitch` and `TraceSwitch` classes provide this feature. Their behavior can be controlled at runtime by either setting an environment variable or a registry entry.

BooleanSwitch

The `BooleanSwitch` class encapsulates a simple Boolean variable, which is then used to control logging.

```
// file=boolean.cs
// compile with: csc /D:DEBUG /r:system.dll boolean.cs
using System;
using System.Diagnostics;
```

```
class MyClass
{
    public MyClass(int i)
    {
        this.i = i;
    }

    [Conditional("DEBUG")]
    public void VerifyState()
    {
        Debug.WriteLineIf(debugOutput.Enabled, "VerifyState Start");

        if (debugOutput.Enabled)
            Debug.WriteLine("VerifyState End");
    }

    BooleanSwitch    debugOutput =
            new BooleanSwitch("MyClassDebugOutput", "Control debug output");
    int i = 0;
}

class Test
{
    public static void Main()
    {
        Debug.Listeners.Clear();
        Debug.Listeners.Add(new TextWriterTraceListener(Console.Out));
        MyClass c = new MyClass(1);

        c.VerifyState();
    }
}
```

In this example, an instance of `BooleanSwitch` is created as a static member of the class, and this variable is used to control whether output happens. If this code is run, it produces no output, but the `debugOutput` variable can be controlled by setting the value in the configuration file for the assembly. This file is named `<assembly-name>.config`, which for this example means it's called `boolean.exe.config`, and it has to be in the same directory as the assembly. Not surprisingly, the config file uses XML to store its values. Here's the config file for the example:

```
<configuration>
    <system.diagnostics>
       <switches>
          <add name="MyClassDebugOutput" value="1" />
       </switches>
    </system.diagnostics>
</configuration>
```

Running the code using this file produces the following result:

```
VerifyState Start
VerifyState End
```

The code in `VerifyState` shows two ways of using the variable to control output. The first usage passes the flag off to the `WriteLineIf()` function and is the simpler one to write. It's a bit less efficient, however, since the function call to `WriteLineIf()` is made even if the variable is false. The second version, which tests the variable before the call, avoids the function call and is therefore slightly more efficient.

TraceSwitch

It is sometimes useful to use something other than a Boolean to control logging. It's common to have different logging levels, each of which writes a different amount of information to the log.

The `TraceSwitch` class defines four levels of information logging. They are defined in the `TraceLevel` enum.

LEVEL	NUMERIC VALUE
Off	0
Error	1
Warning	2
Info	3
Verbose	4

Each of the higher levels implies the lower level; if the level is set to `Info`, `Error` and `Warning` will also be set. The numeric values are used when setting the flag via an environment variable or Registry setting.

The `TraceSwitch` class exposes properties that tell whether a specific trace level has been set, and a typical logging statement would check to see whether the appropriate property was set. Here's the previous example, modified to use different logging levels.

```
// compile with: csc /r:system.dll file_1.cs
using System;
using System.Diagnostics;

class MyClass
{
    public MyClass(int i)
    {
        this.i = i;
    }

    [Conditional("DEBUG")]
    public void VerifyState()
    {
        Debug.WriteLineIf(debugOutput.TraceInfo, "VerifyState Start");

        Debug.WriteLineIf(debugOutput.TraceVerbose,
            "Starting field verification");

        if (debugOutput.TraceInfo)
            Debug.WriteLine("VerifyState End");
    }

    static TraceSwitch    debugOutput =
        new TraceSwitch("MyClassDebugOutput", "Control debug output");
    int i = 0;
}
```

```
class Test
{
    public static void Main()
    {
        Debug.Listeners.Clear();
        Debug.Listeners.Add(new TextWriterTraceListener(Console.Out));
        MyClass c = new MyClass(1);

        c.VerifyState();
    }
}
```

User-Defined Switch

The `Switch` class nicely encapsulates getting the switch value from the Registry, so it's easy to derive a custom switch if the values of `TraceSwitch` don't work well.

The following example implements `SpecialSwitch`, which implements the `Mute`, `Terse`, `Verbose`, and `Chatty` logging levels:

```
// compile with: csc /r:system.dll file_1.cs
using System;
using System.Diagnostics;

enum SpecialSwitchLevel
{
    Mute = 0,
    Terse = 1,
    Verbose = 2,
    Chatty = 3
}

class SpecialSwitch: Switch
{
    public SpecialSwitch(string displayName, string description) :
        base(displayName, description)
    {
    }
```

```
public SpecialSwitchLevel Level
{
    get
    {
       return((SpecialSwitchLevel) base.SwitchSetting);
    }
    set
    {
        base.SwitchSetting = (int) value;
    }
}
public bool Mute
{
    get
    {
        return(base.SwitchSetting == 0);
    }
}

public bool Terse
{
    get
    {
        return(base.SwitchSetting  >= (int) (SpecialSwitchLevel.Terse));
    }
}
public bool Verbose
{
    get
    {
        return(base.SwitchSetting  >= (int) SpecialSwitchLevel.Verbose);
    }
}
public bool Chatty
{
    get
    {
        return(base.SwitchSetting  >=(int) SpecialSwitchLevel.Chatty);
    }
}
```

```
     protected new int SwitchSetting
    {
        get
        {
            return((int) base.SwitchSetting);
        }
        set
        {
            if (value < 0)
                value = 0;
            if (value > 4)
                value = 4;

            base.SwitchSetting = value;
        }
    }

}

class MyClass
{
    public MyClass(int i)
    {
        this.i = i;
    }

    [Conditional("DEBUG")]
    public void VerifyState()
    {
    Console.WriteLine("VerifyState");
        Debug.WriteLineIf(debugOutput.Terse, "VerifyState Start");

        Debug.WriteLineIf(debugOutput.Chatty,
            "Starting field verification");

        if (debugOutput.Verbose)
            Debug.WriteLine("VerifyState End");
    }

    static SpecialSwitch    debugOutput =
        new SpecialSwitch("MyClassDebugOutput", "application");
    int i = 0;
}
```

```
class Test
{
    public static void Main()
    {
        Debug.Listeners.Clear();
        Debug.Listeners.Add(new TextWriterTraceListener(Console.Out));
        MyClass c = new MyClass(1);

        c.VerifyState();
    }
}
```

This switch can be controlled with the same config file as the other example.

CHAPTER 38

The Command Line Compiler

THIS CHAPTER DESCRIBES the command-line switches that can be passed to the compiler. Options that can be abbreviated are shown with the abbreviated portion in brackets ([]).

The /out and /target options can be used more than once in a single compilation, and they apply only to those source files that follow the option.

Simple Usage

In the simple use, the following command-line command might be used:

```
csc test.cs
```

This will compile the file test.cs and produce a console assembly (.exe) that can then be executed. Multiple files may be specified on the same line, along with wildcards.

Response Files

The C# compiler supports a response file that contains command-line options. This is especially useful if there are lots of files to compile, or complex options.

A response file is specified merely by listing it on the command line:

```
csc @<responsefile>
```

Multiple response files may be used on a single command line, or they may be mixed with options on the command line.

Default Response File

To avoid having to specify lots of assemblies, the compiler looks for a csc.rsp file. If it finds one in the current directory, it will use that file as if it had been specified with the "@" syntax. If the file does not exist in the current directory, it will next look in the directory where csc.exe lives.

Command-Line Options

The following tables summarize the command-line options for the C# compiler. Most of these options can also be set from within the Visual Studio IDE.

Error Reporting Options

COMMAND	DESCRIPTION
`/warnaserror[+|-]`	Treat warnings as errors. When this option is on, the compiler will return an error code even if there were only warnings during the compilation
`/w[arn]:<level>`	Set warning level (0-4)
`/nowarn:<list>`	Specify a comma-separated list of warnings to not report
`/fullpaths`	Specify the full path to a file in compilation errors or warnings

Input Options

COMMAND	DESCRIPTION
`/addmodule:<file>`	Specify modules that are part of this assembly
`/codepage:<id>`	Use the specified code page id to open source files
`/nostdlib[+|-]`	Do not import the standard library (`mscorlib.dll`). This might be used to switch to a different standard library for a specific target device
`/recurse:<filespec>`	Search subdirectories for files to compile
`/lib:<file list>`	Specify additional directories to search for references
`/noconfig`	Don't auto-include csc.rsp file
`/r[eference]:<file>`	Specify metadata file to import

Output Options

COMMAND	DESCRIPTION
`/o[ptimize] [+|-]`	Enable optimizations
`/out:<outfile>`	Set output filename
`/t[arget]:module`	Create module that can be added to another assembly
`/t[arget]:library`	Create a library instead of an application
`/t[arget]:exe`	Create a console application (default)

Output Options (Continued)

COMMAND	DESCRIPTION
/t[arget]:winexe	Create a Windows GUI application
/filealign:n	Specify the alignment used for output file sections
/baseaddress:<addr>	Specify the library base address

Processing Options

COMMAND	DESCRIPTION
/debug:{full|pdbonly}	Emit debugging information. Full allows connecting to a running instance.
/incr[emental] [+|-]	Perform an incremental build
/checked[+|-]	Check for overflow and underflow by default
/unsafe[+|-]	Allow "unsafe" code
/d[efine]:<def-list>	Define conditional compilation symbol(s)
/doc:<file>	Specify a file to store XML DocComments into
/win32res:<resfile>	Specify a Win32 resource file
/win32icon:<iconfile>	Specify a Win32 icon file
/res[ource]:<file>[,<name>[,<MIMEtype]]	Embeds a resource into this assembly
/linkres[ource] :<file>[,<name>[,<MIMEtype]]	Link a resource into this assembly without embedding it

Miscellaneous

COMMAND	DESCRIPTION
/? or /help	Display the usage message
/nologo	Do not display the compiler copyright banner
/bugreport:<file>	Create report file
/utf8output	Output compiler messages in UTF8 format.
/main:<classname>	Specify the class to use for the Main() entry point

CHAPTER 39

C# Compared to Other Languages

THIS CHAPTER WILL COMPARE C# to other languages. C#, C++, and Java all share common roots, and are more similar to each other than they are to many other languages. Visual Basic isn't as similar to C# as the other languages are, but it still shares many syntactical elements.

There is also a section of this chapter that discusses the .NET versions of Visual C++ and Visual Basic, since they are also somewhat different than their predecessors.

Differences Between C# and C/C++

C# code will be familiar to C and C++ programmers, but there are a few big differences and a number of small differences. The following gives an overview of the differences. For a more detailed perspective, see the Microsoft white paper, "C# for the C++ Programmer."

A Managed Environment

C# runs in the .NET Runtime environment. This not only means that there are many things that aren't under the programmer's control, it also provides a brand-new set of frameworks. Together, this means a few things are changed.

- Object deletion is performed by the garbage collector sometime after the object is no longer used. Destructors (a.k.a. finalizers) can be used for some cleanup, but not in the way that C++ destructors are used.

- There are no pointers in the C# language. Well, there are in `unsafe` mode, but they are rarely used. References are used instead, and they are similar to C++ references without some of the C++ limitations.

- Source is compiled to assemblies, which contain both the compiled code (expressed in the .NET intermediate language, IL) and metadata to describe that compiled code. All .NET languages query the metadata to determine the same information that is contained in C++ `.h` files, and the `include` files are therefore absent.

- Calling native code requires a bit more work.

- There is no C/C++ Runtime library. The same things—such as string manipulation, file I/O, and other routines—can be done with the .NET Runtime and are found in the namespaces that start with `System`.

- Exception handling is used instead of error returns.

.NET Objects

C# objects all have the ultimate base class `object`, and there is only single inheritance of classes, though there is multiple implementation of interfaces.

Lightweight objects, such as data types, can be declared as structs (also known as value types), which means they are allocated on the stack instead of the heap.

C# structs and other value types (including the built-in data types) can be used in situations where objects are required by boxing them, which automatically copies the value into a heap-allocated wrapper that is compliant with heap-allocated objects (also known as reference objects). This unifies the type system, allowing any variable to be treated as an object, but without overhead when unification isn't needed.

C# supports properties and indexers to separate the user model of an object from the implementation of the object, and it supports delegates and events to encapsulate function pointers and callbacks.

C# provides the `params` keyword to provide support similar to varags.

C# Statements

C# statements have high fidelity to C++ statements. There are a few notable differences:

- The `new` keyword means "obtain a new instance of." The object is heap-allocated if it is a reference type, and stack or inline allocated if it is a value type.

- All statements that test a Boolean condition now require a variable of type `bool`. There is no automatic conversion from `int` to `bool`, so "`if (i)`" isn't valid.

- `Switch` statements disallow fall-through, to reduce errors. `Switch` can also be used on string values.
- `Foreach` can be used to iterate over objects and collections.
- `Checked` and `unchecked` are used to control whether arithmetic operations and conversions are checked for overflow.
- Definite assignment requires that objects have a definite value before being used.

Attributes

Attributes are annotations written to convey declarative data from the programmer to other code. That other code might be the runtime environment, a designer, a code analysis tool, or some other custom tool. Attribute information is retrieved through a process known as reflection.

Attributes are written inside of square brackets, and can be placed on classes, members, parameters, and other code elements. Here's an example:

```
[CodeReview("1/1/199", Comment="Rockin'")]
class Test
{
}
```

Versioning

C# enables better versioning than C++. Because the runtime handles member layout, binary compatibility isn't an issue. The runtime provides side-by-side versions of components if desired, and correct semantics when versioning frameworks, and the C# language allows the programmer to specify versioning intent.

Code Organization

C# has no header files; all code is written inline, and while there is preprocessor support for conditional code, there is no support for macros. These restrictions make it both easier and faster for the compiler to parse C# code, and also make it easier for development environments to understand C# code.

In addition, there is no order dependence in C# code, and no forward declarations. The order of classes in source files is unimportant; classes can be rearranged at will.

Missing C# Features

The following C++ features aren't in C#:

- Multiple inheritance
- Const member functions or parameters. Const fields are supported.
- Global variables
- Typedef
- Conversion by construction
- Default arguments on function parameters

Differences Between C# and Java

C# and Java have similar roots,[1] so it's no surprise that there are similarities between them. There are a fair number of differences between them, however. The biggest difference is that C# sits on the .NET Frameworks and Runtime, and Java sits on the Java Frameworks and Runtime.

Data Types

C# has more primitive data types than Java. The following table summarizes the Java types and their C# analogs:

C# TYPE	JAVA TYPE	COMMENT
`sbyte`	`byte`	C# byte is unsigned
`short`	`short`	
`int`	`int`	

1. Along with C, C++, and Pascal, they belong to the "curly brace" family of languages.

(Continued)

C# TYPE	JAVA TYPE	COMMENT
long	long	
bool	Boolean	
float	float	
double	double	
char	char	
string	string	
object	object	
byte		unsigned byte
ushort		unsigned short
uint		unsigned int
ulong		unsigned long
decimal		financial/monetary type

In Java, the primitive data types are in a separate world from the object-based types. For primitive types to participate in the object-based world (in a collection, for example), they must be put into an instance of a wrapper class, and the wrapper class put in that collection.

C# approaches this problem differently. In C#, primitive types are stack-allocated as in Java, but they are also considered to derived from the ultimate base class, `object`. This means that the primitive types can have member functions defined and called on them. In other words, the following code can be written:

```
using System;
class Test
{
    public static void Main()
    {
        Console.WriteLine(5.ToString());
    }
}
```

The constant `5` is of type `int`, and the `ToString()` member is defined for the `int` type, so the compiler can generate a call to it and pass the `int` to the member function as if it were an object.

This works well when the compiler knows it's dealing with a primitive, but doesn't work when a primitive needs to work with heap-allocated objects in a collection. Whenever a primitive type is used in a situation where a parameter of type `object` is required, the compiler will automatically box the primitive type into a heap-allocated wrapper. Here's an example of boxing:

```
using System;
class Test
{
    public static void Main()
    {
        int v = 55;
        object o = v;       // box v into o
        Console.WriteLine("Value is: {0}", o);
        int v2 = (int) o;   // unbox back to an int
    }
}
```

In this code, the integer is boxed into an `object` and then passed off to the `Console.WriteLine()` member function as an object parameter. Declaring the object variable is done for illustration only; in real code, `v` would be passed directly, and the boxing would happen at the call site. The boxed integer can be extracted by a `cast` operation, which will extract the boxed `int`.

Extending the Type System

The primitive C# types (with the exception of `string` and `object`) are also known as value types, because variables of those types contain actual values. Other types are known as reference types, because those variables contain references.

In C#, a programmer can extend the type system by implementing a custom value type. These types are implemented using the `struct` keyword and behave similarly to built-in value types; they are stack allocated, can have member functions defined on them, and are boxed and unboxed as necessary. In fact, the C# primitive types are all implemented as value types, and the only syntactical difference between the built-in types and user-defined types is that the built-in types can be written as constants.

To make user-defined types behave naturally, C# structs can overload arithmetic operators so that numeric operations can be performed, and conversions so that implicit and explicit conversions can be performed between structs and other types. C# also supports overloading on classes as well.

A `struct` is written using the same syntax as a `class`, except that a struct cannot have a base class (other than the implicit base class `object`), though it can implement interfaces.

Classes

C# classes are quite similar to Java classes, with a few important differences relating to constants, base classes and constructors, static constructors, virtual functions, hiding, and versioning, accessibility of members, `ref` and `out` parameters, and identifying types.

Constants

Java uses `static final` to declare a class constant. C# replaces this with `const`. In addition, C# adds the `readonly` keyword, which is used in situations where the constant value can't be determined at compile time. `Readonly` fields can only be set through an initializer or a class constructor.

Base Classes and Constructors

C# uses the C++ syntax both for defining the base class and interfaces of a class, and for calling other constructors. A C# class that does this might look like this:

```
public class MyObject: Control, IFormattable
{
    public MyObject(int value)
    {
        this.value = value;
    }
        public MyObject()  : base(value)
    {
    }
    int value;
}
```

Static Constructors

Instead of using a static initialization block, C# provides static constructors, which are written using the `static` keyword in front of a parameterless constructor.

Virtual Functions, Hiding, and Versioning

In C#, all methods are non-virtual by default, and `virtual` must be specified explicitly to make a function virtual. Because of this, there are no final methods in C#, though the equivalent of a final class can be achieved using `sealed`.

C# provides better versioning support than Java, and this results in a few small changes. Because versioning is specified explicitly in C#, the addition of a virtual function in a base class will not change program behavior. Consider the following:

```
public class B
{
}
public class D: B
{
    public void Process(object o) {}
}
class Test
{
    public static void Main()
    {
        D d = new D();
        d.Process(15);     // make call
    }
}
```

If the provider of the base class adds a process function that is a better match, the behavior will change:

```
public class B
{
    public void Process(int v) {}
}
public class D: B
{
    public void Process(object o) {}
}
class Test
{
    public static void Main()
    {
        D d = new D();
        d.Process(15);     // make call
    }
}
```

In Java, this will now call the base class's implementation, which is unlikely to be correct. In C#, the program will continue to work as before.

To handle the similar case for virtual functions, C# requires that the versioning semantics be specified explicitly. If `Process()` had been a virtual function in the derived class, Java would assume that any base class function that matched in signature would be a base for that virtual, which is unlikely to be correct.

In C#, virtual functions are only overridden if the `override` keyword is specified. See Chapter 11, "Versioning," for more information.

Accessibility of Members

In addition to `public`, `private`, and `protected` accessibility, C# adds `internal`. Members with `internal` accessibility can be accessed from other classes within the same project, but not from outside the project.

Operator Overloading

C# allows the user to overload most operators for both classes and structs so that objects can participate in mathematic expressions. C# does not allow overloading more complex operators such asmember access, function invocation, assignment, or the `new` operator because overloading these can make code much more complicated.

Ref and Out Parameters

In Java, parameters are always passed by value. C# allows parameters to be passed by reference by using the `ref` keyword. This allows the member function to change the value of the parameter.

C# also allows parameters to be defined using the `out` keyword, which functions exactly the same as `ref`, except that the variable passed as the parameter doesn't have to have a known value before the call.

Enumerations

The C# enum type is akin to the C++ enum type and is used similarly. Implicit conversions between an enum and its underlying type are more restricted, however.

Identifying Types

Java uses the `GetClass()` method to return a `Class` object, which contains information about the object on which it is called. The `Type` object is the .NET analog to the `Class` object and can be obtained in several ways:

- By calling the `GetType()` method on an instance of an object
- By using the `typeof` operator on the name of a type
- By looking up the type by name using the classes in `System.Reflection`

Interfaces

While Java interfaces can have constants, C# interfaces cannot. When implementing interfaces, C# provides explicit interface implementation. This allows a class to implement two interfaces from two different sources that have the same member name, and it can also be used to hide interface implementations from the user. For more information, see Chapter 10, "Interfaces."

Properties and Indexers

The property idiom is often used in Java programs by declaring get and set methods. In C#, a property appears to the user of a class as a field, but has a get and set accessor to perform the read and/or write operations.

An indexer is similar to a property, but instead of looking like a field, an indexer appears as an array to the user. Like properties, indexers have get and set accessors, but unlike properties, an indexer can be overloaded on different types. This enables a database row that can be indexed both by column number and by column name, and a hash table that can be indexed by hash key.

Delegates and Events

When an object needs to receive a callback in Java, an interface is used to specify how the object must be formed, and a method in that interface is called for the callback. A similar approach can be used in C# with interfaces.

C# adds delegates, which can be thought of as type-safe function pointers. A class can create a delegate on a function in the class, and then that delegate can be passed off to a function that accepts the delegate. That function can then call the delegate.

C# builds upon delegates with events, which are used by the .NET Frameworks. Events implement the publish-and-subscribe idiom; if an object (such as a control) supports a click event, any number of other classes can register a delegate to be called when that event is fired.

Attributes

Attributes are annotations written to convey declarative data from the programmer to other code. That other code might be the runtime environment, a designer, a code analysis tool, or some other custom tool. Attribute information is retrieved through a process known as reflection.

Attributes are written inside of square brackets, and can be placed on classes, members, parameters, and other code elements. Here's an example:

```
[CodeReview("1/1/199", Comment="Rockin'")]
class Test
{
}
```

Statements

Statements in C# will be familiar to the Java programmer, but there are a few new statements and a few differences in existing statements to keep in mind.

Import vs. Using

In Java, the `import` statement is used to locate a package and import the types into the current file.

In C#, this operation is split. The assemblies that a section of code relies upon must be explicitly specified, either on the command line using `/r`, or in the Visual Studio IDE. The most basic system functions (currently those contained in `mscorlib.dll`) are the only ones imported automatically by the compiler.

Once an assembly has been referenced, the types in it are available for use, but they must be specified using their fully qualified name. For example, the regular expression class is named `System.Text.RegularExpressions.Regex`. That class name could be used directly, or a `using` statement could be used to import the types in a namespace to the top-level namespace. With the following using clause

```
using System.Text.RegularExpressions;
```

the class can be specified merely by using `Regex`. There is also a variant of the `using` statement that allows aliases for types to be specified if there is a name collision.

Overflows

Java doesn't detect overflow in conversions or mathematical expressions.

In C#, the detection of these can be controlled by the `checked` and `unchecked` statements and operators. Conversions and mathematical operations that occur in a `checked` context will throw exceptions if the operations generate overflow or other errors; such operations in an `unchecked` context will never throw errors. The default context is controlled by the `/checked` compiler flag.

Unsafe Code

Unsafe code in C# allows the use of pointer variables, and it is used when performance is extremely important or when interfacing with existing software, such as COM objects or native C code in DLLs. The `fixed` statement is used to "pin" an object so that it won't move if a garbage collection occurs.

Because unsafe code cannot be verified to be safe by the runtime, it can only be executed if it is fully trusted by the runtime. This prevents execution in download scenarios.

Strings

The C# string object can be indexed to access specific characters. Comparison between strings performs a comparison of the values of the strings rather than the references to the strings.

String literals are also a bit different; C# supports escape characters within strings that are used to insert special characters. The string "`\t`" will be translated to a tab character, for example.

Documentation

The XML documentation in C# is similar to Javadoc, but C# doesn't dictate the organization of the documentation, and the compiler checks for correctness and generates unique identifiers for links.

Miscellaneous Differences

There are a few miscellaneous differences:

- The >>> operator isn't present, because the >> operator has different behavior for signed and unsigned types.
- The `is` operator is used instead of `instanceof`.
- There is no labeled break statement; `goto` replaces it.
- The `switch` statement prohibits fall-through, and `switch` can be used on string variables.
- There is only one array declaration syntax: `int[] arr`.
- C# allows a variable number of parameters using the `params` keyword.

Differences Between C# and Visual Basic 6

C# and Visual Basic 6 are fairly different languages. C# is an object-oriented language, and VB6 has only limited object-oriented features. VB.NET adds additional object-oriented features to the VB language, and it may therefore be instructive to also study the VB.NET documentation.

Code Appearance

In VB, statement blocks are ended with some sort of `END` statement, and there can't be multiple statements on a single line. In C#, blocks are denoted using braces {}, and the location of line breaks doesn't matter, as the end of a statement is indicated by a semicolon. Though it might be bad form and ugly to read, in C# the following can be written:

```
for (int j = 0; j < 10; j++) {if (j == 5) Func(j); else return;}
```

That line will mean the same as this:

```
for (int j = 0; j < 10; j++)
{
    if (j == 5)
        Func(j);
    else
        return;
}
```

This constrains the programmer less, but it also makes agreements about style more important.

Data Types and Variables

While there is a considerable amount of overlap in data types between VB and C#, there are some important differences, and a similar name may mean a different data type.

The most important difference is that C# is more strict on variable declaration and usage. All variables must be declared before they are used, and they must be declared with a specific type—there is no `Variant` type that can hold any type.[2]

Variable declarations are made simply by using the name of the type before the variable; there is no `dim` statement.

Conversions

Conversions between types are also stricter than in VB. C# has two types of conversions: implicit and explicit. Implicit conversions are those that can't lose data—that's where the source value will always fit into the destination variable. For example:

```
int    v = 55;
long x = v;
```

Assigning `v` to `x` is allowed because `int` variables can always fit into `long` variables.

Explicit conversions, on the other hand, are conversions that can lose data or fail. Because of this, the conversion must be explicitly stated using a cast:

```
long    x = 55;
int v = (int) x;
```

Though in this case the conversion is safe, the `long` can hold numbers that are too big to fit in an `int`, and therefore the cast is required.

If detecting overflow in conversions is important, the `checked` statement can be used to turn on the detection of overflow. See Chapter 15, "Conversions," for more information.

---

2. The `object` type can contain any type, but it knows exactly what type it contains.

Data Type Differences

In Visual Basic, the integer data types are `Integer` and `Long`. In C#, these are replaced with the types `short` and `int`. There is a `long` type as well, but it is a 64-bit (8-byte) type. This is something to keep in mind, because if `long` is used in C# where `Long` would have been used in VB, programs will be bigger and much slower. `Byte`, however, is merely renamed to `byte`.

C# also has the unsigned data types `ushort`, `uint`, and `ulong`, and the signed byte `sbyte`. These are useful in some situations, but they can't be used by all other languages in .NET, so they should only be used as necessary.

The floating point types `Single` and `Double` are renamed `float` and `double`, and the `Boolean` type is known simply as `bool`.

Strings

Many of the built-in functions that are present in VB do not exist for the C# string type. There are functions to search strings, extract substrings, and perform other operations; see the documentation for the `System.String` type for details.

String concatenation is performed using the `+` operator rather than the `&` operator.

Arrays

In C#, the first element of an array is always index 0, and there is no way to set upper or lower bounds, and no way to `redim` an array. There is, however, an `ArrayList` in the `System.Collection` namespace that does allow resizing, along with other useful collection classes.

Operators and Expressions

The operators that C# uses have a few differences from VB, and the expressions will therefore take some getting used to.

VB OPERATOR	C# EQUIVALENT
`^`	None. See `Math.Pow()`.
`Mod`	`%`
`&`	`+`
`=`	`==`

VB OPERATOR	C# EQUIVALENT
`<>`	`!=`
`Like`	None. `System.Text.RegularExpressions.Regex` does some of this, but it is more complex.
`Is`	None. The C# `is` operator means something different.
`And`	`&&`
`Or`	`||`
`Xor`	`^`
`Eqv`	None. `A Eqv B` is the same as `!(A ^ B)`.
`Imp`	None

Classes, Types, Functions, and Interfaces

Because C# is an object-oriented language,[3] the class is the major organizational unit; rather than having code or variables live in a global area, they are always associated with a specific class. This results in code that is structured and organized quite differently than VB code, but there are still some common elements. Properties can still be used, though they have a different syntax and there are no default properties.

Functions

In C#, function parameters must have a declared type, and `ref` is used instead of `ByRef` to indicate that the value of a passed variable may be modified. The `ParamArray` function can be achieved by using the `params` keyword.

Control and Program Flow

C# and VB have similar control structures, but the syntax used is a bit different.

3. See Chapter 1, "Object-Oriented Basics," for more information.

If Then

In C#, there is no Then statement; after the condition comes the statement or statement block that should be executed if the condition is true, and after that statement or block there is an optional else statement.

The following VB code

```
If size < 60 Then
    value = 50
Else
    value = 55
    order = 12
End If
```

can be rewritten as

```
if (size < 60)
    value = 50;
else
{
    value = 55;
    order = 12;
}
```

There is no ElseIf statement in C#.

For

The syntax for for loops is different in C#, but the concept is the same, except that in C# the operation performed at the end of each loop must be explicitly specified. In other words the following VB code

```
For i = 1 To 100
    ' other code here
Next
```

can be rewritten as

```
for (int i = 0; i < 10; i++)
{
    // other code here
}
```

For Each

C# supports the `For Each` syntax through the `foreach` statement, which can be used on arrays, collections classes, and other classes that expose the proper interface.

Do Loop

C# has two looping constructs to replace the `Do Loop` construct. The `while` statement is used to loop while a condition is true, and `do while` works the same way, except that one trip through the loop is ensured even if the condition is false. The following VB code

```
I = 1
fact = 1
Do While I <= n
    fact = fact * I
    I = I + 1
Loop
```

can be rewritten as:

```
int I = 1;
int fact = 1;
while (I <= n)
{
    fact = fact * I;
    I++;
}
```

A loop can be exited using the `break` statement, or continued on the next iteration using the `continue` statement.

Select Case

The `switch` statement in C# does the same thing as `Select Case`. This VB code

```
Select Case x
    Case 1
        Func1
    Case 2
        Func2
    Case 3
        Func2
    Case Else
        Func3
End Select
```

can be rewritten as:

```
switch (x)
{
    case 1:
        Func1();
        break;
    case 2:
    case 3:
        Func2();
        break;
    default:
        Func3();
        break;
}
```

On Error

There is no `On Error` statement in C#. Error conditions in .NET are communicated through exceptions. See Chapter 4, "Exception Handling," for more details.

Missing Statements

There is no `With`, `Choose`, or the equivalent of `Switch` in C#. There is also no `CallByName` feature, though this can be performed through reflection.

Other .NET Languages

Visual C++ and Visual Basic have both been extended to work in the .NET world.

In the Visual C++ world, a set of "Managed Extensions" have been added to the language to allow programmers to produce and consume components for the Common Language Runtime. The Visual C++ model allows the programmer more control than the C# model, in that the user is allowed to write both managed (garbage-collected) and unmanaged (using `new` and `delete`) objects.

A .NET component is created by using keywords to modify the meaning of existing C++ constructs. For example, when the `__gc` keyword is placed in front of a class definition, it enables the creation of a managed class and restricts the class from using constructs that cannot be expressed in the .NET world (such as multiple inheritance). The .NET system classes can also be used from the managed extensions.

Visual Basic has also seen considerable improvements. It now has object-oriented concepts such as inheritance, encapsulation, and overloading, which allow it to operate well in the .NET world.

In addition to the Microsoft languages, a large number of third-party languages have been announced for the .NET platform. See `http://www.gotdotnet.com` for more information.

CHAPTER 40

C# Resources and Futures

THIS CHAPTER PROVIDES some resources for learning more about C# and some ideas about how C# will evolve in the future.

C# Resources

A number of C# resources have appeared on the Web. The following sections list some of them.

MSDN

`http://msdn.microsoft.com/net`

This is the main Microsoft site for all things .NET. It has news, articles, columns,[1] and sample code.

GotDotNet

`http://www.gotdotnet.com`

GotDotNet is a Microsoft-operated community site. It has some of the same content as the MSDN site, but it also has a user-contribution area.

Csharpindex

`http://www.csharpindex.com`

Csharpindex is an index site that categories a number of different C# sites.

---

1. You might be interested in the "Working with C#" column.

C-Sharp Corner

`http://www.c-sharpcorner.com`

C-Sharp Corner is a site dedicated only to C#. It's somewhat like GotDotNet, but it deals only with C#, not the whole .NET universe.

DotNet Books

`http://www.dotnetbooks.com`

If there's an existing, new, or upcoming book about C# or other .NET topics, it will probably be listed here.

C# Futures

The C# compiler specification has been submitted for standardization to the European Computer Manufacturers Association (ECMA). The standardization process is underway in Technical Committee 39, the same group that standardized ECMAScript (often known as JavaScript or JScript). In addition to the C# language, a subset of the Common Language Runtime, known as the CLI, is undergoing standardization in the same committee.

The goal is to standardize enough of the language and runtime so that useful programs can be written, roughly analogous to what is available with C++ and the C++ Runtime Library. Current specifications from this process are available at `http://msdn.microsoft.com/net/ecma`.

There are some features under consideration for future versions of the C# language. The most interesting one is generic types, which is also known as "parameterized" types. C++ templates are a specific implementation of generics.

Generics allow an author to write one version of a collection class and have it work correctly for any type of object. The standard collection classes in `System.Collections` do work for any object, but there are several disadvantages to this approach.

Since the type stored by collection classes is `object`, the compiler has no way of knowing the actual type of an object stored in a collection class. A user can write something like:

```
ArrayList arr = new ArrayList();
arr.Add("Hello");
foreach (int value in arr) {…}
```

but the compiler has no way of knowing that `arr` only contains strings and that the `foreach` could never work correctly, so this error will only be found at runtime. In other words, the current collection classes are runtime type-safe, but not compile-time type-safe.

Another issue has to do with performance. Because the objects are stored as values of type `object`, value types will be boxed, which requires some additional overhead. A generic implementation of `ArrayList` would allow an `int` to be stored without any boxing overhead.

Currently, the work with generics is at a "research project" level, so it's not clear what the actual implementation will be, but it seems likely that the genericity will show up at the IL level, and it will be the responsibility of the JIT to create a type-specific implementation of the generic type for each unique usage.

Index

Symbols

B

D

E

F

G

J

K

L

N

O

P

Q

R

S

T

U

V

W

X

About Apress

Apress, located in Berkeley, CA, is an innovative publishing company devoted to meeting the needs of existing and potential programming professionals. Simply put, the "A" in Apress stands for the "Author's Press™." Apress' unique author-centric approach to publishing grew from conversations between Dan Appleman and Gary Cornell, authors of best-selling, highly regarded computer books. In 1998, they set out to create a publishing company that emphasized quality above all else, a company with books that would be considered the best in their market. Dan and Gary's vision has resulted in over 30 widely acclaimed titles by some of the industry's leading software professionals.

Do You Have What It Takes to Write for Apress?

Apress is rapidly expanding its publishing program. If you can write and refuse to compromise on the quality of your work, if you believe in doing more then rehashing existing documentation, and if you're looking for opportunities and rewards that go far beyond those offered by traditional publishing houses, we want to hear from you!

Consider these innovations that we offer all of our authors:

- **Top royalties with *no* hidden switch statements**
  Authors typically receive only half of their normal royalty rate on foreign sales. In contrast, Apress' royalty rate remains the same for both foreign and domestic sales.
- **A mechanism for authors to obtain equity in Apress**
  Unlike the software industry, where stock options are essential to motivate and retain software professionals, the publishing industry has adhered to an outdated compensation model based on royalties alone. In the spirit of most software companies, Apress reserves a significant portion of its equity for authors.
- **Serious treatment of the technical review process**
  Each Apress book has a technical reviewing team whose remuneration depends in part on the success of the book, since they too receive royalties.

Moreover, through a partnership with Springer-Verlag, one of the world's major publishing houses, Apress has significant venture capital behind it. Thus, we have the resources to produce the highest quality books *and* market them aggressively.

If you fit the model of the Apress author who can write a book that gives the "professional what he or she needs to know™," then please contact one of our Editorial Directors, Gary Cornell (gary_cornell@apress.com), Dan Appleman (dan_appleman@apress.com), Karen Watterson (karen_watterson@apress.com), or Jason Gilmore (jason_gilmore@apress.com) for more information.

Apress Titles

ISBN	LIST PRICE	AUTHOR	TITLE
1-893115-01-1	$39.95	Appleman	Dan Appleman's Win32 API Puzzle Book and Tutorial for Visual Basic Programmers
1-893115-23-2	$29.95	Appleman	How Computer Programming Works
1-893115-97-6	$39.95	Appleman	Moving to VB.NET: Strategies, Concepts and Code
1-893115-09-7	$29.95	Baum	Dave Baum's Definitive Guide to LEGO MINDSTORMS
1-893115-84-4	$29.95	Baum, Gasperi, Hempel, and Villa	Extreme MINDSTORMS
1-893115-82-8	$59.95	Ben-Gan/Moreau	Advanced Transact-SQL for SQL Server 2000
1-893115-99-2	$39.95	Cornell/Morrison	Programming VB.NET: A Guide for Experienced Programmers
1-893115-85-2	$34.95	Gilmore	A Programmer's Introduction to PHP 4.0
1-893115-17-8	$59.95	Gross	A Programmer's Introduction to Windows DNA
1-893115-62-3	$39.95	Gunnerson	A Programmer's Introduction to C#, Second Edition
1-893115-10-0	$34.95	Holub	Taming Java Threads
1-893115-04-6	$34.95	Hyman/Vaddadi	Mike and Phani's Essential C++ Techniques
1-893115-79-8	$49.95	Kofler	Definitive Guide to Excel VBA
1-893115-50-X	$34.95	Knudsen	Wireless Java: Developing with Java 2, Micro Edition
1-893115-75-5	$44.95	Kurniawan	Internet Programming with VB
1-893115-19-4	$49.95	Macdonald	Serious ADO: Universal Data Access with Visual Basic

ISBN	LIST PRICE	AUTHOR	TITLE
1-893115-06-2	$39.95	Marquis/Smith	A Visual Basic 6.0 Programmer's Toolkit
1-893115-22-4	$27.95	McCarter	David McCarter's VB Tips and Techniques
1-893115-76-3	$49.95	Morrison	C++ For VB Programmers
1-893115-80-1	$39.95	Newmarch	A Programmer's Guide to Jini Technology
1-893115-81-X	$39.95	Pike	SQL Server: Common Problems, Tested Solutions
1-893115-20-8	$34.95	Rischpater	Wireless Web Development
1-893115-93-3	$34.95	Rischpater	Wireless Web Development with PHP and WAP
1-893115-24-0	$49.95	Sinclair	From Access to SQL Server
1-893115-94-1	$29.95	Spolsky	User Interface Design for Programmers
1-893115-59-3	$59.95	Troelsen	C# and the .Net Platform
1-893115-16-X	$49.95	Vaughn	ADO Examples and Best Practices
1-893115-83-6	$44.95	Wells	Code Centric: T-SQL Programming with Stored Procedures and Triggers
1-893115-95-X	$49.95	Welschenbach	Cryptography in C and C++
1-893115-05-4	$39.95	Williamson	Writing Cross-Browser Dynamic HTML
1-893115-78-X	$49.95	Zukowski	Definitive Guide to Swing for Java 2, Second Edition
1-893115-92-5	$49.95	Zukowski	Java Collections

Apress Titles Publishing SOON!

ISBN	AUTHOR	TITLE
1-893115-96-8	Jorelid	Architecting a Servlet and JSP Based Application
1-893115-56-9	Kofler/Kramer	MySQL
1-893115-87-9	Kurata	Doing Web Development: Client-Side Techniques
1-893115-54-2	Trueblood/Lovett	Data Mining and Statistical Analysis Using SQL

To order, call (800) 777-4643 or email `sales@apress.com`.

Apress™

The Ultimate .NET Resource

Apress is committed to helping developers with all their .NET needs. Whether you're looking for information on C#, or how to make the transition from earlier versions of Visual Basic to VB.NET, or just looking for general .NET information, Apress will be there. Check out our .NET area on www.apress.com for more .NET news and information. And, while you're there, see how readers of our books can register for our free electronic .NET update program to their books.

ISBN: 1-893115-59-3 $59.95
ISBN: 1-893115-97-6 $39.95
Andrew Troelsen
C# and the .Net Platform
Dan Appleman
Moving to VB.NET:
Strategies, Concepts, and Code
Gary Cornell & Jonathan Morrison
Programming VB.NET:
A Guide for Experienced Programmers
.NET Developer Series
Eric Gunnerson
A Programmer's Introduction to C#, Second Edition
a! Apress
ISBN: 1-893115-99-2 $39.95
ISBN: 1-893115-62-3 $39.95

Books for professionals by professionals™

www.apress.com

Available at bookstores nationwide or from Springer-Verlag New York, Inc. at 1-800-777-4643; fax 1-212-533-3503.
Contact us for more information at sales@apress.com.

Promotion #L2443